The Routledge Course in Translation Annotation

The Routledge Course in Translation Annotation: Arabic-English-Arabic is a key coursebook for students and practitioners of translation studies. Focusing on one of the most prominent developments in translation studies, annotation for translation purposes, it provides the reader with the theoretical framework for annotating their own, or commenting on others', translations.

The book:

- presents a systematic and thorough explanation of translation strategies, supported throughout by bidirectional examples from and into English
- features authentic materials taken from a wide range of sources, including literary, journalistic, religious, legal, technical and commercial texts
- brings the theory and practice of translation annotation together in an informed and comprehensive way
- includes practical exercises at the end of each chapter to consolidate learning and allow the reader to put the theory into practice
- culminates with a long annotated literary text, allowing the reader to have a clear vision of how to apply the theoretical elements in a cohesive way

The Routledge Course in Translation Annotation is an essential text for both undergraduate and postgraduate students of Arabic-English translation and of translation studies.

Ali Almanna is Assistant Professor of Translation in the Department of Foreign Languages, Translation Section, at the University of Nizwa, the Sultanate of Oman.

The Routledge Course in Translation Annotation
Arabic-English-Arabic

Ali Almanna

LONDON AND NEW YORK

First published 2016
by Routledge
2 Park Square, Milton Park, Abingdon, Oxon OX14 4RN

and by Routledge
711 Third Avenue, New York, NY 10017

Routledge is an imprint of the Taylor & Francis Group, an informa business

© 2016 Ali Almanna

The right of Ali Almanna to be identified as author of this work has been asserted by him in accordance with sections 77 and 78 of the Copyright, Designs and Patents Act 1988.

All rights reserved. No part of this book may be reprinted or reproduced or utilised in any form or by any electronic, mechanical, or other means, now known or hereafter invented, including photocopying and recording, or in any information storage or retrieval system, without permission in writing from the publishers.

Trademark notice: Product or corporate names may be trademarks or registered trademarks, and are used only for identification and explanation without intent to infringe.

British Library Cataloguing in Publication Data
A catalogue record for this book is available from the British Library

Library of Congress Cataloging-in-Publication Data
A catalog record for this book has been requested

ISBN: 978-1-138-91307-3 (hbk)
ISBN: 978-1-138-91309-7 (pbk)
ISBN: 978-1-315-66558-0 (ebk)

Typeset in Times New Roman
by Apex CoVantage, LLC

Contents

Acknowledgments   viii

Introduction   1

1 **Annotation – defining matters**   6

   Place of annotation and related issues 6
   Annotation and related issues 8
   Quality from different perspectives 13

2 **Annotation and global strategies**   37

   Strategies and translation brief 37
   Skopos 40
   Readership 41
   Text typology 41
   Genre 42
   Discussion 43
   Evaluating researchers' strategic decisions 44

3 **Annotating translation strategies**   54

   Local Strategies 55
   J. P. Vinay and J. Darbelnet (1958/1995) 56
   J. C. Catford (1965) 61
   J. L. Malone (1988) 64
   M. Baker (1992/2011) 71

4 **Annotating grammatical issues**   82

   Grammatical equivalence 82
   Number 84

Active versus passive 86
Tense versus aspect 90
Modality 93

5 Annotating lexical and phraseological choices 103

Lexical choice 103
Multiword units 109
    Metaphor 110
    Simile 112
    Idioms 114
    Collocation 117

6 Annotating aspects of cohesion 125

Cohesion versus coherence 126
Reference 127
Substitution 128
Ellipsis 130
Conjunction 133
Lexical cohesion 137
Thematic progression 138
Parallelism and continuity of tenses/aspects 143

7 Annotating register 150

Field of discourse 151
    The process 151
    Participants 152
    Circumstances 153
Tenor of discourse 157
    Formality versus informality 157
    Personalization versus impersonalization 157
    Accessibility versus inaccessibility 157
    Politeness: Social distance versus standing 158
Mode of discourse 161

8 Annotating pragmatic, semiotic and stylistic aspects 168

Aspects of pragmatics 169
Aspects of semiotics 175
Aspects of stylistics 180

9 Annotating cultural and ideological issues 190

Culture 190
Ideology 197

10 Annotation into action 210

Introduction 210
Rationale 211
Language role and register 211
Text type and genre 212
Readership 214
Purpose of translation 214
Global strategy 215
Translation 215
Annotation 217
References 224

References 226
Index 239

Acknowledgments

In addition to my students, both past and present, whose challenges and difficulties in annotating their own translation and commenting on others' I have attempted to address, I would like to thank my colleagues at the Dept. of Translation (College of Arts, University of Basra) and at the Foreign Languages Dept. (College of Arts and Sciences, University of Nizwa) for their meticulous feedback on the manuscript.

My special thanks are due to Fred Pragnell and Mike Hall, who offered valuable insights into and guidance on the many and varied aspects of the linguistic and analytical challenges of translating Arabic.

Further, I would like to thank the BA and MA students of Arabic< >English translation over the years at the University of Durham (UK), the University of Westminster (UK), the University of Nizwa (the Sultanate of Oman) and the University of Basra (Iraq) whose translation projects with their permission have been used as a major source of translation examples used in this book.

Finally, the author and publisher would like to thank Sayyab Books Ltd for permission to reproduce material from Muḥammed Khuḏayyir's story حكايات يوسف *Joseph's Tales*, 'Abdul-Raḥmān al-Rubai'ī's story ذلك الأنين *Groaning*, Karīm 'Abid's story غرام السيدة (ع) *The Passion of Lady A*, Muḥsin Al-Ramlī's story البحث عن قلب حيّ *Search for a Live Heart*, Abdul-Sattār Nāṣir's story ثلاث قصص ليست للنشر *Three Stories Not for Publishing* and Haifā' Zangana's story مثوى *Dwelling*.

Introduction

The Routledge Course in Translation Annotation: Arabic-English-Arabic is an academic textbook. The book is initially designed for those whose mother tongue is either Arabic or English and who have some knowledge in both linguistics and translation theories. As such, the intended readership for this book is postgraduate (MA and PhD students) and advanced BA students along with their translation instructors throughout the world. PhD students in translation and intercultural studies may also benefit from this book. Further, students of applied linguistics and contrastive studies may well benefit from the book. Nowadays, there are a great number of universities in the UK, United States, Canada, Australia and the Arab world that encourage MA students to translate and annotate their own translation in place of writing theses. The book is aimed at:

- raising awareness of the pitfalls specific to Arabic-English translation;
- increasing translators' competence in both translation practice and translation annotation; and
- developing and honing translators' competences (be they linguistic, translational, contrastive or evaluative).

The number of translation programmes grows exponentially worldwide at academic institutions, and teaching translation theories in a direct link with the actual act of translation (practice) has moved to centre stage in the translator education, particularly in the UK and the United States, but also worldwide. Despite this, translation students, in particular those who work on the language pair (Arabic-English), commonly complain about the scarcity of relevant translational data, in view of the fact that the entire Arab world often use one language pair (English-Arabic) in translation studies and translation practice. Further, despite the large number of translation programmes (at both the undergraduate and postgraduate levels) worldwide, very few academic publications take the language pair (Arabic-English) as their focus. Here are some:

- *English-Arabic/Arabic-English Translation: A Practical Guide* by Basil Hatim published by Saqi Books in 1997.
- *Thinking Arabic Translation* by James Dickins *et al*. published by Routledge in 2002.

2 *Introduction*

- *Translating Irony: An Interdisciplinary Approach with English and Arabic as a Case in Point* by Raymond Chakhachiro published by Sayyab Books Ltd in 2011.
- *Advanced Issues in Arabic-English Translation Studies* by Mohammed Farghal published by Kuwait University Press in 2012.
- *Arabic-English-Arabic Legal Translation* by Hanem El-Farahaty published by Routledge in 2014.

Unlike some of the publications mentioned, this book is in both directions (out of Arabic and into Arabic) and does not confine itself to a particular text type or a perspective. This book is different because it does not only conduct a linguistic analysis of translated texts at different levels, but it deals with theoretically informed perspectives from a practical point of view. That is, it employs current translation theories and other related perspectives and approaches to inform the actual act of translating based on ample textual data taken from authentic examples.

The idea of this book initially grew out of my students' clear need for a coursebook on translation annotation, as there is little published material on how to annotate their own translation and comment on others'.

The key features of the book

- It provides the readers (be they translation students or translation researchers) with a theoretical framework for annotating their own translation.
- It links some translation theories with the actual work of translators (be they trainees or professionals).
- It strikes a balance between theory and practice by linking theoretical claims to authentic translational data, thereby helping translation trainees/students annotate their own translations.
- It provides the readers with precise definitions of the terms that focus on the various processes and stages of the mechanisms of annotation and their relation with other terms in the field.
- It provides the readers with a list of recommended readings and resources for each of the topics under discussion.
- It provides the readers (be they students or instructors) with a range of supporting exercises.

The organization of the book

The organization followed in this book is a top-down one, starting from the macro level (such as text type, genre, readership and the like) to micro level such as local strategies (Chapter 3), grammar (Chapter 4) and lexical and phraseological choices (Chapter 5). Due to the strong tie between some local strategies discussed in Chapter 3 (such as transposition, modulation reordering, and so on) and grammar, grammatical issues are discussed before lexical and phraseological issues. However, the organization of Chapters 5 through 9 is largely hierarchical. The discussion starts with issues such as lexical and phraseological choices (Chapter 5) and grows in complexity, thus discussing issues such as textuality (Chapter 6), register (Chapter 7), pragmatics, semiotics and stylistics (Chapter 8) and culture and ideology (Chapter 9) – all these issues being viewed through the prism of translation. Finally, a text is translated and annotated (Chapter 10) in an attempt to provide the readers with a clear vision on how to annotate a whole text by integrating together and applying the theoretical elements presented in this book.

Notes on how to use the book

The book user, depending on his/her area of interest, expertise, research question(s) and so on, can select the chapters that respond to what they are looking for. For example, if they would like to translate a text from language *A* to language *B* and annotate it from, let us say, a pragmatic perspective, then they can go to Chapter 8 in this book and start familiarizing themselves with the area. However, sometimes translation students want to translate texts and annotate them from different perspectives, without confining themselves to a particular perspective. Then, in this case, they need to examine the entire book in search of forming a holistic picture on the main areas that may be annotated while translating.

Two key notations are employed when discussing translational data in this work:

- **comment**, which is used when commenting on others' translations (be they published or translated by others for the purpose of the current study);
- **annotation**, which is used to refer to the translations suggested by the author of this book.

The course is intended to fit into an academic timetable lasting 1 year. Each chapter needs at least 6 hours. Some of the assignments provided at the end of each chapter, apart from the first chapter as it focuses on defining the key terms, will be done at home whether individually or in group, depending on task *per se*. However, some other practical activities can be done in class under the supervision of the instructor. Instructors are also invited to adapt the examples and exercises that suit their individual purposes. Once a given topic is explained and understood, alternative texts can easily be used by both instructors and students.

Unless stated otherwise, the original texts and translations offered by others appear in the book in the way they do in the original publication, without any postediting on the author's part.

Each chapter has a wealth of features, such as an overview under the title *'In this chapter . . .'* outlining the main points and key terms as well as illustrative examples and some suggested activities.

The book does not confine itself to one direction but focuses on translations in both directions: translating from Arabic into English and *vice versa*. It features original materials taken from a wide range of sources, including:

- literary texts
- journalistic texts
- religious texts
- legal texts

4 *Introduction*

- technical texts
- advertisements

Further, materials related to this course can be obtained directly from *The Routledge Course in Translation Annotation* website at www.routledge.com/cw/almanna. The materials include:

- PowerPoint slides
- Further reading links
- Further assignments
- More research questions
- Further annotated texts

Main abbreviations used in the book

SL	source language
ST	source text
SLC	source language culture
TL	target language
TT	target text
TLC	target language culture

Transliteration system

The following Arabic transliteration system has been consistently employed throughout this book:

Arabic	Transliteration	Arabic	Transliteration
ء	ʾ	ط	ṭ
ب	b	ظ	ẓ
ت	t	ع	ʿ
ث	th	غ	gh
ج	j	ف	f
ح	ḥ	ق	q
خ	kh	ك	k
د	d	ل	l
ذ	dh	م	m
ر	r	ن	n
ز	z	ة/ـة	h
س	s	و	w
ش	sh	ي	y
ص	ṣ	ا / ى	a
ض	ḍ		

Vowels

Arabic		Transliteration
َ	fatḥah	a
ِ	kasrah	i
ُ	ḍammah	u
ا	alif	ā
ي	yaa'	ī
و	waaw	ū

Notes

- In the case of (ّ) *shaddah,* a consonant is doubled.
- The names of Arab authors whose works have been published in English are spelled as they appear on the publication without applying this transliteration system.
- Any Arab names that appear in quotations follow the transliteration system of the reference quoted and not the one listed here.
- Some names remain as they commonly appear in English and are not transliterated to avoid confusion: Mahfouz, Mohammed Choukri and so on.

1 Annotation – defining matters

> **In this chapter...**
>
> In this chapter, an attempt is made to reach a precise definition of the term 'annotation' focusing on the various processes and stages of the annotating mechanisms and such related terms as 'commenting', 'assessing', 'revising', 'editing', 'proofreading' and so forth on the one hand and placing the terms concerned in their right place according to Holmes's map. Further, another attempt will be made to show that annotation, like other translation activities, is characterized by subjectivity. The question that will be implicitly addressed in this chapter is: Can subjectivity be kept to a minimum?
>
> **Key issues**
>
> - Annotation
> - Assessment
> - Comment
> - Criticism
> - Evaluation
> - Reviewing
> - Revision
> - Subjectivity
> - Textual profile

Place of annotation and related issues

The whole discipline is divided into two main branches, viz. 'pure translation studies' and 'applied translation studies' (Holmes 1970/2004: 172–185; also discussed in Toury 1995; Baker and Malmkjær 1998; Munday 2001/2008/2012; Hatim 2001; Hatim and Munday 2004; Chakhachiro 2005 among others). The former deals with theoretical and descriptive studies, whereas the latter focuses on issues, such as translator training, translator aids and translation criticism. The

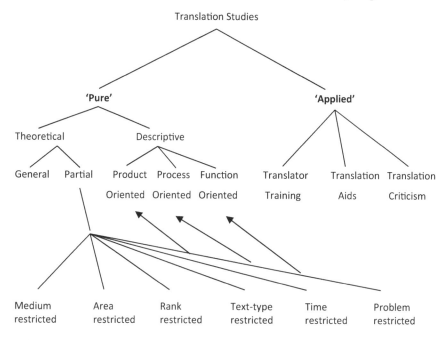

Holmes's basic map of translation studies (Toury 1995: 10)

figure above, received later from Gideon Toury (1995: 10), clearly shows these categories.

As the central focus of this study is on annotation, comment and other related issues, such as reviewing, assessment, evaluation and so on, attention is intentionally centred on applied translation studies, in particular translation criticism in the sense Holmes (1970/2004: 181–183) uses the term. As far as translation criticism is concerned, it is further subdivided by Holmes into revision, evaluation and reviews of translation. What is of greater importance, here, is that translation criticism (be it revision, evaluation or review) is retrospective in nature, and so are annotation and comment our main concern in the current study. Translation criticism utilizes principles of contrastive analysis, yet it is not aimed at studying differences between two languages. Rather, it focuses on equivalence or 'matches' and 'mismatches' between the source text (ST) and target text (TT). In spite of using similar principles and concerning themselves with the relationship between the ST and TT, the use of revision is concerned with the 'whys', whereas translation criticism concentrates on the 'whats' and 'hows' (Chakhachiro 2005: 227–228).

Building on the premise that translation criticism is conducted retrospectively, one cannot avoid adopting parameters that may be considered mainly subjective when conducting annotation, comment or comparative analysis (cf. Lauscher 2000; Reiss 2000; House 2001; Chakhachiro 2005). However, the reviewers' comments

8 *Annotation – defining matters*

and translators' annotations need to be systematic in order to control their own subjectivity and achieve consensus about an outcome.

Annotation is different from revision, reviewing, proofreading, editing, assessment or evaluation in the sense that annotation is conducted by the translator him/herself while facing a particular problem. The purpose of annotation is to defend the choices made by the translator; hence the importance of sensitizing trainee translators to the existence of such controversial issues and the local strategies that may be invoked to accommodate them. In the main body of the translation, the ST and TT can appear on facing pages, with notes at the bottom of the page (footnotes) or at the end (endnotes), but they do not have to. It seems likely that the majority of the notes will be on the translation side (be they on translation strategies, language role, aspects of pragmatics, aspects of textuality, cultural aspects, stylistic aspects or semiotic aspects; see next chapters in this book). However, the original text may be annotated also, especially with regard to grammatical difficulties or ambiguities.

When the text has already been translated, especially if it has been translated more than once, the annotations may also provide examples of the other translated versions. It is entirely appropriate to refer to translation theories where this provides a clue to the justification of a certain approach. An annotated translation should have a brief introduction presenting the text, indicating its interest and explaining what kinds of difficulties it might present. Getting this introduction just right is important: A short background to the original text and its author needs to be given by the translator prior to embarking on the actual act of annotating. Further, when the ST is in any way uncertain, an explanation needs to be provided of which text has been used or how it was determined. This applies particularly to older texts but not exclusively so. The introduction might well address the problem of what a translation is, dealing with some theoretical points and suggesting particular problems inherent in translating between the two languages concerned or dealing with the text type (for more details, see next chapter).

Annotation and related issues

Linguistically speaking, annotation derives from the verb 'annotate', which means to add explanatory notes, supply a work with critical commentary or explanatory notes or provide interlinear explanations for words or phrases. Its synonyms include 'comment' (cf. Longman Dictionary of Contemporary English 1987/1995: 33). However, in this study, a distinction is made between the term 'annotation' and its synonym 'comment'. While 'comment' is used when commenting on others' translations, 'annotation' is used to refer to the critical notes offered by translators on their own translations. Further, annotation should not be confused with a translation with a lot of footnotes and/or endnotes. As such, annotation can be envisaged as a reflection. To sum up, annotation for translation purposes is used to explain the decisions taken by the translator. Obviously, therefore, they should not be used sparingly in this case, as the absence of a note might be taken as indicating that a difficulty or obscurity had not been properly understood.

When doing translation-oriented analysis in order to annotate one's own translation or comment on somebody's translation, one needs to distinguish between obligatory features and optional features. Obligatory features involve choices that must be followed by the translator in order to satisfy the rules imposed by the target language (TL) system, without which the translation will be ungrammatical. However, optional features represent cases in which the translator can exercise real choice by deciding on one translation option rather than another/others. Annotation is needed by translators when translating a segment that leaves them with more than one option to follow. In this case, the translator starts a series of actions, including analyzing the ST, highlighting the elements that need to be reflected in the TT and prioritizing among the competing elements. Hence the need for annotation to persuade their readers that they are aware of other options but opted for this particular local strategy or a combination of many local strategies in rendering the text at hand for a particular reason. Annotation is a common method of reflection.

With regard to revision, scholars' views on revision can be reduced to two main perspectives:

1   the revision should be conducted by a person other than the translator (cf. Dickins *et al.* 2002; Samuelsson-Brown 2004; Chakhachiro 2005; British Standards Institution; Mossop 2007a, 2007b; Robert 2008 among others) and
2   the revision should be conducted by the translator him/herself (cf. Sedon-Strutt 1990; Sager 1994; Yi-yi Shih 2006; Mossop 2007a among others).

Building on the assumption that everybody agrees a translator has to check his/her own work before submitting it to a client and/or translation project manager, this binary subdivision is rather fake and ambiguous.

As for identifying the *persona* of the reviser, it is strictly connected to identifying the moment in time at which the revision process has to be carried out; in other words 'who' is the reviser also depends and is interrelated with the discussion on at 'which level' of the translation process revision is expected to take place. According to the BSEN15038:2006 standard (British Standards Institution 2006: 11), revising translation is a compulsory stage in a professional and quality-oriented translation process at its macro level, and it should be conducted by a person other than the translator. Mossop (2007a: 6) speaks of two types of revision: unilingual and comparative revision. When conducting a unilingual revision, the reviser focuses on the TT as a text in its own right in order to determine any unidiomatic and incorrect use of language, any textual errors and the like and only checks with the ST occasionally. This procedure is similar, to a certain degree, to what an editor does (see editing later in this section). When conducting a comparative revision, the reviser, however, checks the TT in terms of accuracy and completeness by comparing it with the ST (cf. Rasmussen and Schojoldager 2011: 90). When the procedure is conducted by the translator him/herself, it is not revision anymore; it is named checking by BSEN15038:2006 standard (British Standards Institution 2006: 11):

> On completion of the initial translation, the translator shall check his/her own work. This process shall include checking that the meaning has been conveyed, that there are no omissions or errors and that the defined service specifications have been met. The translator shall make any necessary amendments.

Checking, in the sense BSEN15038:2006 standard uses the term, is labeled 'self-assessment' by Santos and Gomes (2006) and 'self-revision' by Mossop (2007a, 2007b). Santos and Gomes (2006: 49) stress: "In essence, every individual performs self-assessment"; here they talk about self-assessment that is conducted by the person on his/her work, so the level of the process is a micro level. This ability of self-assessing, as they indicate, "may contribute to the self-construction of a trajectory that allows him/her to overcome obstacles". Self-assessment "is a competency that is worth constructing" in order to sidestep a "spontaneous assessment" with a view to having "an intentional control system regarding one's performances" (Santos and Gomes: Ibid.).

Regardless of the term used, there are two different procedures at the macro level of the translation process: one is conducted by the translator him/herself and the other is conducted later by a person other than the translator. In translation studies, a variety of terms have been used to refer to these two procedures. The former has been termed 'checking' (Graham 1989; Samuelsson-Brown 2004; British Standards Institution 2006), 'self-revision' (Sedon-Strutt 1990; Yi-yi Shih 2006; Mossop 2007a, 2007b), 'self-correction' (Mizon and Dieguez 1996) and 'self-assessment' (Santos and Gomes 2006), while the latter has been termed 'revision' (Sager 1994; Brunette 2000; Lauscher 2000; Dickins *et al.* 2002; Chakhachiro 2005; Yi-yi Shih 2006), 'other-revision' (Mossop 2007a, 2007b), 'bilingual revision' (Horguelin and Brunette 1998 cited in Robert 2008) and 'revision of translation' (Sedon-Strutt 1990). However, in the current study, they are termed 'checking' and 'revision', respectively.

The processes of revision, whether conducted by the translator him/herself, that is, checking, or conducted by other than the translator, that is, revision, involve a qualitative, heuristic decision making (cf. Wilss 1996; Chakhachiro 2005).

Having distinguished between revision (i.e., a procedure conducted by someone other than the translator) and checking (i.e., a procedure conducted by the translator him/herself), now let us turn our focus of attention towards other terms, such as 'assessment' and 'evaluation'. 'Assessment' and 'evaluation' have been used by a great number of scholars as synonyms of each other, although this has not been clearly indicated (cf. Maier 2000: 137). Lauscher (2000: 162) roughly defines "evaluation as a procedure in which an evaluating person compares an actual target text to a more or less implicit, 'ideal' version of the target text, in terms of which the actual target text is rated and judged". In the light of the definition provided by Lauscher, this procedure "consists of three elements which influence judgement: the evaluating subject, the object, the model target text" (Ibid.).

Annotation – defining matters 11

Annotation, revision and evaluation/assessment share the fact that they are all bidirectional and, also, require the person who annotates/comments/revises/assesses to comprehend the content of the ST, identify the challenges that a translator may face and be aware of the available local strategies that a translator may opt for.

However, they differ in their own purpose. The purpose of annotation, as stated, is to defend the choices made by the translator. However, the evaluation/assessment seeks "to measure the degree of efficiency of the text with regard to the syntactic, semantic and pragmatic function of ST within the cultural frame and expressive potentials of both source language and target language" (Al-Qinai 2000: 499). Revision, for its turn, is part of a quality-control process, aiming at ensuring translation quality (cf. Chackachiro 2005: 225). Also, revision differs from assessment/evaluation in the sense that revision always occurs during the translation process at its macro level, while assessment/evaluation may happen during the translation process at its macro level or at times after submitting the translated text to the translation teacher, translation project manager, client and so on. When the client him/herself evaluates the TT by comparing it with the ST, the process is called validation (cf. Robert 2008). The text can only be validated if it has been assessed and evaluated as 'fit for purpose', 'adequate', 'appropriate', 'faithful' or in line with the specs for the job as commissioned.

Further, revision, proofreading and editing are different in the sense that revision is a bidirectional process on bilingual texts while both proofreading and editing are unilingual. Proofreaders normally concern themselves with language-related issues, such as spelling, punctuation, grammar and so on. By contrast, what concerns editors is how to achieve the "optimum orientation" of the proofread and revised TT to live up to the target reader's expectations (Graham 1983: 104) by exploiting the lexical, syntactic and stylistic norms of the TL to the fullest. In this regard, Mossop (2007a: 120) lists four criteria that should be taken into account by translation editors. They are posed in the form of questions that editors should ask themselves:

1 Are there some parts of the text which will not be of interest to the target readership?
2 Do several paragraphs have to be eliminated to make the text fit into the allotted space?
3 Is the writing lively and interesting? A translation may be accurate, idiomatic and authentic, but nevertheless make for rather dull reading.
4 Is the content appropriate to the genre? (Mossop 2007a: 120)

In his list of criteria, in particular the first one, it seems that Mossop, focusing on the translation of governmental papers to be used in the workings of institutions and departments, does not concern himself with literary texts. However, in an attempt to distinguish between editing and rewriting, Mossop (2007a: 30) rightly comments:

> When editing, you start from an existing text and make changes in its wording. Sometimes, however, the existing text is so badly written that it is easier

to abandon the existing wording and re-express the text's content with newly composed sentences and possibly a new text structure. This is rewriting.

It is worth noting here that rewriting occurs when the person does his/her job without any reference to the ST. Otherwise, this approach is termed retranslation not rewriting. As such, terms such as 'annotation', 'checking', 'revision', 'proofreading', 'editing', 'validation', 'rewriting', 'retranslation' and 'assessment/evaluation' can be defined in the current chapter by paying special attention to the following points as shown in Table 1.1:

1. the person conducting the procedure: the same person as the original translator or a different or more senior translator;
2. the time of conducting the procedure: during the translation process at its micro or macro level;
3. the level of the translation process: macro level or micro level;
4. whether referring to the original text or not; and
5. the purpose of the procedure.

Procedure	Person	Timing	Level	With or without the ST	Purpose
Checking	The translator	During	Micro	With	To go through the translation checking issues related to language, consistency, accuracy, completeness, comprehension, style, strategy and presentation in an attempt to improve the TT prior to submitting it
Revision	Not the translator: reviser	During	Macro	With	To ensure translation quality as part of an overall quality-control process
Proofreading	Not the translator: proofreader	During	Macro	Without	To reduce the number of linguistic errors in the TT, such as spelling, punctuation, grammar, consistency and the like
Editing	Not the translator: editor	During	Macro	Without	To achieve optimum orientation of the proofread and revised translated text to live up to the target reader's expectations (cf. Graham 1983: 104; Belhaaj 1998: 85)

Validation	Not the translator: client	After	No matter	With	To check that all contents have been transferred accurately
Rewriting	Not the translator: editor	During	Macro	Without	To produce a better text in terms of readability, living up to the target reader's expectations
Retranslation	Another translator	During	Macro	With	To produce a better translation in terms of accuracy and acceptability
Assessment/ evaluation	Not the translator: assessor or evaluator	During/ after	No matter	With	To measure the degree of efficiency of the TT with regard to the syntactic, semantic and pragmatic function of the ST within the cultural frame and expressive potentials of both the SL and TL
Annotation	The translator	During/ after	Micro	With	To explain with the aim of defending the choices made by the translator

Quality from different perspectives

It is worth noting that the actual practice of translation quality differs from one person to another, according to his/her linguistic, translational and communicative competences as well as his/her background, skills and experiences. As such, quality can be judged differently from different perspectives – quality from a critic's perspective, quality from a TL reader's perspective, quality from a publisher's perspective, quality from an editor's perspective and quality from a researcher's perspective. This entails that annotations and comments can be judged differently, too.

As people are different in perceiving world reality, in their tolerance to the pressure exerted on them, in their reaction to such pressure and in their beliefs, feelings, cultural background, ideologies, attitudes, mentality, idiosyncrasies, experiences and skills, such a selection among available strategies is subjective rather than objective, being ascribed to people's ideology, idiolect, competences, experiences, skills and social and religious background. In this regard, Al-Rubai'i (1996: 56) rightly comments that

> the elements of subjectivity can never be avoided neither in monolingual communication nor in bilingual communication involving translation. But the presence of subjectivity should not annul the necessity of translation criticism [. . .].

The translation process in this chapter is envisaged as a dynamic activity, achieved by a number of people, not a process performed by the translator only.

14 *Annotation – defining matters*

To show that in spite of the number of steps and procedures that may be taken to avoid subjectivity, the elements of subjectivity still impose themselves, a research corpus consisting of an original Arabic text and its English different versions will be used here. The ST ذلك الأنين *Dhālik al-Anīn 'Groaning'* was written by 'Abdul-Raḥmān al-Rubaiʿī. The text was translated first by an Arab professional translator holding a PhD degree in linguistics and translation, and then it was retranslated by an English native speaker holding an MA in linguistics who has translated some literary works from Arabic into English. So this supposedly gave them the first hand experience in bringing issues related to translation into the fore, and this put them in better situations to discuss and uncover the larger cultural context of problems with which translators constantly grapple. The participants who voluntarily and happily agreed to take part in the translation of this text are six people: an Arab translator (henceforth called First Translator), an English translator (henceforth called Second Translator), a reviser whose mother tongue is English and mastering Arabic (henceforth called Reviser) and three native speakers of English to express their own impressions on the draft translations without referring to the ST (henceforth called Native Speakers). By way of clarification, let us consider the following example quoted from research corpus:

ST

حلمان تداخلا مع حلمك في أن أحدا قد إغتالني وذهبت، سدد إلي إطلاقات مسدسه ونخرني نخرا، وكنت تصرخين لعل أحدا يأتي ولكن صراخك يتردد في واد لا رائحة فيه لآدمي.

Textual Profile:

- **First Translation:**

Two dreams intervened into your dream. Someone killed me. He pointed his gun towards me and all the bullets went straight through me. You were crying for help but your cry resounded through a valley where no human being was around.

- **Second Translation:**

Two dreams intervened into your dream. Someone killed me and you (??) went away. He pointed his gun towards me and filled me full. You were crying for help but your cry resounded through a valley where there was no human being.

- **First Translator's Comments:**

  - Man wakes from a dream about falling into a pit then has another dream about snakes and a spider. 'Then two dreams intervened into your dream' . . . then I got shot. This is followed by the narration of events of the man with his partner (wife?) at a funeral

and then in the desert with crows. The end! There seems to be no resolution to the story of the man waking up.
- Suggestion: You (went away and) were crying for help but your cry resounded through a valley where there was no human being.
- Question: He pointed his gun towards me and *filled me full*?

- **Second Translator's Comments:**

Wonderfully ingenious! It's a pity we cannot ask Sigmund Freud for his interpretation.

Two dreams intervened into your dream. Someone killed me and you went away. He pointed his gun towards me and filled me full of holes. You were crying for help but your cry resounded through a valley where there was no human being.

- **Final Translation of Both Translators:**

Two dreams intervened into your dream. Someone killed me and you went away. He pointed his gun towards me and filled me full of holes. You were crying for help but your cry resounded through a valley where there was no human being.

- **Reviser's Version:**

Two dreams intertwined into your dream in that someone had assassinated me, but you left. He pointed his gun at me and filled me full of holes. You were screaming perhaps someone would come, but your scream resounded through a valley where there was no trace of anyone.

- **Reviser's Comments:**

The ST is vague here in that we, as the audience, do not know what she was screaming. The other translations had cleared this up, stating, 'you were crying for help', but in actuality, she was screaming something and there was a possibility that someone would hear and come.

- **Native Speaker's Impression:**

Impression one:

Final translation of both translators is the better, however, "You were crying for help but your cry resounded through a valley where there were no human beings" would be more correct.

Impression two:

Unsure of the 1st correction [in the reviser's version] as both verbs have different meanings. Disagree with 2nd change – a hyphen would suit better.

16 *Annotation – defining matters*

> 3rd and 4th changes would depend on context. Agree with 5th amendment. Change 'full of' to 'with'. Agree with 'screaming', though not with the rest of the 6th amendment. Agree with the 7th change.
>
> **Impression three:**
>
> Collocation problems. Foreign word patterns, for example 'Dreams intervened', 'pointed gun towards me', 'filled me full of holes', 'there was no human being', 'your scream resounded'.

In selecting the native speakers to act as readers here, the following points were taken into account to guarantee the effectiveness of such a step. These are (1) how seriously they take their task (i.e., the significance of their work depends on the seriousness with which they deal with the process of validation of one prose over another), (2) whether they appreciate literature, in general and foreign literature in particular and (3) whether they are well trained in appreciating the series of events and their developments in a particular activity in one culture and accommodating these events in their own cultural environment. This is in line with Venuti's (n.y.) view that translations need to read "with an eye out for the translator's work, with the awareness that the most a translation can give you is an insightful and eloquent interpretation of a foreign text, at once limited and enabled by the need to address the receiving culture" (www.wordswithoutborders.org). This, in particular, requires them, in the first place, to comprehend the processes of the events and their developments in the source language (SL) cultural environment and then imaginatively compare them to corresponding events and their developments in a particular activity but in a different cultural environment, that is, their own cultural environment. So the readers in general and the selected readers herein in particular heavily rely on their reaction in such an exercise. Failing to do so may indicate that they may not have a complete understanding of the community being represented or, indeed, may have preconceived notions about the particular society that are quite at variance, if not in conflict, with the realities of the situation. In a very successful rendering, we do not expect readers to react in a similar way as do the original receivers for whom the ST is originally intended.

With regard to the person in charge of assessing/evaluating others' versions and comments, s/he should be a person who is able to weigh out the selected readers' impressions by comparing the ST with the TT concerning the points raised by the selected readers. Such ability requires him/her to possess or be trained in specific competences, such as translational, linguistic, communicative, cultural and technical competence, not to mention his/her translating experience in the domain under consideration (see BSEN-15038 European Quality Standard for Translation Services, paragraph 3.2.2, 2006: 7). Otherwise, only the readers' comments on the TL itself, such as grammar, punctuation and so on can be appreciated.

To further demonstrate how the same text can be translated differently, justified differently and defended differently, let us consider the following extracts quoted from 'Abdul-Raḥmān al-Rubai'ī's story ذلك الأنين *Dhālik al-Anīn 'Groaning'*.

Method of presentation of analysis

Prior to presenting the ST along with the first translation and the second translation, a short background to the ST and its author is given. This is then followed by an analysis of both translations. In the analysis of the text in this chapter, first, the ST is presented. Then a structured discussion follows in an attempt to form a textual profile that can be consulted by the researcher (in the current study) and the person in charge of translation quality control in a real-life situation. The final version will be presented according to the textual profile constructed for each text segment, irrespective of the researcher's opinion. Whenever necessary, particularly in the event of unsettled issues, the final version is followed by the researcher's comments. These comments are presented here to show that the practice of translation quality is a never-ending activity and differs from one person to another (according to his/her linguistic, translational and communicative competences as well as his/her background, skills and experience) and from one perspective to another (be it a translator, publisher, editor, target language reader, researcher and so on).

Further, the ST is divided into smaller parts containing a sentence or a group of related sentences reflecting a complete idea. This is to make the task of the analysis easier and enable the reader to follow the thread of argumentation more easily. As for the two translations that were sent to the native speakers to provide the researcher with their impressions, they are referred to henceforth as the 'final translation of both translators' and 'reviser's version'. However, when they were sent to the native speakers, they were named 'first translation' and 'second translation', respectively. This is to avoid any connotation that might be associated with the word 'reviser'. The discussion of these unsettled issues, which follows the presentation of the ST along with the first translation and the second translation, will be presented as follows:

- the source text (ST);
- the first translation;
- the second translation;
- the first translator's comments (if any);
- the second translator's comments (if any);
- the final translation of both translators;
- the reviser's version;
- the reviser's comments (if any);
- the native speakers' impression;
- the final version;
- the researcher's comments;
- the suggested version.

About the author

The text is written by the leading Iraqi writer 'Abdul-Raḥmān al-Rubai'ī. After studying painting in Baghdad, 'Abdul-Raḥmān al-Rubai'ī worked as director of the Iraqi Cultural Centre in Beirut and Tunisia. His publications include

18 *Annotation – defining matters*

السيف والسفينة *al-Saīf wa al-Safīnah* 'The Sword and the Ship', a collection of short stories (1966), الظل في الرأس *al-Ẓil fī al-Raā's* 'The Shadow in the Head', a collection of short stories (1986), الوشم *al-Washim* 'The Tattoo', a novel (1972), عيون في الحلم *'Uyūn fī al-Ḥilim* 'Eyes in the Dream', a collection of short stories (1974), and ذاكرة المدينة *Dhākirat al-Madīnah* 'The Memory of the City', a collection of short stories (1975), among others.

About the story

The story ذلك الأنين *Dhālik al-Anīn* 'Groaning' was published in 2009 in a collection of short stories under the title *'Modern Iraqi Short Stories'*. The text used in this chapter comes from the first part of the story, which is divided into two unrelated parts by the writer, who numbers but does not name them. The first part is built on three dreams narrated by the main character. In the first dream, he was being chased by strange beasts with open jaws. The place was filled with rocks and pits. When he fell into one of them, he was surrounded by hooded men wielding axes, trying to prevent him from getting out of the pit. In the second dream, he imagined himself in a large, cold and desolate room. On the bare floor, there was a nest of small snakes intertwined around one another because of the cold, but he was not afraid, as he assured himself that they were just house snakes. However, his calm turned into panic when he saw a large spider. The spider in the dream was so large that it survived the attack with the hammer until it finally breathed its last. In his third dream, somebody opened fire on him and killed him while his partner was screaming for help, but her screams resounded in vain through the valley before them. It is clear that the story embodies the main character's sufferings that are reflected clearly in his dreams or, more accurately, his nightmares. These three dreams may be understood as implicit references to the sufferings of Iraqis during Saddam Hussein's regime. The language is referential, focusing on the message itself and its implicit references.

Example 1:

ST:

أستفيق من حلمي، أشعل المصباح المنضدي، ثم أسكب من زجاجة الماء في الكأس، أكرع الماء بسرعة لأبعد عن حلقي التخشب واليبوسة

- **First Translation:**

I woke up from my dream, switched on the table lamp, poured a glass of water from the bottle, drank it quickly to moisten my dry throat.

- **Second Translation:**

I woke up from my dream, switched on the table lamp, poured a glass of water from the bottle and sipped it quickly to moisten my rough, parched throat.

- **First Translator's Comments:** no comment.
- **Second Translator's Comments:** no comment.
- **Final Translation of Both Translators:**

I woke up from my dream, switched on the table lamp, poured a glass of water from the bottle and sipped it quickly to get rid of the dryness and roughness from my throat.

- **Reviser's Version:**

I awaken from my dream, switch on the table lamp, pour a glass of water from the bottle and sip it quickly to relieve my throat of dryness and roughness.

- **Reviser's Comments:**

In some cases the changes that I made follow the ST more closely, such as the verb tense in the beginning paragraphs. The ST author chose to use the present tense, therefore the verb tense should be, in the best of circumstances, mirrored in the TT.

1   'relieve' collocates with 'dry throat' while 'get rid of' does not (see Note 2).

- **Native Speaker's Impression:**

Impression One:

The final version of both translators is the better English, although *'I awoke from my dream'* would have been more correct.

Impression Two:

Like both translations, though the difference in tenses should be noted.

Impression Three:

1st one sounds natural. 2nd one has grammatical mistakes. The first one is in the past tense, whereas the second one states 'I awaken' which means to wake someone up as opposed to 'awake' which is the correct form. Also, word usage is strange – 'relieve my throat' sounds foreign. We'd say 'soothe my throat'. Also, we wouldn't say 'roughness' of the throat, rather we would say 'hoarseness'.

Final Version:

I wake up from my dream, switch on the table lamp, pour a glass of water from the bottle and sip it quickly to soothe my throat of dryness and hoarseness.

Comment

(a) Here, had the translators/reviser paid extra attention to the stylistic features, such as the length of the sentences, the thematic progression and the parallelism in the extract, they could have come up with a translation that reflects all these stylistic features. The first two sentences in the ST استفيق من حلمي، أشعل المصباح المنضدي '*I wake up from my dream + I switch on the table lamp*' are produced as two independent sentences joined by a comma, indicating that there is no time span between the two events. However, the third sentence ثم أسكب من زجاجة الماء '*then, I pour from the bottle*' is used with a connector ثم '*then*', thereby generating a sort of feeling that there is probably a time span between the act of pouring a glass of water and the preceding two acts, waking up and switching on the lamp. This is completely lost in the final translation offered by the two translators and the reviser's version, who opted for a series of sequences of events. From a textual point of view, there is a strong relationship between the syntactic structures and the pace of events (cf. Shen 1987). As such, the way in which the syntactic units are presented in the text, whether subordinated or coordinated to one another and whether with connectors, punctuation marks and so on, should be taken into account, as it has "a role to play in determining the pace of the processes involved" (Shen 1987: 185).

(b) As for the translation of the original verb بَعَدَ '*lit. to distance*', it was translated differently by the parties involved in translating the extract: the first translator (*to 'moisten' my throat*), the second translator (*to 'moisten' my throat*), both translators (*to 'get rid of' the dryness and roughness from my throat*), the reviser (*to 'relieve' my throat*) and one of the readers (*to 'soothe' my throat*). In fact, taking into account the context in which it is used and the co-text as well as the collocation chains used by the original writer, one would suggest '*get rid of*', as it reflects more effectively the idiom of the original Arabic. Also, one would stick to '*roughness*' instead of '*hoarseness*', as the latter usually refers to roughness of voice, not throat.

Suggested Version:

I wake up from my dream; I switch on the table lamp. Then, I pour a glass of water from the bottle; I sip it so quickly to get rid of the dryness and roughness in my throat.

Example 2:

ST:
ثم سقطت في إحداها، لم أعد قادرا على الخروج، قوة ساعدي لم تسعفني، وعندما أفلحت أحاط بي رجال ملثمون يتبادلون كلمات مبهمة ويستحثون بعضهم عليّ،

Annotation – defining matters 21

- **First Translation:**

Then I fell into one of them. I was unable to get out. The strength of my forearm did not help me, but when I made it, I was surrounded by veiled men exchanging obscure words and encouraging some of them to attack me.

- **Second Translation:**

Then I fell into one of them and was unable to get out. The strength of my forearm did not help me, and when I had some luck, I was surrounded by hooded men exchanging strange words and urging one another on to attack me.

- **First Translator's Comments:** no comments.
- **Second Translator's Comments:** no comments.
- **Final Translation of Both Translators:**

Then I fell into one of them and was unable to get out. The strength of my forearm did not help me, and when I did have some luck, I was surrounded by hooded men exchanging strange words and urging one another on to attack me.

- **Reviser's Version:**

Then I fell into one of them; unable to get out. The strength of my forearm did not help me. When I did make it out, hooded men surrounded me exchanging strange words, urging one another to attack me.

- **Reviser's Comments:**

The other translations had changed the agent of the sentence from 'hooded men surrounded me' to 'I was surrounded by hooded men'. There is no need to switch to passive voice in English when the Arabic used active voice, which in most cases is much stronger and powerful.

- **Native Speaker's Impression:**

Impression One:

Final translation of both translators is the better English, but *'urging one another to attack me'* would have been more grammatically correct.

Impression Two:

Like both versions, though the amendments made in the reviser's version make the paragraph flow well.

> **Impression Three:**
>
> Both sound pretty well the same meaning but the final translation of both translators would be better for a literature book. It reads to me as being more descriptive.

Final Version:

Then I fell into one of them and was unable to get out. The strength of my forearm did not help me, and when I did have some luck, some hooded men surrounded me exchanging strange words, urging one another to attack me.

Comment

(a) Here, it is worth noting that passive and active voices in transitivity choices are not identical. Rather, they have different functions and effects and reflect different points of view and ideologies. In this regard, Ghazala (2011: 101) comments:

> Active and passive are two different styles of language, both grammatically and semantically. They have different meanings and perform different actions and functions in language. They are not identical in the sense of being interchangeable, for they enact completely different function. Their occurrence and existence in language grammar as two different forms entails their independence from one another. Also, since they have different forms, functions and implications, they have to be considered as two different styles.

The ST actor of the material processes in the fifth, sixth and seventh clauses in the example, ... أحاط بي رجال ملثمون is sharply determined by the original writer, viz. رجال ملثمون, *'hooded men'*. As such and as long as the TL stylistically accepts the active form in such a context, there is no need to change it into a passive form.

(b) The length of the sentences and the way they are presented in the ST should be taken into account in translating the above extract (cf. Ghazala 2011: 164). In his first three sentences, the original writer strongly insists on his ideas by producing unconnected, short, past-tense sentences, one after another. Such types of sentences "could be heard as an insistent hammering home of the point hammer-blow by hammer-blow" (Haynes 1995: 32). However, he subordinates the last two clauses by using the connector عندما *'when'*. The complexity and simplicity of the structures of language used in the text reflect the degree of formality that, in turn, determines, among other elements, the tenor of discourse. The attention that is given to the structures of language by the writer and/or speaker can be measured by way of formality versus informality: a lot of "attention leads to more care in writing and this marks the text as possessing a higher degree of formality and signals a more distant relationship between sender and receiver(s)" (Bell 1991: 186). As such, this formality, as opposed to informality, that in a way or another influences the tenor of discourse needs to be taken into account by translators when rendering the text at hand.

(c) As for the translation of the third sentence قوة ساعدي لم تسعفني *'the strength of my forearm did not help me'*, one can opt for a less literal translation and complete restructuring of the sentence to offer an idiom more familiar to the target readership and yet still in keeping with the ST register, such as *'my arm was not strong enough to help me get out'*.

Suggested Version:

Then, I fell into one of them; I was unable to get out. My arm was not strong enough to help me get out. When I did have some luck, some hooded men surrounded me exchanging strange words, urging one another to attack me.

Example 3:

ST:

كل واحد منهم يحمل فأسا ينزلها عليّ، كلما إقتربت من الخروج، آلاتهم الحادة هذه أقابلها بيدي، قاتلتهم، قاتلتهم، حتى مضوا عني، فجأة كفوا، تبادلوا كلمات ثم إنسحبوا، بعدها صحوت.

- **First Translation:**

Every one of them was holding an ax pointing it towards me to hit me with whenever I was close to getting out. I defended myself against their sharp tools by my hands. I fought them; I fought them until they left me. Suddenly, they stopped. They exchanged some words and withdrew. Then I woke up.

- **Second Translation:**

They were all holding axes pointing down towards me to hit me with whenever I was close to getting out. I warded off their sharp weapons with my hands. I fought them; I fought them until they left me. Suddenly, they stopped. They exchanged some words and then withdrew. At this point I woke up.

- **First Translator's Comments:** no comments
- **Second Translator's Comments:** no comments
- **Final Translation of Both Translators:**

They were all holding axes pointing down towards me to hit me with whenever I was close to getting out. I warded off their sharp weapons with my hands. I fought them; I fought them until they left me. Suddenly, they stopped. They exchanged some words and then withdrew. At this point I woke up.

24 *Annotation – defining matters*

> - **Reviser's Version:**
>
> *Every one of them wielded an axe bringing it down upon me whenever I came close to getting away. I met their sharp weapons with my hands. I fought them; I fought them until they left me be. Suddenly, they had stopped. They exchanged some words, then withdrew. At this point I woke up.*
>
> - **Reviser's Comments:** no comments
> - **Native Speaker's Impression:**
>
> Impression one:
>
> Neither translation is correct. How would you defend against axes with bare hands? In both translations 'I fought them until they left me. Suddenly, they stopped' surely they would have stopped & then left.
>
> Impression two:
>
> Prefer the reviser's version with amendments, though the 5th amendment should be 'let me be'
>
> Impression three:
>
> 2nd one more concise, better choice of words. Language is more idiomatic. Examples of more idiomatic, 'wielding an axe', 'getting away' however the phrase 'warded off' in the 1st one sounds more idiomatic. Also, 'pointing down towards me' and 'bringing down upon me' both sound foreign. I think 'aimed at my head' 'directed towards the direction of my head', 'directed towards me' all sound more natural.

Final Version:

Every one of them wielded an axe bringing it down upon me whenever I came close to getting away. I warded off their sharp weapons with my hands. I fought them; I fought them until they left – they had stopped suddenly. They exchanged some words, then, withdrew. At this point, I woke up.

Comment

(a) Attention should be paid to the consistency of verb tenses. In the ST, a combination of both past (or perfect) tense, expressed by صحوت، انسحبوا، تبادلوا، كفوا، مضوا، قاتلتهم، اقتربت and present (or imperfect) tense, expressed by verbs such as أقابل, يحمل, ينزل and so on, is used. However, the emphasis in the original sentences is on the completion of the action, except in the first sentence, where the emphasis is put on the continuity of the action in a specific period of time, which is expressed by an implicit كان plus a verb in the present يحمل 'lit. *to carry*'. Such a shift in aspect from a past tense to a present tense in the ST should be taken into consideration by the translation controller, as it does produce a change in time reference and continuity, which in turn will affect the pragmatic communicative effect.

(b) The ambiguity in the ST that is raised due to the illogical sequences of events ... قاتلتهم، قاتلتهم، حتى مضوا عني، فجأة كفوا can be disambiguated when being read aloud as if being uttered in a spoken mode of discourse. Only then can one conceptualize how to affect the transfer to the TT – hence the use of a hyphen, the past perfect tense in English to emphasize the time sequence of the events described and the marked positioning of the adverb *'suddenly'* at the end of the clause.

(c) In the ST, there is an example of repetition قاتلتهم، قاتلتهم *'I fought them; I fought them'*. This repetition in such a text type should be paid extra attention by translators. It is normally used by writers and/or speakers for different functions, effects and purposes. In this regard, Ghazala (2011: 175) rightly comments,

> in texts where a high degree of accuracy is demanded (e.g. religious [or legislative] texts), or a close cognitive reading and conceptualisation is expected (e.g. literary texts), attendance to the style of repetition is a must.

Suggested Version:

Every one of them was wielding an axe bringing it down upon me whenever I came close to getting away. I warded off their sharp weapons with my hands. I fought them; I fought them until they left – they had stopped suddenly. They exchanged some words, then, withdrew. At this point, I woke up.

Example 4:

ST:

كأس ماء أخرى والحمى في الرأس والإرتجاف يقتلع الجسد. هذا هو حلمي الأول وعندما عدت للنوم دخلت في حلم آخر. كأنه كان ينتظرني ما أن إنطبقت أجفاني حتى جاءني، خلتني في غرفة واسعة. تغط بالبرودة والوحشة

- **First Translation:**

Another glass of water, fever in the head, the shivers ripped the body apart. This was my first dream. When I went back to sleep, I dreamt once more. It seemed as if the dream was waiting for me. It came to me as soon as I closed my eyelids. I imagined myself in a large cold and desolate room.

- **Second Translation:**

Another glass of water, fever in the head and a shiver ripped through the body. This was my first dream. When I went back to sleep, I had another dream. It seemed as if the dream had been waiting for me. It came to me as soon as I closed my eyelids. I imagined myself in a large cold and desolate room.

- **First Translator's Comments:** no comments
- **Second Translator's Comments:** no comments
- **Final Translation of Both Translators:**

Another glass of water, a fever in the head and a shiver ripped through the body. This was my first dream. When I went back to sleep, I had another dream. It seemed as if the dream had been waiting for me. It came to me as soon as I closed my eyelids. I imagined myself to be in a large cold and desolate room.

- **Reviser's Version:**

Another glass of water, a fever in my head; a shiver running through my body. This was my first dream; when I went back to sleep, I entered into another – as if the dream had been waiting for me. No sooner had I closed my eyelids than it came to me. Alone, in a spacious room plunged in chilliness and gloom.

- **Reviser's Comments:**

The room is the agent in the sentence and the subject of the verb 'plunged'.

- **Native Speaker's Impression:**

Impression one:

The reviser's version is the better English, although *'I had a fever in my head; a shiver ran through my body'*. & *'No sooner had I closed my eyes, it came back to me. I was alone, in a spacious room'* would read more correctly.

Impression two:

Sentences in the reviser's translation up to the 3rd amendment are my preference. 3rd amendment could work but should say 'another dream' rather than just 'another'. Both penultimate sentences work. Prefer the original final sentence in the final translation of both translators, though also like the incorporation of the word 'alone'.

Annotation – defining matters 27

Impression three:

2nd one smoother both contain certain amount of strangeness. Examples of strangeness, 'fever in the head', 'close my eyelids', 'plunged in chilliness and gloom'.

Final Version:

Another glass of water, a fever in my head; a shiver running through my body. This was my first dream. When I went back to sleep, I had another dream as if it had been waiting for me. No sooner had I closed my eyes than it came to me. I imagined myself to be alone in a large cold and desolate room.

Comment

(a) Here, to respond to the marked use of the nominal structure, particularly in the first three sentences in the ST, which are written in a poetic style كأس ماء أخرى والحمى في الرأس والإرتجاف يقتلع الجسد, it is felt that it is necessary to avoid the use of verbs in these sentences as suggested by the first native speaker: *I had a fever in my head; a shiver ran through my body* (see native speaker's comments). This is because the successive series of nominalizations in a narrative fictional text like this short story injects it, in addition to remarkable neutrality, indirectness and particular attitudinal connotations, with a special poetic style. By contrast, the insertion of these verbs will change the whole tone of these sentences into less abstract, less formal and less depersonalized, thereby stripping away its poetic overtone. In his comments on the differences between the nominal and verbal forms, Ghazala (2011: 203) states:

> Each type of style has its functions and implications. Among other things, nominalisation may imply neutrality, authority, indirectness, ideological or attitudinal connotations, etc. Verbalisation, on the other hand, involves action, activity, process, directness, subjectivity, etc.

(b) Also, attention should be paid to verb aspects, in particular the fourth one هذا هو حلمي الأول 'lit. *this is my first dream*'. The emphasis in the original sentence is on the completion of the action, as there is an implicit كان that can be elicited from the context and co-text.

Suggested Version:

Another glass of water . . . a fever in my head . . . a shiver running through my body. This was my first dream. When I went back to sleep, I had another dream; it

28 *Annotation – defining matters*

was as if it had been waiting for me. No sooner had I closed my eyes than it came to me. I imagined myself to be in a large, cold and desolate room.

Example 5:

ST:

ولم يكن على جسدي أيّ غطاء وعلى أرضية الغرفة العارية حزمة أفاع صغيرة ملتفة حول بعضها بفعل البرد ولم تستطع أن تغادر مكانها أو تفك إلتفاتها المحكم،

- **First Translation:**

I was not wearing any clothes. On the naked ground of the room, there was a bundle of small snakes folded tightly around one another because of the cold. They were unable to leave their place or unfold themselves.

- **Second Translation:**

I was not wearing any clothes. On the bare floor of the room, there was a nest of small snakes tightly intertwined around one another because of the cold. They were unable to leave where they were or to disentangle themselves.

- **First Translator's Comments:** no comments
- **Second Translator's Comments:** no comments
- **Final Translation of Both Translators:**

I was not wearing any clothes. On the bare floor of the room, there was a nest of small snakes tightly intertwined around one another because of the cold. They were unable to leave where they were or to disentangle themselves.

- **Reviser's Version:**

I was not wearing any clothes. On the bare floor of the room, a nest of small snakes intertwined around one another because of the cold. They were unable to leave their spot or to disentangle themselves.

- **Reviser's Comments:** no comments.
- **Native Speaker's Impression:**

Impression one:

Both translations are nearly correct but: – "I was not wearing any clothes. On the bare floor of the room, a nest of small snakes intertwined around one another. Because of the cold, they were unable to leave their spot or to disentangle themselves". Would read more correctly.

Impression two:

Agree with the change made in the reviser's translation. Otherwise, no suggestions here.

Impression three:

Both sound strange but the 2nd one is smoother. Instead of 'I was not wearing any clothes', we'd say, 'I was stark naked', 'I was completely naked'. Also, 'bare floor of the room', 'unable to leave their spot' sound strange.

Final Version:

I was not wearing any clothes. On the bare floor of the room, a nest of small snakes intertwined around one another because of the cold. They were unable to leave their spot or to disentangle themselves.

Comment

(a) Here, the original writer deliberately opts for the word غطاء 'lit. *cover*', instead of ملابس 'i.e. *clothes*' in an attempt to invoke different imaginations and/or images in the mind of his readers. However, such an open invitation is completely lost when the two translators as well as the reviser resorted to changing it into *'clothes'*. Had they accounted for such an open invitation and its effects on the target reader, they could have suggested a translation, such as *'Nothing was covering my body'*.

(b) As for the unmarked collocation in the ST, أرضية عارية, it is reflected in the TT as *'bare floor'*, which is also unmarked collocation.

Suggested Version:

Nothing was covering my body. On the bare floor of the room, a nest of small snakes intertwined around one another because of the cold. They were unable to leave their place or to disentangle themselves.

Example 6:

ST:

ثم إشتعلت نار في موقد يتوسط الغرفة وتعالى لهبها وعندما تسرب الدفء الى المكان أخذت الأفاعي تتحرك ثم إنسابت على أرضية الغرفة. كل واحدة مضت الى جهة، وتحت سريري دخل بعضها،

- **First Translation:**

Then a fire was lit in a fireplace in the middle of the room and the flames grew higher. When warmth was felt into the place, the snakes started to move, crept along the floor, and went into different directions. Some of them entered under my bed.

- **Second Translation:**

Then a fire was lit in a hearth in the middle of the room and the flames rose up. When warmth spread through the place, the snakes started to move and slithered across the floor all in different directions. Some of them went under my bed.

- **First Translator's Comments:** no comments
- **Second Translator's Comments:** no comments
- **Final Translation of Both Translators:**

Then a fire was lit in a hearth which was situated in the middle of the room and the flames rose up. When warmth spread through the place, the snakes started to move and slithered across the floor all in different directions. Some of them went under my bed.

- **Reviser's Version:**

Then a fire was lit in a hearth situated in the middle of the room – its flames rising. When the warmth spread to their spot, the snakes started moving and slithered across the floor each in a different direction. Some of them went under my bed.

- **Reviser's Comments:**

'rising' not 'rising up', which is redundant in that there is no way to 'rise down'.

- **Native Speaker's Impression:**

Impression one:

The reviser's version is the more correct.

Impression two:

Change in tense should be noted with the first alteration – either version works well. Prefer the original of the final translation of both translators translation here, though 'throughout' could perhaps be considered rather than 'through'. Again, a change in tense should be considered with regards to the 3rd change. Agree with the last change in the reviser's translation. A hyphen is all that is needed to join the final 2 sentences. See commas added in blue on both translations.

Impression three:

2nd one better – yes but still a bit strange, 'the warmth spread to their spot'.

Then a fire was lit in a hearth situated in the middle of the room – its flames rising. When the warmth spread throughout the place, the snakes started moving and slithered across the floor, each in a different direction. Some of them went under my bed.

Comment

Here, there is an example of unmarked collocation in the ST, تعالى لهبها. To reflect such an unmarked collocation in the TT on the one hand and to produce an idiomatic literary rendering on the other, one can opt for verbs such as *'flare'* or *'leap'*, as they collocate well with the noun *'flame'*.

Suggested Version:

Then, a fire was lit in a hearth situated in the middle of the room – its flames flaring. When the warmth spread throughout the place, the snakes started to move and slithered across the floor, each in a different direction. Some of them went under my bed.

Example 7:

ST:

لم أكن خائفا، كنت أتمدد بإطمئنان وأنا أردد مع نفسي: إنها أفاعي بيوت وقد سمعت أنها لا تلدغ أحدا من السكان وعندما أغادر سريري سأضع وسط الغرفة كأسا فيها ماء وملح آنذاك لن تقربني.

- **First Translation:**

I was not afraid. I was lying in peace and kept saying to myself: They are domestic snakes. I've heard that they don't bite any of the residents. When I leave my bed, I'll put a glass of water and salt in the middle of the room. Then they won't come near me.

- **Second Translation:**

I was not afraid. I was lying calmly and kept saying to myself: They are house snakes. I've heard that they don't bite people. When I leave my bed, I'll put a glass of water and salt in the middle of the room. Then they won't come near me.

- **First Translator's Comments:** no comments
- **Second Translator's Comments:** no comments
- **Final Translation of Both Translators:**

I was not afraid. I was lying calmly and kept saying to myself: They are house snakes. I've heard that they don't bite people. When I leave my bed,

32 *Annotation – defining matters*

> *I'll put a glass of water and salt in the middle of the room. Then they won't come near me.*
>
> - **Reviser's Version:**
>
> *I was not afraid. I was lying calmly while repeating to myself: They are house snakes. I've heard that they don't bite people. When I leave my bed, I'll put a glass of water and salt in the middle of the room then they won't come near me.*
>
> - **Reviser's Comments:**
>
> Here is a great example of واو الحال that should be translated as 'while' and not as 'and'.
>
> - **Native Speaker's Impression:**
>
> **Impression one:**
>
> Both translations are correct.
>
> **Impression two:**
>
> Disagree with the change. Speech marks required (I was not afraid. I was lying calmly while repeating to myself: "They are house snakes".). Only a hyphen is needed to connect the final 2 sentences in the final translation of both translators.
>
> **Impression three:**
>
> Same effect. Not really a difference. 'Kept saying' and 'repeated to myself' are both idiomatic. They both follow the same style of describing the situation.

Final Version:

I was not afraid. I was lying calmly while repeating to myself: "They are house snakes. I've heard that they don't bite people". When I leave my bed, I'll put a glass of water and salt in the middle of the room – then, they won't come near me.

Comment

(a) The original writer does not opt for a full stop to separate the first two sentences. Instead, he uses a comma, indicating an implicit connector بل, i.e. *'rather'*. To speed up the pace of events slightly on the one hand and reflect such an implicit connector on the other, a semicolon instead of a full stop can be used.

(b) As indicated by the second native speaker (see impressions), quotation marks are required as long as direct speech is used: *I was lying calmly while repeating to myself: "They are house snakes. I've heard that they don't bite people"*. Unlike Arabic, which does not pay attention to the use of inverted commas for direct speech, English uses inverted commas as well as capitalization to distinguish between the two modes of speech. In this regard, Hatim (1997b: 136) comments that "the choice between direct and indirect speech is available in Arabic. A system of punctuation has been 'imported' by certain Arab neo-rhetoricians from English and other European languages". However, in Arabic, cohesion "is maintained through text syntax and semantics, and not by the use of marks that artificially set off parentheses" (Ibid.).

Suggested Version:

I was not afraid; I was lying calmly while repeating to myself: "They are house snakes. I've heard that they don't bite people". When I leave my bed, I'll put a glass of water and salt in the middle of the room — then, they won't come near me.

Example 8:

ST:

لكنى فجأة أبصرت عنكبوتا كبيرا، شعرت بالقرف والخوف منه، وإنقلب هدوئي الى ذعر، كان يتحرك داخل بيته وإمتدت يدي لتلتقط مطرقة لا أدري من جاءني بها، ووجدتني أهب من مكاني وأظل أضرب العنكبوت حتى أحلته الى نزق تنز بالدم والقيح.

- **First Translation:**

All of a sudden, I saw a big spider. I was disgusted and frightened. My calm turned into panic. It was moving into its web. My hand extended to pick a hammer that came to me from nowhere. I rushed from my bed and went on hitting it, and made it bleed and produce pus.

- **Second Translation:**

All of a sudden, I saw a large spider. I was disgusted and frightened. My calm turned into panic. It was moving inside its web. My hand reached out to pick a hammer that someone or other had brought me. I rushed from my bed and went on hitting it until I changed it to a mess exuding blood and pus.

- **First Translator's Comments:** no comments
- **Second Translator's Comments:** no comments
- **Final Translation of Both Translators:**

All of a sudden, I saw a large spider. I was aghast and frightened. My calm turned into panic. It was moving inside its web. My hand reached out to pick up a hammer that someone or other had brought me. I rushed from my bed and went on hitting it until I changed it to a mess exuding blood and pus.

- **Reviser's Version:**

All of a sudden, I saw a large spider. I felt disgusted and frightened. My calm turned into panic as it moved inside its web. My hand reached out to pick up a hammer that someone or other had brought me. I rushed from my spot and continued hitting it until I knocked it senseless.

- **Reviser's Comments:**

This is easily the most difficult word of this short story. The other two translators felt that the ST had a typo in نزق where they felt it should have read نزف. I did some research into the word and found that it meant 'to be lightheaded, frivolous, reckless'. Then I realized, after talking to the English scholar, that the spider in the story was so large that it survived the attack, that the protagonist had just 'knocked it senseless'.

- **Native Speaker's Impression:**

Impression one:

The reviser's translation is more correct, however, hitting a spider with a hammer would have killed it not knocked it senseless.

Impression two:

Disagree with 1st amendment [in the reviser's version], agree with the 2nd. Replace 'inside' with 'along'. Disagree with 4th and 6th amendments, though agree with the 5th. Changed 'rushed from' to 'jumped out of' and 'changed it to' to 'reduced it to'.

Impression three:

Both sound foreign. 'Someone or other', 'went on hitting' 'change it to a mess exuding . . . ', "Rushed from my spot', 'Knocked it senseless' for a spider?

Final Version:

All of a sudden, I saw a large spider. I felt disgusted and frightened. My calm turned into panic as it moved inside its web. My hand reached out to pick up a hammer that someone or other had brought me. I jumped out of my place and continued hitting it until I knocked it senseless.

Comment

(a) Here, the original writer simply says: مطرقة لا أدري من جاءني بها, that is, *'a hammer that I didn't know who had brought me'*. However, those involved in the process of translating this extract opted to modify the original version slightly, thereby shifting the focus, which is, in the original, on the narrator, not on the person who brought the hammer, as suggested by the second translator and the reviser: *'a hammer that someone or other had brought me'*, or on the process of bringing it as suggested by the first translator: *'a hammer that came to me from nowhere'*.

(b) Another challenging issue is the lexical item نزق. Looking up its meaning in a good bilingual dictionary, such as Al-Mawrid, one might find out it means *'rashness, impetuousness, heedlessness, thoughtlessness, frivolity, recklessness, lightheadedness'* and the like. However, all these equivalents suggested by the dictionary make no sense in such a context. It is a real decision-making test for all parties involved in rendering the extract. Luckily enough, I had the chance to consult the original writer, who made it clear there was a misprint here and that the word should indeed read مزق 'i.e. *tear, rip or rift'*. As such, it becomes obvious what is exactly meant by the original writer by the whole sentence حتى احلته مزق تنز بالدم والقيح '*lit. until I changed it to torn pieces, exuding blood and pus'* is that the spider in the story was so large that it survived the attack with the hammer until finally it breathed its last, and its physical appearance as a spider almost disappeared due to the act of hitting it with a hammer. Taking these elements into account, one may suggest something like: *'until it emitted the last breath, turning into tiny pieces, exuding blood and pus'*. More idiomatically, one may come up with a rendering like *'until I reduced it to a bloody pulp'* or, more prosaically and economically, something like *'until I knocked it out'*.

Suggested Version:

All of a sudden, I saw a large spider. I felt disgusted and frightened. My calm turned into panic as it was moving inside its web. My hand reached out to pick up a hammer that I didn't know who had brought me. I jumped to my feet and continued hitting it until I reduced it into a bloody pulp.

The discussion of these examples has shown that the elements of subjectivity can never be avoided either in the actual act of translating done by the translator him/herself or in the stage of posttranslation done by the reviser, proofreader, editor or translation quality controller.

Further reading

Al-Qinai, J. (2000). "Translation Quality Assessment: Strategies, Parameters & Procedures," *Meta*, Vol. 45 (3), pp. 497–519.

Al-Rubai'i, A. (2005). *Translation Criticism*. Durham, UK: Durham Modern Languages Series.

Baker, M., & Malmkjær, K. (eds.). (1998). *Routledge Encyclopedia of Translation Studies* (1st ed.). London/New York: Routledge.

British Standards Institution. (2006). *Translation Services: Service Requirements (BSEN-15038 European Quality Standard for Translation Services)*. London: BSI.

Brunette, L. (2000). "Towards a Terminology for Translation Quality Assessment: A Comparison of TQA Practices," *The Translator*, Vol. 6 (2), pp. 169–182.

Chakhachiro, R. (2005). "Revision for Quality," *Perspectives Studies in Translation*, Vol. 13 (3), pp. 225–238.

Mossop, B. (2007a). *Revising and Editing for Translators*. Manchester: St. Jerome Publishing.

———. (2007b). "Empirical Studies of Revision: What We Know and Need to Know," *The Journal of Specialised Translation* [on-line serial], Vol. 8, pp. 5–20. www.jostrans.org

Reiss, K. (2000). *Translation Criticism – The Potentials & Limitations*. Manchester and New York: St. Jerome Publishing & American Bible Society. Translated into English by Erroll F. Rhodes.

Sager, J. C. (1989). "Quality and Standards – The Evaluation of Translations". In C. Picker (ed.), *The Translator's Handbook* (2nd ed.), pp. 91–102. London: Aslib.

Sedon-Strutt, H. (1990). "The Revision of Translation Work – Some Observations," *Language International*, Vol. 2 (3), pp. 28–30.

Yi-yi Shih, C. (2006). "Revision from Translator's Point of View: An Interview Study," *Target*, Vol. 18 (2), pp. 295–312.

Companion website and online resources

http://cw.routledge.com/textbooks/translationstudies/
www.est-translationstudies.org/

2 Annotation and global strategies

In this chapter . . .

The previous chapter focused on the various processes and stages of the assessment mechanisms and such related terms as 'annotating', 'revision', 'editing', 'proofreading' and so on. Further, an attempt has been made to show that assessment and annotation are so related that in order to be a good annotator, one has to be a good assessor/evaluator. In this chapter, an attempt is made to focus on the main factors translators need to take into account while adopting their global strategies, such as the purpose of translation, text type, genre, readership and the like.

Key Issues:

- Genre
- Global strategies
- Language function
- Readership
- Skopos
- Text typology
- Translation brief

Strategies and translation brief

In translation studies, strategies (also labeled methods, procedures and techniques) have been investigated by a great number of scholars and theorists (cf. Vinay and Darbelnet 1958/1995; Nida 1964; Malone 1988; Newmark 1988; Baker 1992/2011; Chesterman 1997/2000 among others).

As long as translation is concerned, translation strategies are defined by Löescher (1991: 8) as conscious procedures adopted by translators to deal with the different types of problems they realize while rendering the text or part of it from one language into another. This means that strategies are problem centred that are consciously applied. Further, they are part of the translation process at its micro level. While translating the text at hand, the translators face different types of problems. To overcome the problems they face, the translators start a serious of actions, such as identifying the source of the problem *per se* (be it lexical, syntactic, textual, cultural to name some), searching for a suitable solution or a combination of many, prioritizing the competing solutions and so on. According to Jääskeläinen (1993: 116), there are two types of translation strategies, local strategies and global strategies. Holding the assumption that translation strategies simply mean changing something, Chesterman (1997/2000) classifies them into three main categories; each category has its own subcategories:

- **Semantic changes**, which include *'synonymy', 'antonymy', 'hyponymy', 'converses', 'trope change', 'abstraction change', 'distribution change', 'emphasis change'* and *'paraphrase strategy'*.
- **Syntactic changes**, which include *'literal translation', 'loan translation', 'transposition', 'unit shift', 'paraphrase structure change', 'clause structure change', 'sentence structure change', 'cohesion change', 'level shift'* and *'scheme change'*.
- **Pragmatic changes**, which include *'cultural filtering', 'explicitness change', 'information change', 'interpersonal change', 'speech act change', 'visibility change', 'coherence change', 'partial translation'* and *'trans-editing'*.

However, there are some nonbehavior strategies that are adopted by translators before starting the actual act of translating called 'global strategies'. To put this differently, a global strategy means the general strategy adopted by the translator to handle the whole text, whether, to use Schleiermacher's (1813/1992: 41–42) ideas, to leave the reader alone as much as possible and move the original author along with his/her text towards the reader, adopting a reader-oriented translation, or the other way round to move the reader towards the original author and his/her text, adopting an original text-/author-oriented translation.

In order to be in a position to decide on the appropriateness of a particular global strategy and exclude others, translators need to consider a number of factors, such as the purpose of translation, intended readership, text type, generic convention and the like. In this regard, Xiao-jiang (2007: 64) holds that it is crucial for translators "to know why a text is translated and what the function of the translated text is". This goes hand in glove with Vermeer's (1989/2004: 223) skopos rule, which requires translators to render the ST in a way that makes it function in the situation in which it is used and with the people who intend to use it in the way they want it to function.

Further, there are other nonverbal factors that superimpose certain directionality on the process of producing the final shape of the TT. These factors include the company's attitude and its publishing policy, the master discourse of translation, the relationship between the source and target cultures, the presence of the ST in a bilingual edition and the like.

In realistic situations, the translators, whether implicitly or explicitly, are sometimes provided by the translation commissioner (be it a client, translation agent, translation project manager, translation quality controller, depending on the company infrastructure) with certain information and/or instructions that would help them in adopting a certain global strategy and excluding others. Such pieces of information or sets of instructions are labeled by Janet Fraser (1996: 73) as the translation brief. As such, the translation brief, also referred to as translation instructions (Nord 1991), can be defined here as a set of instructions or pieces of information sometimes prepared by the translation project manager (such as the medium over which the text will be transmitted and the time and place of text reception), while at other times they are supposedly to be driven by translators themselves (such as the function of the text, the translation purpose, the genre aims and properties and so on). Taking into account the different circumstances of each translation task, the translation brief may include:

- the purpose of translation (skopos);
- the readership;
- the text function;
- the genre aims and properties;
- the medium over which the text will be transmitted; and
- the time and place of text reception, and the like (for more details, see Nord 1997; Munday 2001/2008/20012; Sharkas 2005, 2009).

Based on the so-called New Rhetoric, Nord (1991: 35–140), in an attempt to analyze the ST on the one hand and formulate the translation brief on the other, proposes her model in a series of *Wh*-questions. By asking themselves these questions, translators will formulate a clear picture on:

- the author of the text (who?);
- the intended readership (to whom?);
- the author's intention (what for?);
- the channel through which the text is communicated – is it in written or spoken form and so forth (by which medium?);
- the place (where?) and the time (when?) of communication (text production and text reception); and
- the motive of communication (why?).

However, in professional settings, as Nord (1997: 47) rightly comments, translators normally do not feel any need for a detailed specification of the translation function(s) because their experience tells them that a particular kind of source text provided by a particular kind of client (perhaps their employer, if they happen to enjoy the benefits of stable employment) is usually, if not stated otherwise, expected to be translated for a particular kind of purpose, including a particular kind (or even specimen) of addressee, medium, format and so on.

Although the translation brief helps translators formulate a clear image of their readership and determine the purpose of the translation, the function of the text in the TL, the commissioner's demands and the time and place of text delivery, it will not tell them directly what global strategy to apply (cf. Nord 1997: 31; Dickins *et al.* 2002: 230; Sharkas 2005: 26). This is precisely what Hervey and Higgins (1992: 14) mean when they write:

> Strategic decisions are decisions which the translator makes before actually starting the translation, in response to such questions as 'what are the salient linguistic characteristics of this text?'; 'what are its principal effects?'; 'what genre does it belong to and what audience is it aimed at?'; 'what are the functions and intended audience of my translation?'; 'what are the implications of these factors?'; and 'Which, among all such factors, are the ones that most need to be respected in translating this particular text?'
> (Hervey and Higgins 1992: 14)

Skopos

To begin with, *skopos* is a Greek word meaning 'purpose', 'aim', 'goal', 'function' and the like. However, in translation studies, it is used to specifically mean 'purpose'. Drawing on the theory of Translational Action introduced by the Finland-based German Justa Holz-Manttari, skopos theory is based on the notion that every action has a purpose, which eventually leads to a result. The purpose (skopos) of any action is what determines the result/product. With this in mind, the proponents of skopos theory hold that the translation purpose is what determines the final shape of the TT (the *translatum*). As such, the skopos helps translators determine whether they adopt an original text-/author-oriented translation, thus safeguarding accuracy, a reader-oriented translation, thereby guaranteeing acceptability, or a translation that stands somewhere between these two types of translation, thus striking a balance between accuracy and acceptability. According to the skopos theory, the purpose of translation is divided into three types (cf. Nord 1997: 27–28; Hatim 2001: 74). They are:

- *The general purpose*: the purpose of the translator, such as gaining reputation, adding something to his/her cultural or social capital, and so on.
- *The communicative purpose*: what is the function of the TT? Is it for persuading people or just for informing them of events?
- *The purpose of the translation strategy*: why do you go for this particular strategy instead of others?

This means that the purpose of translation along with other factors superimposes certain directionality on the process of translation, thus shaping the product, the TT. For example, the translator may resort to certain decisions and choices when translating a text for publication purposes, whereas the same translator may well opt for different decisions and choices when translating the same text for, say, pedagogical purposes. In this respect, Hatim and Mason (1997: 11) hold: "Translators' choices are constrained by the brief for the job which they have to perform, including the purpose and status of the translation and the likely readership and so on". Further, through the nexus of translation, the communicative purpose sometimes changes from a persuasive purpose to an informative one, as in translating a political speech.

Readership

Prior to embarking on the actual act of translating, translators need to live up to the TL readers' expectations. To do so, they need to take into account a number of fundamental decisions concerning the levels of acceptability, readability, naturalness. Further, translators need to take into account the intended readers' levels of education and familiarity with the topic discussed, event narrated, entities referred to and so on. Through careful reading and analysis, translators can make some guesses as to the degree of formality as opposed to informality, generality as opposed to specificity, accessibility as opposed to inaccessibility, explicitness as opposed to implicitness, and so on. Actually, translators as special readers do not have direct access to the cognitive environment of their target readers, but they rely on certain beliefs and assumptions as well as their own intuitions (Gutt 1991: 112). For example, in order to produce an acceptable and readable TT, the translator needs to opt for a number of local strategies that would guarantee acceptability and readability, such as reordering the SL syntactic structures to be in line with the linguistic and stylistic norms of the TL, altering the way information is packaged to conform to the demands of the text type and the generic conventions, unpacking an implicit message and so on. In this regard, Baker (1992: 219) rightly comments:

> Whether a text is judged acceptable or not does not depend on how closely it corresponds to some state in the world, but rather on whether the reader finds the presented version of reality believable, homogenous or relevant.

Text typology

Further, it is important that translators give due attention to the text type prior to adopting the most appropriate global strategy to apply. Traditionally, text types are categorized according to their subject matter. Thus, texts are classified into literary, legislative, technical, scientific and so on. It is considered a legislative text, for instance, when it shares certain characteristics such as the frequency of occurrence of certain lexical items and expressions with other legislative texts. To elaborate, let us have a look at the following example quoted from a treaty between the State of Bahrain and the government of the United States of America:

Article 9

For the purposes of this Treaty, an investment dispute is a dispute between a Party and a national or company of the other Party Ø arising out of or Ø relating to an investment authorization, an investment agreement or an alleged breach of any right Ø conferred, Ø created or Ø recognized by this Treaty with respect to a covered investment.

According to the subject matter-based taxonomy, it is a legislative text because it shares certain characteristics with other legislative texts, such as the use of certain punctuation (as in *'Treaty'*, *'Party'*), lexical repetition (such as *'treaty'*, *'investment'*, *'dispute'* and *'party'*), prepositional phrases (*'for the purpose of'* and *'with respect to'*), long and complex sentences (a long compound complex sentence), whiz deletion (such as the deletion of *'which is'* in the above sentence marked by Ø), syntactic discontinuities and the like.

Although these linguistic features are of crucial importance to the language user to identify the text type, there is a substantial difficulty in working with such a text typology, in particular when we come to the act of defining a particular text type (Bell 1991: 202). In this regard, Bell (Ibid.: 203) is of a view that in defining a text type according to such a text typology, there will be some degree of overlapping that "suggests that content, *per se*, is inadequate as discriminator" (Ibid.). Such a classification may "work with some highly ritualized genres (some types of poetry, for example) but not in the case of the majority of texts where again, and now at the formal level, there is overlap" (Ibid.).

Being influenced by the German psychologist Karl Bühler, who classified language functions into three types, namely *'expressive'*, *'informative'* and *'vocative'*, Katharina Reiss (1977/1989: 105–115) divided texts into three types: *'informative'*, *'expressive'* and *'operative'*. Approached from a completely different perspective, Hatim and Mason (1990, 1997) designed a model of text typologies in translation. In their model, texts are divided into three main types, *'exposition'* (be they descriptive, narrative or conceptual), *'argumentation'* (be they counter-argumentative or through-argumentative) and *'instruction'* (be they with options or without).

What is of paramount importance for translation annotators is that they familiarize themselves with one of the classifications proposed by different scholars and adopt it while annotating their own translations.

Genre

Another factor that needs to be given full consideration by translators prior to adopting a particular global strategy is 'genre'. The term 'genre' is often used by some people in a similar sense to 'text type'. Subject matter, which is used by some scholars (see previous) to distinguish text types, cannot be used as a criterion for describing genres because the same topic can be touched and discussed in different genres. Genre is defined by Swales (1993: 58) as "a class of communicative events, the members of which share some set of communicative purposes". This entails that there should be some conventions and norms that would determine the features of a given genre. In any society, individual texts are produced and perceived according to the norms and conventions formed over time by virtue of the recurrence of certain institutionalized properties (for more details, see Swales 1993). To put this differently, genre can be envisaged as conventionalized forms of text that reflect the functions and aims of each sociocultural activity, thus providing the language user with precise references and indications of the relevant social occasions of a community at a given time. In a direct link to translation, these generic conventions, on the one hand, help translators expect the lexical items, syntactic structures, register, style, content, intended readers and the like which are normally used in such a genre (cf. Kress 1985: 19; Hatim and Mason 1990: 69–70; Bayar 2007: 137). There are many different ways to categorize human communications. Dickins and colleagues (2002: 178–179) made a distinction among five broad categories of genre. They are:

- The first category comprises **literary genres** (such as poetry, fiction, drama and the like), which belong to a 'big' genre in which the world is created autonomously through imaginative texts sharing certain characteristics, such as containing features of expression and having, to a certain degree, a weak relationship with the real world.
- The second category covers **religious genres**. Unlike literary genres, "the subject matter of religious texts implies the existence of a spiritual world that is not fictive, but has its own external realities and truths" (p. 178). Further, they are characterized by the heavy use of archaic words and expressions and formal syntactic structure, in particular in Arabic.
- The third category comprises **philosophical genres**, which deal with a world of ideas. They are characterized by the fact that text producers do not experience a complete freedom in writing up their own texts, but rather they are restricted within the bounds of 'standards of rationality' (p. 179).
- The fourth category comprises **empirical genres**, which deal with sociocultural experiences in the real world as being mapped and recorded by observers. They are characterized by being objective and less informative.
- The fifth category comprises **persuasive genres**. This category covers a huge number of genres and sub-genres whose ultimate objective is to persuade readers/hearers to agree with a stated opinion, point of view or belief on the one hand and sometimes to convince them to take an action on the other.

Discussion

By way of illustration, let us consider the following example (adapted from www.lobotero.com) along with two different implicit translation briefs:

Translation brief 1:

Translate the following short text into Arabic to be published in one of the local antigovernment newspapers.

Translation brief 2:

Translate the following short text to be used by first-year students in class to learn about the differences between Arabic and English syntactic structures.

ST:

It is believed that the central government in the capital Baghdad is now dominated by some Arabs, while some other Arabs feel marginalized. However, Iraq's Kurdish minority enjoys a strong autonomy in the north of the country, with its own government and security forces.

Before translating:

- What is the purpose of translation?
- What is the text type?
- What is the genre?
- Who is your reader?
- What is the general atmosphere?
- What else?

In an attempt to decide the most appropriate global strategy to apply, translators are required to ask themselves these questions among other questions, depending on the circumstances of each translation task.

Suggested translation according to translation brief 1:

TT1:
بينما يعتقد بعض العرب أنهم مهمَّشون وأن حكومة المركز في العاصمة بغداد يُهيمن عليها طائفة من العرب، فإن الكرد – الذين يعدّون أقلية – يتمتعون في شمال البلاد بحكم ذاتي متين وحكومة وقوات أمنية مستقلة.

Suggested translation according to translation brief 2:

TT2:
يُعتقد أن حكومة المركز في العاصمة بغداد مُهيمن عليها من قبل بعض العرب، بينما يشعر بعض العرب الآخرين بأنهم مهمَّشون. لكن الأقلية الكردية العراقية تتمتع في شمال البلاد بحكم ذاتي قوي وحكومة وقوات أمنية.

Taking into account translation brief 1 (translating the text to be published in one of the local antigovernment newspapers), one may well suggest a reader-oriented translation by living up to the target reader's expectations. As a result, the relationship between the original text and the translation will be quite weak, as priority is given in such a type of translation to acceptability, naturalness and readability at the expense of accuracy. By contrast, motivated by translation brief 2 (translating the text to be used by first-year students in class to learn about the differences between Arabic and English syntax), one may well opt for a text-/author-oriented translation in which the syntactic structure of the original text is given a front seat, thus shortening the distance between the original text and the translation and having a strong relationship between them.

Evaluating researchers' strategic decisions

In evaluating researchers' strategic decisions, the term 'adequacy' comes to the surface. Adequacy is achieved when translators take into account the translation brief (i.e., the purpose of translation, text type, readership, etc.) before adopting their global strategy (reader-oriented, text-/author-oriented or a translation that lies somewhere between these two types). Then their local strategies (addition, omission, manipulation, etc.; see next chapter for more details on local strategies) need to be in line with their global strategy adopted earlier.

Global strategies and annotation 45

Now let us have a look at some of the strategic decisions provided by translation students as part of their MA translation projects done at different universities in the UK.

Student 1:

> In accordance with the target readership, the aim was to achieve a receptor-oriented TT. This was achieved by approaching the source text (ST) communicatively (Newmark 1988: 46–48). Communicative translation can be defined as trying to replicate the effect that the ST has on the original readers in the TT on the target readerships. In contrast, semantic translation, which is more or less literal translation, focuses on the words of the ST and their equivalents (Newmark 1988: 46–48, 2012: 70–72).
>
> In doing so, various techniques have been used to produce a fluent, natural and idiomatic TT. These include translation by addition (Dickins *et al.* 2002: 23–24); semantic repetition (Dickins *et al.* 2002: 59); omission (Baker 2011: 42); amplification (Vinay and Darbelnet 1995, cited in Munday 2012: 89); explicitation (Vinay and Darbelnet 1995, cited in Munday 2012: 90) and modulation (Vinay and Darbelnet 1995, cited in Munday 2012: 88). However, it is worth mentioning that some instances were approached semantically when semantic translation produced a more natural TT than communicative translation.
>
> For example, Hoffmann, Bergmann and Smith define an 'exclusionary riot' or 'exclusionary violence' as "one-sided, nongovernmental form of collective violence against an ethnic group that occurs . . . ethnic group (usually the minority)" (2002: 12). When communicative translation was used to translate 'exclusionary violence', it produced الإخلاء القسري. However, الإخلاء القسري is usually used in Arabic to refer to an 'exclusionary violence' exercised by an official body, such as the government (Ohchr.org 2014). Accordingly, the approach had to be changed in order to produce an accurate TT. Hence, it was translated semantically into العنف الإقصائي. In other words, it can be said that the overall approach to translation is greatly dependent on the 'principle of equivalent effect' (Nida 1964, cited in Venuti 2000: 129), whether that is achieved through communicative or semantic translation. The principle of equivalent effect states that the 'relationship' between the receptor and the target text should match that which is between the original receptor and source text (Nida 1964, cited in Venuti 2000: 129).

Comment:

As can be seen, the researcher has adopted a receptor-oriented translation, that is Newmark's (1988) communicative translation. To this end, she has resorted to a number of local strategies, such as 'addition', 'omission', 'amplification', 'explication' and 'modulation' among others. In adopting her global strategy, the researcher has taken into account the TL readers' expectations only. To be more persuasive, she could have touched on the purpose of translation, text type, genre, register, language function (for more details, see Chapter 10 in this book).

Student 2:

> Considering that the readers are specialists and not lay public, they are expected to have some background information about the topic of the article. I therefore decided to follow the 'foreignisation' approach advocated by Schleiermacher (Fawcett 1997: 116). According to this approach, the translation is closer to the ST and its culture rather than to the TT culture. Bearing this in mind, I translated the term 'the third Reich' literally, for example, as الرايخ الثالث, without giving any further explanation, in compliance with the 'foreignisation' approach. This however did not prevent me from giving extra but necessary information on other occasions. For example, when translating the term 'the Guilford Bombings', I added some extra information about it in order to make sure that the TT readers will understand this culture-specific concept. The addition of this information was necessary for understanding because this is a culture-specific term. This is perhaps not in line with the 'foreignisation' approach, but it does not affect the fact that the text still reads foreign. Because of the methodological approach I chose to follow, it was acceptable to paraphrase some of the culture-specific terms for which I could find an equivalent, since according to Schleiermacher's approach, it is not necessary for the TT to be completely arabicised; it is acceptable for it to seem more or less foreign. In some other theories, this is also known as exoticism. In brief, as I approached this translation, I chose to apply a combination of translation theories, rather than to adhere strictly to one approach. I thus varied my choices according to each instance.

Comment:

Here, the researcher has adopted a text-/author-oriented translation, Venuti's (1995) foreignization. However, when dealing with culture-specific terms and expressions, she has resorted to adding extra information to clarify the terms/expressions for the TL reader. So her global strategy is a combination of both a text-/author-oriented translation, that is foreignisation and reader-oriented translation or domestication. In her justification to do so, she has given full consideration to the TL readers and their expectations. Again, to be more persuasive, she could have touched on issues, such as the purpose of translation, text type, genre, register, language function prior to adopting her global strategy.

Student 3:

> Generally, it is agreed among translation theorists and teachers as well as professional translators that literal translation is the strategy to be adopted while dealing with legal documents, in particular legislative texts, such as agreements, treaties, contracts and so forth. In such a type of translation, the ST word order, tenor and layout are reflected as far as possible in the TT (Hatim 1997b). Further, priority is always given to the ST accuracy, all-inclusiveness and clarity at the expense of the TT naturalness. This is because such documents are characterized by a high degree of authoritativeness, they are text oriented rather than audience or writer oriented (for more details, see Newmark 1981, 1988: 39–44), hence the preference of literal translation. Accordingly, I adopted the literal translation strategy as the general strategy in the course of translating this document into Arabic. However, fluency and keeping the legal and formal features of the Arabic document distinctive, as well as preserving the ST intended meaning were my ultimate concern. In other words, I found it crucial to make the TT readable, fluent and accepted by the reader as long as doing so would not affect the ST intended meaning. Venuti (1995: 1) states that "A translated text, whether prose or poetry, fiction or nonfiction, is judged acceptable by most publishers, reviewers, and readers when it reads fluently". Therefore, it was crucial, in some cases, to adopt some other strategies along with the literal strategy. This is in line with Farghal and Shunnaq (1999: 161) who state that "the approach to translating legal texts is literal translation. Unless there is a good reason to do otherwise, translators must adhere to source text word order, meaning, style, etc.". [. . .]
>
> Moreover, it was essential, in some contexts, to opt for addition while dealing with the segment of the text at hand for the purpose of achieving more readable and fluent TT as long as it does not change the meaning. This finely tunes with Dickins *et al.* (2002: 24) who state that "addition is a fairly common feature of Arabic/English translation and is therefore worth specifically identifying". For instance, frequently adding the emphatic particle "إنّ!", the connector "وكذلك" as well as "و" to the TT would help in hanging the segments of the text together, thereby producing more coherent and cohesive text. Also, it is sometimes essential to add words or phrases to the TT in order to avoid possible ambiguity and to make the TL more readable. [. . .] In addition, I opted, in some sentences, to change the word order with a view to make the Arabic structure more grammatical and natural.

Comment:

Here, having taken into account the text type, which deals with legislation, the researcher has adopted a literal translation that gives priority to issues such as 'accuracy', 'all-inclusiveness' and 'clarity' at the expense of 'acceptability' and 'readability'. However, in an attempt to make the TT readable, fluent and acceptable without affecting the ST intended meaning, he has opted for certain local strategies, such as addition, which is inconsistent with his global strategy, thereby affecting the adequacy of his translation.

Student 4:

> The target text (TT) is aimed at educated Arabic-speaking individuals simply interested in politics in general and in military analysis and warfare in particular, and to Lebanese researchers studying the military behaviours of non-state actors and the response of the states to the ongoing changes. It is also mainly addressed to Hezbollah leaders who are interested in knowing a different point of view regarding the 2006 July war and actually looking at it from a different perspective. It is mostly intended to inform them of how others view this war and to reveal to Hezbollah leaders how these two authors view Hezbollah and assess this war. The TT can also be addressed to human rights activists and students of political sciences, mainly in the Middle East.
>
> Before getting into the overall strategy of translation, I would like to shed light on the issue of ideology that was a challenging factor when translating this type of texts. It is worth noting that ideology constitutes an actor within Bruno Latour's Actor-Network Theory (2005: 9) that studies 'how social actors create social networks' (Tyulenev 2013: 164) that are 'intertwined with other actor-networks, influenced by them, but not compelled by them' (Bogic 2010: 182). While translating, I came across terms that oppose my ideology, being a Lebanese and a pro-resistance person. Terms such as "Israeli Defense Force" and "Israeli borders" were very ideologically challenging, but considering that I did not want to change the authors' viewpoint, I preferred to transfer them as they are, being a supreme interest to the target readers, over letting my ideology interfere. Moreover, at certain points, the authors refer to Hezbollah fighters as defenders at times and attackers at other times, and the same goes for the Israeli soldiers, depending on who is attacking a certain position and who is defending it, so I chose to stick to the text and translate each as mentioned in the source text. [. . .]
>
> On another level, it is worth noting that the ST was filled with footnotes, some of which extended to several pages. Some included references to further readings, so I chose to omit them entirely, as these references are most likely not to be available in Arabic, and others included further information about certain points in the text, and I also chose to omit them due to the word limit restraint, especially that omitting them does not affect the fluency and cohesion of the ST. [. . .]

Global strategies and annotation 49

> Considering that the genre of the text is military and analytical, I faced many problems in finding the adequate equivalences in the TT that are familiar to the target readers and that seem quite natural in a way that makes the TT read as a text originally written in Arabic and not as a translation. In most of the text, I resorted to Venuti's foreignization strategy (1995: 17–42) mainly to bring the readers to the authors by preserving the latter's viewpoint and clarifying it to the target readers, so I translated "Israeli Defense Force" as "جيش الدفاع الإسرائيلي" (see footnote 61) and "Israeli border" as "الحدود الإسرائيلية" (see footnote 63). [. . .]
>
> Although the overall strategy adopted was foreignization, coupled with formal equivalence and word-for-word translation, I could not but resort to Venuti's domestication strategy (Venuti 1995: 17–42) to translate certain terms by adapting them to the TT, as they would have seemed rather awkward and unfamiliar to the target readers had they not been adapted. [. . .]

Comment:

As can be observed, the researcher, having given full consideration to nonverbal elements such as the intended readership (educated Arabs who are interested in politics, military analysis and warfare; Lebanese researchers who focus on studying the military behaviours of nonstate actors; Hezbollah leaders; and human rights activists and students of political sciences), ideological issues and their influence on forming the final shape of the TT, the text type and its genre, which is military and analytical, she has adopted a text-/author-oriented translation. However, in an attempt to live up to the TL readers' expectations, she has opted for a reader-oriented translation whenever necessary.

Student 5:

> Attempts have been made to produce the TT as equivalent as possible to the original in terms of meaning and effect. Thus, the free translation method has mostly been used in translating the ST in order "to reproduce the original's impact on the target audience" (Shuttleworth 1997: 73) in addition to accomplishing the orientation of dynamic equivalence which seeks receptor response (Nida 1969 [sic; 1964]). Furthermore, great attention has been paid to approaches such as communicative translation (Newmark 1981/1988), and idiomatic translation (Larson 1984). [. . .]
>
> While translating, attention has also been paid to the religious and social background of the target readership. For example, the avoidance of translating literally "the tithing law says you will never have enough money," because this

contradicts with the target readership's religious background as they believe that only God grants people money, wealth, etc. (note no. 81). Moreover, rhetorical devices such as redundancy "synonymy" and extraposition "defined as changing elements positions in a sentence" (Sadiq 2008: 45–46), are used for the sake of the TT fluency. [. . .]

As far as the TT clarity is concerned, introductions about the philosophers and scholars the author quoted in the ST are made in the footnotes. In confirming the correspondence of the general theme of the ST with the target readership's beliefs and religious background, verses from the Glorious Quran are quoted in several parts in TT and are found in the footnotes.

Although the ST is easy to be understood, there are some difficulties with regard to rendering its meaning into the TL if someone tries to maintain the same message and effect in the TT. In order to take into account the effect and the response of the audience in such a text, translators have to be attentive when choosing the appropriate equivalent translation.

Comment:

As can be seen, the researcher has given full consideration to the TL readers, in particular their own religious and social background, without any references to other nonverbal elements, such as the translation purpose, generic conventions, text-type demands and so on. Further, in an attempt to reproduce the original's impact on the TL audience, the researcher, in his strategic decision, has used different terminologies referring to various approaches, such as 'free translation', Nida's 'dynamic equivalence', Newmark's 'communicative translation' and Larson's 'idiomatic translation' without a serious attempt to differentiate among these types of equivalents or at least define them.

Further reading

Baker, M. (1992/2011). *In Other Words: A Coursebook on Translation*. London/New York: Routledge.

———, & Malmkjær, K. (1998). *Routledge Encyclopaedia of Translation Studies*. London/New York: Routledge.

Bell, R. T. (1991). *Translation and Translating: Theory and Practice*. London/New York: Longman.

Dickins, J., Hervey, S., & Higgins, I. (2002). *Thinking Arabic Translation*. London/New York: Routledge.

Farghal, M. (2012). *Advanced Issues in Arabic-English Translation Studies*. Kuwait: Kuwait University Press.

Jääskeläinen, R. (1993). "Investigating Translation Studies." In S. Tirkkonen-Condit & J. Laffling (eds.), *Recent Trends in Empirical Translation Research*, pp. 99–116. Joensuu: University of Joensuu, Faculty of Arts.

Munday, J. (2001/2008/2012). *Introducing Translation Studies: Theories and Applications*. London/New York: Routledge.

Newmark, P. (1988). *Approaches to Translation*. New York: Prentice Hall.
Nord, C. (1991). *Text Analysis in Translation: Theory, Methodology, and Didactic Application of a Model for Translation-Oriented Text Analysis* (1st edition) (C. Nord & P. Sparrow, Trans.). Amsterdam: Rodopi.
Nord, C. (1997). *Translating as a Purposeful Activity: Functionalist Approaches Explained*. Manchester: St. Jerome Publishing.
Pym, A. (2010). *Exploring Translation Theories*. London/New York: Routledge.
Sharkas, H. (2009). "Translation Quality Assessment of Popular Science Articles: Corpus Study of the Scientific American and Its Arabic Version," *Trans-com*, Vol. 2 (1), pp. 42–62.
Swales, J. (1993). *Genre Analysis. English in Academic & Research Settings*. Cambridge: Cambridge University Press.
Venuti, L. (1995). *The Translator's Invisibility: A History of Translation*. London/New York: Routledge.
Vermeer, H. J. (1989/2004). "Skopos and Commission in Translational Action." Translated by A. Chesterman in A. Chesterman (ed.), *Readings in Translation Theory*, pp. 173–187. Helsinki: OyFinnLectura Ab. Reprinted in L. Venuti (ed.), *The Translation Studies Reader* (2nd ed.), pp. 227–238. London/New York: Routledge.

Companion website and online resources

http://cw.routledge.com/textbooks/translationstudies/
www.est-translationstudies.org/

Assignment 1: *Instructors*: Select an English or Arabic text (depending on your students' translation directionality whether they translate out of Arabic or into Arabic) from BBC (no more than 500 words). Then ask them to translate the text to be published in one of the local newspapers and to write on their global strategy.

Assignment 2: *Students*: Select an English text (no more than 500 words) and translate it for publication in one of the local newspapers in your country. Before embarking on the actual act of translating the text, adopt the most appropriate global strategy. In no more than 100 words, tell us in your introduction about your expected readers and the purpose of translation.

Assignment 3: *Students*: Select an Arabic text (no more than 500 words) and translate it to a professional level. Before embarking on the actual act of translating the text, adopt the most appropriate global strategy. In no more than 400 words, tell us in your introduction why you have opted for this particular global strategy and why you have chosen this text and author (rationale).

Assignment 4: *Students*: Select a legislative text (no more than 500 words) and translate it to a professional level. Before embarking on the actual act of translating the text, adopt the most appropriate global strategy. In no more than 400 words, tell us in your introduction about the effect of the text type on your global strategy.

Assignment 5: *Instructors*: Discuss with your students the strengths and weaknesses of the following strategic decision taken by an MA student:

Strategic decision

When translating the ST into English, I confronted several issues, for examples, difficulties in or features of the ST, which hindered the fluency of the translation process. As a translator, I had to stop and think of solutions to overcome them. To start with, the ST lacks punctuation marks, the use of which would have composed a fluent text in the source language. The ST contains less than 190 commas, although it comprises about 10 thousand words. Furthermore, the ST has several paragraphs with no punctuation marks, except one full stop. Following what Newmark (1981) proposed in his book, *Approaches to Translation*, I modified the syntactic structure of the ST by making use of the English punctuation marks to separate each idea from another. He also contended that punctuation is "A powerful cohesive factor" (p. 178). Thus, I used it to help the TT readers comprehend what they were reading so that they would know what is what in the text.

Almost any translation process incorporates two essential techniques that help translators produce fine translations. These two techniques are 'translation by omission' and 'translation by addition'. Regarding the former technique, to omit a word or phrase from the ST shows that its meaning is not vital in the TT. This technique is applied "fairly frequently" when the two languages involved in translation are Arabic and English, in particular when the text is translated from Arabic into English which is a very succinct language (Dickins *et al.* 2002: 23). The author kept repeating several words and phrases in the ST, which were redundant. For example, although the author already mentioned at the beginning of his memoire that Kathmandu is the capital of Nepal, he repeated that piece of information throughout the ST. Another type of repetition is that the author made use of noun-doublets in the ST, like 'الملابس والثياب', 'التزويق والتزيين', 'حذرا متوقيا' and 'مداخل أو نوافذ'. However, because English is a succinct language, I opted to delete any word or phrase that would be redundant and make the TT prosaic.

In the ST, there was some incorrect information. I decided to correct them, for I believe that the author might have written them by mistake. I also believe that correcting the ST information would cause no offense to the author. That is because I corrected some informative phrases written in Urdu (for example see footnotes no. 153, 246 and 391).

Furthermore, I transliterated and italicised all of these words in the TT, except some, like 'sheikh', 'imam', 'kiblah', 'muezzin' and 'azan'.

Regarding the culturally specific words, the word 'الأخ' plus other words of the same root were repeated several times. Besides its straightforward meaning, it carries two other meanings in Arabic, in the Islamic culture in particular.

The author included a number of literary devices in his memoir. For example, he used metaphors, similes, proverbs and idiomatic expressions to keep his readers interested in the description of what he experienced in

Global strategies and annotation 53

Kathmandu. Otherwise, the ST would have been boring. As a translator, I had to find equivalent literary devices in English, which would work efficiently and be natural in the TT.

One of the critical decisions I opted for is that I did not translate some Arabic and Urdu phrases in the ST, which the author had seen written on, for example, walls and graves. I just incorporated them in the TT. That is because I want the TT readers to visualise what the author saw in his visit to Kathmandu.

The Routledge Course in Translation Annotation website at www.routledge.com/cw/almanna contains:

- A video summary of the chapter
- PowerPoint slides
- Further reading links
- Further assignments
- More research questions
- Further annotated texts

3 Annotating translation strategies

In this chapter...

In this chapter, special attention will be paid to translation strategies and how to annotate and comment on them in the actual act of translating. To this end, ample authentic data drawn from existing translation will be used to drive home relevant theoretical constructs. Further, in this chapter and henceforth, a distinction will be made between two key terms, namely *'comment'*, i.e., commenting on others' translations, and *'annotation'*, i.e., annotating one's own translations.

Key issues

- Adaptation
- Addition
- Amplification versus reduction
- Borrowing
- Calque
- Diffusion versus condensation
- Divergence versus convergence
- Equation
- Equivalence
- Lexical creation
- Literal translation
- Local strategies
- Modulation
- Omission
- Reordering
- Shift
- Substitution
- Transposition

Local strategies

As stated in the previous chapter, strategies (also labeled methods, procedures and techniques) have been touched on by a great number of scholars, theorists and translation teachers (cf. Vinay and Darbelnet 1958/1995; Nida 1964; Malone 1988; Newmark 1988; Baker 1992/2011; Chesterman 1997/2000; Dickins *et al.* 2002 among others). In this chapter, special attention will be paid to local strategies, the strategies adopted by translators when facing a particular problem and trying to do their best to sort it out. In this chapter, only three classifications – Vinay and Darbelnet's (1958/1995), Malone's (1988) and Baker's (1992/2011) – will be given full consideration. Adopting a particular local strategy may well lead to a type of shift; hence the importance of casting some light in this chapter on types of *'shift'* (be they level shifts or category shifts) proposed by Catford (1965).

The question that comes to mind in this connection is: how do we annotate our local strategies? Is there any particular way? In fact, as mentioned in the first chapter, annotation is a subjective exercise, depending on the person and his/her competences. However, translation students who have no experience can follow this, but they do not have to:

- **State their local strategy, as in:**

I (have) opted for . . .
I (have) resorted to . . .
I (have) translated . . . into . . .
I (have) used . . .
I (have) added . . .
I (have) deleted . . .

- **State the reason, as in:**

This is because . . .
The main reason behind this is . . .

- **State the type of the local strategy or shift, as in:**

This is an example of 'translation by addition', 'translation by omission', 'translation by paraphrase', etc.
This is an example of 'class shift', 'unit shift', 'intra-system shift', 'level shift', etc.

- **Elaborate if they can**

- **Refer to another researcher's opinion in order to make their own annotation externally coherent, as in:**

In this regard, Dickins et al. (2002: 59) state that . . .
In this respect, Baker (1992/2011) holds that . . .

56 *Annotating local strategies*

By way of explanation, let us consider the following example (Ghazala 2012: 10):

ST:
No one is sure whether, from Israel's current perceived position of strength, he [Netanyahu] genuinely wants a lasting peace that would give the Palestinians a proper state. He leaves room for maneuver. He is flexible to a point of opportunism.

TT:
وفي ظل سطوة الموقف الإسرائيلي في الوقت الراهن، فلا أحد يعرف بشكل قاطع ما إذا كان حقاً يريد سلاماً دائماً يمنح بموجبه الفلسطينيين دولةً حقيقيةً أم لا. إذ إنه عادة ما يترك باب المناورة مفتوحًا فهو مرن إلى حدّ الانتهازية.

Annotation

Local Strategy I have opted for the addition of the phrase عادة ما *'usually'*.

Why This is to make the text read smoothly on the one hand, and lay emphasis on the regularity and frequency of the action as a matter of routine on the other.

Elaboration It is worth noting that unlike English that has to express the regularity and frequency of an action grammatically, Arabic can express them lexically when they are relevant (cf. Baker 1992/2011). Languages differ widely in the way they map various aspects of world experiences.

External coherence In this regard, Baker (1992: 84) rightly comments:

> Languages that have morphological resources for expressing a certain category such as number, tense or gender have to express these categories regularly; those that do not have morphological resources for expressing the same categories do not have to express them except when they are felt to be relevant.

J. P. Vinay and J. Darbelnet (1958/1995)

Strategies, or procedures, as these authors label them, are divided into two main types: 'direct translation', which is subdivided into three types – 'borrowing', 'calque' and 'literal translation' – and 'oblique translation', which is subclassified into four types: 'transposition', 'modulation', 'equivalence' and 'adaptation' (Vinay and Darbelnet 1958/1995: 84–91).

In what follows, an attempt will be made to touch on each type on the one hand and draw a comparison with other local strategies proposed by other scholars on the other.

Borrowing

It is a local strategy referring to the process of transferring a lexical item into the TL directly because of, for instance, a gap in the TL lexicon or to add an element of local colour (Vinay and Darbelnet 1958/1995: 85). To elaborate, religious words like إمام, جهاد, حج, and the like are loaned in English as *'hijj'*, *'jihad'*, *'Imam'* and so on. By contrast, sports words like *'goal'*, *'corner'*, *'penalty'*, *'off side'*, *'linesman'* and so on are loaned in Arabic as گول, كورنر, بنلتي/بلنتي, أوفسايد, لاين مان. Further, this strategy is sometimes expanded to include terms already have equivalents in the TL, as in *'bank'*, *'telephone'*, *'cassette'*, *'mobile'* and so on, whose equivalents in Arabic are respectively مصرف, هاتف, شريط, جوال/نقال/خليوي/محمول. By way of explanation, let us consider the following example (quoted from NIDO ® 1 PLUS; emphasis in the original):

ST:

NIDO ® 1 PLUS is not a breast-milk substitute but a milk specially suited to healthy young children from 1 to 3 years.

TT:

نيدو واحد بلس، ليس بديلا لحليب الأم، بل تركيبة حليب مناسبة للأطفال الأصحاء من عمر 1–3 سنوات.

> **Comment**
>
> Here, the translator has decided to translate the word *'one'* into واحد and to borrow the lexical item *'plus'* although they are both parts of the same product name.

Calque, or 'through-translation', as it is labeled by Newmark (1988), is a type of borrowing whereby an expression form is borrowed from another language, and then the components of the borrowed expression are translated literally. Vinay and Darbelnet (1958/1995) hold that, like borrowing, many calques with time become "an integral part of the language" and with some "semantic change" could turn into false friends (85). There are two types of calque according to Vinay and Darbelnet:

(i) a lexical calque, which "respects the syntactic structure of the TL while introducing a new mode of expression". Examples of lexical calques from English into Arabic include translating *'to play a role'* into يلعب دورًا, *'part-time job'* into دوام بوقت جزئي, *'skyscraper'* into ناطحة السحاب, *'recycling'* into إعادة تدوير, *'weekend'* into عطلة نهاية الأسبوع, *'nonviolence'* into لا عنف, *'nonacademic'* into لا أكاديمي, *'Anglo-American'* into أنجلو أمريكي, *'amphibian'* into برمائي and so on. On the other hand, examples of calques from Arabic into English include translating القشّة التي قصمت ظهر البعير into *'mother of battles'*, أم المعارك into *'straw that broke the camel's back'* and so on.

(ii) a structural calque, which "introduces a new construction", such as placing the pronoun before its antecedent, that is, the noun to which the pronoun refers, or using the forced passive voice *'by-*structure', such as من قبل or

58 *Annotating local strategies*

من جانب in Arabic, as in the following example cited in and translated by Fred Pragnell (2003: 90–91):

ST:

وفي إجراء قوبل بمعارضة مريرة من جانب حكومة الأقلية التي يرئسها (.sic) المحافظون وافق البرلمان على اقتراح من جانب الديمقراطيين الاجتماعيين المعارضيين يدعو لوقف إسهامات الدانمرك في المستقبل في برنامج البنية الأساسية لحلف شمال الأطلسي حتى إشعار آخر.

TT:

In a measure which was met by bitter opposition from the minority government headed by the Conservatives, Parliament agreed on a proposal from the Social Democratic opposition calling for a halt to Denmark's future contributions to the NATO infrastructure programme until further notice.

Literal translation refers to the capability of transferring the ST expression, phrase, sentence and so on into the TT literally without any change apart from those required by the TL grammar. By way of illustration, let us consider this example cited in and translated by Fred Pragnell (2003: 8–9):

ST:

بدأ خبراء قطاع الكهرباء والطاقة تنفيذ خطة لترشيد الطاقة بإحلال الغاز الطبيعي محل السولار والمازوت في تشغيل محطات التوليد لتوفير السولار للتصدير.

TT:

Experts of the electricity and energy sector have begun carrying out a project for the proper use of energy by substituting natural gas for solar and fuel oil in the operation of power stations to save the solar for export.

Comment

As can be seen, the translator has opted for a literal translation in rendering this journalistic text. Such a translation, although it is literal, is acceptable, makes sense and does not change the meaning of the message. This is in line with Vinay and Darbelnet (1958/1995), who hold that a literal translation, which is a type of direct translation, should be avoided only if

(i) it changes the meaning;
(ii) it is meaningless;
(iii) it is 'structurally impossible';
(iv) it does not correspond to anything in the target-language 'metalinguistic experience';
(v) it does have a correspondence in the TL but within a different register (87).

They add that when translators feel the outcome is unacceptable, they could have recourse to one of the four procedures of oblique translation, 'transposition', 'modulation', 'equivalence' and 'adaptation'.

Transposition refers to a change of one part of speech for another without changing the meaning. Vinay and Darbelnet comment that for a stylistic reason, the transposed materials might have a different impact; thus they advise translators to opt for transposition only if "the translation [. . .] obtained fits better into the utterance, or allows a particular nuance of style to be retained" (89). By way of explanation, let us consider the following example (quoted along with its published translation from Axe: Deodorant Body Spray):

ST:
Shake well before use. Hold can upright and spray away from face and body. Note that the spray is released upwards from the top of the cap.

TT:
رجّ العبوة جيداً قبل الاستعمال. امسك العبوة بشكل عمودي وقم برش البخاخ بعيداً عن الوجه والجسم. يجب ملاحظة أن البخاخ ينطلق نحو الأعلى من قمة الغطاء.

> **Comment**
>
> As can be seen, while translating the preceding extract, the translator has opted for a number of local strategies, including 'obligatory transposition' and 'optional transposition' in the sense that Vinay and Darbelnet (1958/1995: 89) use the terms. The translator, in addition to obligatorily changing the adverb *'upright'* to a prepositional phrase, that is بشكل عمودي 'lit. *in a vertical form*', has optionally resorted to changing the verb *'spray'* to a weak verb قم 'lit. *stand*' plus a prepositional phrase برش 'lit. *by spraying*' although s/he could use the verb رش 'lit. *spray*'.

Modulation refers to "a variation of the form of the message, obtained by changing point of view" (89). For stylistic reasons, to avoid repetition or for other reasons, translators at times opt to use an antonym plus a negation element, change the passive form into active form or *vice versa*, change a concrete noun to an abstract one or reorder the cause-effect sequence and so forth. Like transposition, modulation, according to Vinay and Darbelnet, could be 'optional' or 'obligatory'. By way of illustration, let us consider the following example (quoted from Alqunayir 2014: 21–22):

ST:
Contrary to what many think, this does not prove that the West has become a godless civilization. Rather, it confirms, as Cox argues, the changing nature of being religious in a post traditional world.

TT:
وعلى عكس ما يظنه الكثيرون، لا تثبت هذه الحقيقة أن الحضارة في الغرب قد أصبحت ملحدة. بل تؤكد كما يقول كوكس، على الطبيعة المتغيرة للتدين في عالم تجاوز التقليدية.

> **Comment**
>
> As can be observed, the translator has opted for changing the point of view when she has translated *'the West has become a godless civilization'* in which *'the West'* is the doer of the action into أن الحضارة في الغرب قد أصبحت where the doer of the action becomes الحضارة and *'the West'* becomes part of the adverb of place في الغرب *'in the West'*. This is an example of modulation, to use Vinay and Darbelnet's (1958/1995: 89) terminology.

Equivalence, in the sense that Vinay and Darbelnet use the term, refers to the possibility of rendering an idiom, proverb, cliché, nominal or adjectival phrase and so on by "using completely different stylistic and structural methods" as long as it is used in the same situation in the interfacing languages, as in the Arabic idiomatic expression على أحرّ من الجمر, which may well be translated into English as *'to be on tenterhooks'*. By way of explanation, let us consider the following example (Alqunayir 2014: 18):

ST:
Islamophobia did not suddenly come into being after the events of 9/11. In many ways, the trauma caused by 9/11 merely helped bring the problem to the surface.

TT:
فالإسلاموفوبيا لم تظهر فجأة للعلن في أعقاب أحداث الحادي عشر من سبتمبر. وإنما ساعدت الصدمة التي أثارتها أحداث الحادي عشر من سبتمبر في نواحٍ متعددة على مجرد دفع تلك المشكلة لتطفو على السطح.

> **Comment**
>
> As can be seen, the idiomatic expression *'to bring something to the surface'* has been translated idiomatically into لتطفو على السطح *'*lit. *to float on the surface'* as they are used in a similar situation in the TL. Had the translator tried another idiomatic expression, such as إبراز تلك المشكلة *'*lit. *causing the problem to stand out'*, there would have been 'equivalence' in the sense that Vinay and Darbelnet (1958/1995: 89) use the term.

Adaptation is a special kind of equivalence, "a situational equivalence"; it is used when the TL culture does not have a similar situation in its experience that could accommodate the situation of the original culture. They suggest "the translators have to create a new situation that can be considered as being equivalent" (91). A good example of adaptation in the sense that Vinay and Darbelnet use the term is when the translator, for instance, changes the proper noun used as a vehicle in a simile like *'he is as rich as Croesus'* into another proper noun such as قارون *'Qārūn'* in Arabic, as in يملك مال قارون *'*lit. *he has Qārūn's wealth'* (for more details, see Almanna 2010: 118–120).

J. C. Catford (1965)

Following Firthian and Hallidayan linguistic models, Catford (1965), in his oft-cited book *'A Linguistic Theory of Translation'*, introduces two types of translation, namely *'formal correspondent'* and *'textual equivalent'*. Formal correspondent is "any TL category (unit, class, element of structure, etc.) which can be said to occupy, as nearly as possible, the 'same' place in the 'economy' of the TL as the given SL category occupies in the SL" (Catford 1965: 27). Textual equivalent, however, is defined by Catford as "any TL text or portion of text which is observed on a particular occasion [. . .] to be the equivalent of a given SL text or portion of text" (27).

In a direct link to local strategies resorted to by translators while dealing with the text at hand, one can touch on shifts that may well occur as a result of adopting a particular local strategy or a combination of many. Catford defines shifts as "departures from formal correspondence in the process of going from the SL to the TL" (73). He argues that there are two main types of translation shifts, namely level shifts and category shifts.

Level shifts

They occur when the SL item at one linguistic level (e.g., lexis) has a TL equivalent at a different level (e.g., grammar). For instance, in English, to emphasize the frequency of the action as a matter of routine, one can express it grammatically by opting for a simple present tense, such as *'She goes to school with her dad'*. However, to emphasize the frequency of the action in Arabic, the only solution is to resort to lexical items/expressions, such as عادة ما *'usually'*, غالبا ما *'often'*, and so on or leave it to the context to see to it.

Category shifts

According to Catford (Ibid.), category shifts are divided into four types:

a. *Structure shifts*

They involve a grammatical change between the structure of the ST and that of the TT. By way of explanation, let us consider the following example (quoted along with its published translation from Air Wick: Oud العود product label):

ST:
Do not spray or place on painted or polished surfaces. Keep out of reach of children. Pressurised containers: Protect from sunlight; do not expose to temperatures exceeding 50 C.

TT:
لا يرش أو يوضع على الأسطح المطلية أو الملمعة. يحفظ بعيدا عن متناول الأطفال. تحفظ العبوة المضغوطة بعيداً عن أشعة الشمس ولا يجب أن تتعرض لدرجات حرارة تزيد عن (50) درجة مئوية.

62 *Annotating local strategies*

> **Comment**
>
> Here, the translator has changed the grammatical structures of the ST from active, expressed by *'do not spray'*, *'place'*, *'keep out'* and *'protect'* into passive, expressed by لا يرش, يوضع, يحفظ and تحفظ. These are examples of structure shifts. Structure shifts, according to Catford (1965: 77), occur when translators resort to arranging lower-rank units (nouns, verbs, adjectives, adverbs, etc.) that form a larger unit (clause or sentence) differently. Structure shifts are the most frequent among the category shifts between Arabic and English. In discussing the translation of an English clause into a Gaelic clause, Catford (77) shows how those lower-rank units (subject, predicate, and complement) are arranged differently in the TT, thus resulting in a structure shift.

b. *Class shifts*

They occur when a SL item is translated into a TL item that belongs to a different grammatical class. Consider the following example (Alqunayir 2014: 12–13):

ST:
Taylor's remark that the debate about Islam and Muslims in Western societies is turning into a crisis of multiculturalism is alarming to say the least.

TT:
إن أقل ما يقال عن ملحوظة تايلور المتعلقة بتحول النقاش حول الإسلام والمسلمين في المجتمعات الغربية إلى أزمة تعددية ثقافية هو أنها مدعاة للقلق.

> **Comment**
>
> Here, a number of shifts occurred in the nexus of translation. To begin with, the verb *'turn'* has been translated into a noun تحوّل. This is an example of 'class shift', to borrow Catford's (1965: 20) terminology. Further, the verb *'alarm'* has been translated into a phrase مدعاة للقلق, thus creating a combination of 'class shift' and 'unit shift' (see what follows).

c. *Unit shifts* or *rank shifts*

They involve changes in rank, such as translating a sentence in one language into a phrase, expression and the like in another. Here is an example extracted from Alqunayir (2014: 12–13):

ST:
Cultural racism arises out of monolithic notions of religious, ethnic, and cultural groups that are seen as united by a central value system with virtually no room for diversity or human agency.

TT:

وتنشأ العنصرية الثقافية من تجانس أفكار جماعات دينية وعرقية وثقافية يُنظر إليها على أنها متحدة وفق منظومة قيم مركزية لا تدع أي مجال تقريبًا للتنوع أو لإظهار فاعلية الإنسان.

> **Comment**
>
> As can be seen, for the sake of naturalness, the translator has opted for the use of the noun تجانس instead of the adjective متجانسة in the translation of *'monolithic notions'*, thus creating a class shift (Catford 1965: 20). Further, the phrase *'with no room'* has been translated into a sentence لا تدع أي مجال *'it does not leave any room'*. This is an example of 'unit shift'.

d. *Intrasystem shifts*

They occur when the SL and TL possess systems that approximately correspond formally as to their constitution but when translators opt for selecting a noncorresponding term/expression/structure in the TL system (80). By way of illustration, let us consider the following example quoted from 'Abdul-Raḥmān al-Rubai'ī's story ذلك الأنين *Groaning* (2009: 163):

ST:

لقد كان حلما إذا؟ آه ما أثقله إنني حي، أتحسس أطرافي ثم أدس يدي في زيق بجامتي لتستقر على قلب يدق بعنف كأنه عائد من مطاردة عاتية، حيوانات خرافية تلاحقني، أشداق مفتوحة، صخور، حفر

TT:

It was a dream then? Oh! How heavy it was! I am still alive, though. I feel my limbs and slip my hand down my pyjama top until it comes to rest on a heart that is throbbing violently as if returning from a furious chase – mythical beasts chasing me, jaws open . . . rocks . . . pits.

> **Annotation**
>
> Here, an intrasystem shift occurs through the nexus of translation where a simple present tense expressed by ما أثقله is translated into a simple past tense in the TL, *'how heavy it was'*. In the original text, the emphasis is on the completion of the action rather than on its continuity or frequency, therefore, it lends itself to a simple past tense in the TT.

Here is another example extracted from (Al-Hinai 2009: 36):

ST:
The duties of the First Minister and Deputy First Minister will include, inter alia, dealing with and co-ordinating the work of the Executive Committee and the response of the Northern Ireland administration to external relationships.

64 *Annotating local strategies*

TT:

ستشمل واجبات الوزير الأول ونائب الوزير الأول، من جملة أمور أخرى، التعامل مع أعمال اللجنة التنفيذية ومع استجابة إدارة ايرلندا الشمالية للعلاقات الخارجية وتنسيقها

> **Comment**
>
> As can be observed, the translator has translated the singular noun *'work'* into a noun in a plural form أعمال *'works'*. This is an example of an intrasystem shift according to Catford (1965).

J. L. Malone (1988)

Malone (1988: 15) provides a list of five local strategies the translator may have recourse to when dealing with the text at hand. These are:

1 Matching: (equation versus substitution);
2 Zigzagging: (divergence versus convergence);
3 Recrescence: (amplification versus reduction);
4 Repackaging: (diffusion versus condensation); and
5 Reordering.

The first eight strategies appear as pairs, that is to say, one is the opposite of the other. For instance, when translating the Arabic noun صوت into English, it is a type of divergence since we have to carefully select the most appropriate equivalent from a potential range of alternatives, such as: *'sound'*, *'voice'*, *'vote'*, *'volume'* and so on. Conversely, translating one of the English nouns into Arabic undergoes converging.

Equation versus substitution

Equation is the most common strategy in dealing with culturally specific words and neologies. Generally speaking, culture-specific words like جهاد, إمام, فلافل, and so on are loaned in English as *'falafel'*, *'Imam'*, *'jihad'*. In reverse, scientific terms, such as *'computer'*, *'camera'*, *'Bluetooth'*, *'Internet'*, *'email'*, *'mobile'*, *'fax'*, *'video'*, *'satellite'*, *'telephone'*, *'cassette'* and so on are loaned in Arabic as كاسيت, تلفون, ستلايت, فيديو, فاكس, موبايل, إيميل, انترنت, بلوتوث, كاميرا, كمبيوتر. This strategy is labeled by Baker (1992: 34) 'translation using a loan word or loan word plus explanation' (see next section for more details).

Another form of equation, which is labeled by Vinay and Darbelnet (1958/1995: 85) as 'calque', is when an expression form is borrowed from another language, and then the components of the borrowed expression are translated literally.

The third type of equation, which is labeled by Farghal and Shunnaq (1999: 29) 'lexical creation', occurs when the translator coins "new lexical items in the TL

Annotating local strategies 65

to stand for SL culture-specific elements", such as *'co-wife'* for الضرة and عيد الحب for *'Valentine's Day'* and so forth.

Substitution, on the other hand, refers to a type of rendering that "may bear little or no morpho-syntactic or semantic relations to the source text" (Taylor 1998: 52). For example, the *idafa*-construction in Arabic is substituted by the *of*-structure, Saxon genitive or adjective-noun expression in English. Consider the following examples:

- بيت الرجل = the man's house
- عملية الترجمة = the process of translation

In the same vein, some adverbs in English are replaced with a prepositional phrase followed by a qualifier in Arabic, as in:

- dramatically = بشكل كبير
- reasonably = بشكل معقول
- surprisingly = بشكل مفاجىء

Further, there are a great number of verbs in Arabic, such as: كلّ, تعب, تحلّى (بالصبر), أجاد, تشاءم, تفاءل, خجل, اقتنع, انزعج, اندهش, جاع, عطش, سئم, ملّ, أسف, غضب, أفلس, فرح, حزن, and the like that are best replaced with a linking verb (verb *to be, feel, become, get,* etc.) plus an adjective in English, as in:

> *be/feel happy, be/feel sad, be/become bored, be/feel thirsty, be/feel/become hungry, be/become surprised, be/become annoyed, be/become content, be/become shy, be/become optimistic, be/become pessimistic, be/become excellent, be patient, be/become tired, be/become weary, be/feel sorry, be/become/get angry, become bankrupt,* etc.

At a more semantic rather than morphosyntactic level, the translator's decision to use a particular strategy will largely depend on:

(a) "How much licence is given to him/her by those who commission the translation"; and
(b) "The purpose of the translation" (Baker 1992: 31).

As such, sometimes in certain contexts, proverbs like

- *There's no place like home.*
- *Cleanliness is next to godliness.*
- *Beggars can't be choosers.*
- *Beauty is in the eye of the beholder.*
- *If you can't beat 'em, join 'em.*
- *Too many cooks spoil the broth.*
- *If it ain't broke, don't fix it*

66 *Annotating local strategies*

can be respectively substituted with

- بلادي وإن جارت عليّ عزيزة.
- النظافة من الإيمان.
- شحاذ ويتشرط.
- لولا الأذواق لبارت السلع.
- اليد التي لا تلاويها، قبّلها.
- السفينة التي يكثر ملاحينها تغرق.
- اِمسكْ مجنونك لا يجيك الأجن منه.

Although in such a strategy the denotative meaning of each individual word is not taken into account, it is still operative, particularly "in general texts, publicity and propaganda, as well as for brief explanation to readers who are ignorant of relevant SL culture" (Newmark 1988: 83).

Divergence versus convergence

Divergence, as hinted, involves the process of selecting the most appropriate equivalent from a potential range of alternatives. When translating Arabic words like محام, شركة, رئيس, نائب, صوت, مكتبة, مدير, and so on into English, we have to select the most suitable equivalent among alternatives available such as *'solicitor/barrister'*, *'company/partnership'*, *'president/chair'*, *'vice/deputy'*, *'sound/voice/vote/volume'*, *'library/bookshop (bookstore)/bookcase'*, *'manager/director'* and so on. Reversely, in translating, for instance, words like خال/عم or خالة/عمة, we converge them into *'uncle'*, *'aunt'* respectively. Dickins and associates (2002: 56) state that when the denotative meaning of the TT word is wider than that of its counterpart in the ST, it is, then, convergence or, as Dickins and associates label it, translating by 'hyperonym' or 'generalization'. However, when the denotative meaning of the TT word is narrower and more specific than the ST word, it is divergence or, as Dickins and colleagues (Ibid.) call it, 'translating by a hyponym' or 'particularization'. By way of illustration, let us consider the following translation offered by a trainee translator:

ST:
Smoking is a hard habit to break because tobacco contains nicotine, which is highly addictive.

TT:
التدخين هو من الأمور التي لا يمكن التخلص منها بسهولة بسبب احتواء التبغ على مادة مسببة للإدمان وهي النيكوتين.

> **Comment**
> Here, the translation offered by the student translator contains a generalizing translation in which the denotative meaning of the lexical item الأمور 'lit. *things*' in the TT is wider and less specific than its counterpart in the

ST, *'habit'*. Baker (1992: 26), in her list of strategies used by professional translators, suffices with the second strategy 'convergence' under the rubric 'translation by a more general word (superordinate)'.

Amplification versus reduction

Amplification, here, implies the process of expanding the ST expression by the addition of some elements to it. Such amplification occurs owing to the fact that

1 the original word is not lexicalized in the TL;
2 the original word is culturally specific;
3 the original verbal sign has a cultural connotation;
4 the original social deixis makes references to gender or social classes;
5 the translator sometimes tries to make up for the loss of the ST effect by creating a similar effect in the TT;
6 the translator sometimes tries to meet the requirements of the TL genre;
7 the translator sometimes for different reasons tries to change emphasis or thematic focus; or
8 it is sometimes used for the purpose of greater comprehensibility.

Nida and Taber (1969: 167) warn against inserting "information indispensable to the understanding of the message" in the body of the text itself. They argue that such pieces of information "may only be part of the general cultural backgrounds shared by the participants in the Source Language". By way of illustration, let us consider these two examples quoted from (Alqunayir 2014: 19–20) in which amplification occurs for different reasons:

ST:
Given the growing complexity of cultural and religious identities in late modernity, multiculturalism has deepened in Western societies and produced new modes of identity and social agency.

TT:
وعلى ضوء التعقيد المتزايد الذي شهدته هويات الثقافة والدين في حقبة الحداثة المتأخرة، تعمقت التعددية الثقافية في المجتمعات الغربية وأنتجت أنماطاً جديدةً للهوية والفاعلية الاجتماعية.

Comment

Here, the translator has opted for amplification twice: first, the relative clause الذي شهدته 'lit. *which witnessed*' has been added, and second the word حقبة 'lit. *period*' has been added to 'late modernity'.

68 *Annotating local strategies*

ST:

Middle Eastern cases have been especially influential in this way. Initial impressions of the lethality of precision guided antitank weapons in the 1973 October War, for example, gave powerful impetus to one of the most sweeping U.S. doctrinal revisions of the Cold War in the development of the Army's Active Defense concept.

TT:

وكان لقضايا الشرق الأوسط تحديداً أثرٌ كبيرٌ في هذا المجال. فقد أعطت الانطباعات الأولية حول فاعلية الأسلحة الموجهة بدقة المضادة للدبابات المستخدمة في حرب أكتوبر 1973، على سبيل المثال، زخماً كبيراً لإحدى المراجعات العقائدية الأمريكية الأكثر جذرية الخاصة بالحرب الباردة في مجال تطوير مفهوم الدفاع النشط الخاص بالجيش.

> **Comment**
>
> Here, to remove any state of confusion, the translator has opted for the addition of the word المستخدمة, for had she not added this lexical item, the sentence might have been understood as *'the antitank missiles precisely guided in October war'* and not in another war.

Reduction, on the other hand, involves the omission of some elements in the TT. Such omission frequently occurs in rendering a text from Arabic into English and *vice versa*. The main reason for such reduction is when the element is not important to the development of the text and omitting it does not harm the author's intentions or alter the text-type focus but, on the contrary, retaining it in the TT might complicate the structure and strike the TL receptor as unusual. Another reason for omitting certain elements is to maintain a desired level of naturalness. By way of illustration, let us consider the following example quoted from 'Izz al-Dīn al-Madanī's story حكاية القنديل *'The Tale of the Lamp'* compiled and translated by Husni and Newman (2008: 26–27):

ST:

فقال الرجل: (نعم يا مولاي السلطان إنه والله قنديل من النحاس).

TT:

'Yes, my lord – a lamp made out of copper'.

> **Comment**
>
> There, the translators, in an attempt to maintain a desired level of naturalness that requires them to coordinate "obligatory and optional information through the choices of explicit or implicit expressions" (Trotter 2000: 199), have opted for deleting the lexical items السلطان *'sultan'* and والله *'by God/ Allah'*. It is of greater importance for the translator to be aware of the common TL conventions and language-specific rules that determine the text naturalness.

> Borrowing terms from norm theory, one can discuss the translation from a different perspective. Guided by 'the initial acceptability norm' (Toury 1995) and 'the expectancy norm' (Chesterman 1997/2000), the translators have yielded to the pressure of eliminating the religious tinge of the text, which they dismiss as alien to TT readers. However, making such a decision has underestimated 'the initial adequacy norm' (Toury 1995) and 'the relation norm' and 'communication norm' (Chesterman 1997/2000; see also Farghal and Almanna 2015).

Diffusion versus condensation

Unlike amplification and reduction, which deal with the addition or omission of some elements for the sake of naturalness, better style, avoidance of repetition and the like as shown, diffusion and condensation are "concerned with phenomenon of linguistically slackening and tightening source text expressions for the target text version, that is, providing more or less elaboration" (Taylor 1998: 56). For instance, some verbs in English need to be diffused in Arabic, as in: *'to bottle'* يبحث في محركات البحث *'to google'*, يلغي صداقة *'to unfriend'*, يُعبّئ في زجاجة and so on. In reverse, some Arabic verbs need to be diffused in English, as in: بسمل *'he said: In the name of God, the most gracious, the most merciful'*, كبّر *'to exclaim 'allāhu akbar''*, and so on. By way of explanation, let us consider the following authentic example quoted from Mahfouz's novel ثرثرة فوق النيل *'Adrift on the Nile'* (1966: 165) translated by Frances E. Liardet (1993: 61):

ST:

وترامى إليه من الحديقة صوت عم عبده لدى رجوعه وهو يبسمل.

TT:

He heard 'Amm Abduh's voice now, from the garden, as he was returning from the prayer. "In the name of God, the Merciful, the Compassionate," he was murmuring.

> **Comment**
>
> In the original text, the religious verb يبسمل verbally means saying بسم الله الرحمن الرحيم needs to be unpacked into full English sentence, as it has no equivalent in the TL. Here, the translator has decided to translate it into '*In the name of God, the Merciful, the Compassionate, he was murmuring*'. This is an example of diffusion in the sense that Malone (1988) uses the term. It is also an example of 'unit shift' or 'rank shift', to borrow terms from Catford (1965).

70 *Annotating local strategies*

Reordering

Reordering, as the name suggests, is a strategy that involves the inversion of ST sequences, such as adjective-noun, verb-adverb, collocation sequences, subject-object sequences and so forth to fit in the TL and read more cogently. In Arabic, for instance, the adjective is preceded by the noun, as in: السيارة الجديدة, but in English it should be the other way round: the adjective is followed by the noun, as in '*the new car*'. Reordering also involves the inversion of the verb-subject sequences while translating, for instance سألني سؤالاً صعبًا into '*he asked me a difficult question*'. As for collocations, it is worth noting that some sequences of collocates (such as '*black and white*', '*day and night*', '*giving and taking*', '*sooner or later*', etc.) require translators to reorder them when translating from English into Arabic or *vice versa*, as in آجلاً أم عاجلاً, أخذ وعطاء, ليل نهار, أبيض وأسود respectively (for more details, see Shama 1978; Trotter 2000). By way of explanation, let us consider these two examples extracted from Muḥsin Al-Ramlī's story البحث عن قلب حيّ *Search for a Live Heart* (2009: 37, 39):

ST:

كيف قلب أمي إذًا! أمي التي تسمرّت عند النافذة ليل نهار .. ترضع السجائر وعيناها الدامعتان ترقبان الطريق.. تراه يترجّل عن كل السيارات المارقة ..

TT:

Oh, my God, what about my mother's heart then – my mother who remains pinned to the window day and night, puffing on cigarettes, her tearful eyes checking the road to see if he's getting out of a passing car . . .

Annotation

(a) This is an example of reordering the sequences of the collocates. In Arabic, when one talks about day-night succession or any similar expressions involving '*day and night*', ليل '*night*' preferably comes before نهار '*day*', while in English the opposite is true. Thus, the adverbial phrase ليل نهار requires the translator to reorder the sequence of its collocates prior to transferring it into the TL. This is because "meaning is first carried in semantic units rather than in syntagmatic patterns"; therefore, "a certain grammatical 'skewing' or rearranging, is often required" (Taylor 1998: 61).

(b) Further, an intrasystem shift, to use Catford's (1965) terminology, occurs through the nexus of translation where a noun in a plural form سيارات '*cars*' is translated into a noun in a singular form '*car*' in the TL.

ST:

ومتى يعود هو؟ (مشيرًا إلى الباب) لتعود إلينا معه الحياة التي نريدها .. أنا وأمي والجيران والنخلة التي زرعناها.

TT:
When will he (pointing at the door) come back so that the life we wish for may thereby be restored to us . . . to my mother, to the neighbours, to me and to the palm tree that we planted together?

Annotation

In English, when a story is narrated from the first-person perspective, such as the first-person narrative, and there are others characters to talk about, the first-person singular pronoun is preferably placed after other pronouns unless the focus is on a negative issue. By contrast, Arabic tends to use the first-person singular pronoun أنا *'I/me'* at the beginning; hence the shift in the word order of أنا وأمي والجيران والنخلة 'lit. *I, my mother, the neighbours and the palm tree'*. Further, due to the relative clause التي زرعناها, which describes the palm tree, the pronoun *'me'* is placed before *'the palm tree that we planted together'*.

M. Baker (1992/2011)

Local strategies are classified by Baker (1992/2011: 23–44) into eight local strategies, namely the following.

Translation by a more general word (superordinate)

It is a local strategy resorted to by translators when dealing with nonequivalence, in particular when the denotative meaning of the TL word is wider and less specific. Consider the following extract quoted from HEAD & SHOULDERS shampoo:

ST:
Apply onto wet hair, wash, rinse. Repeat if required.

TT:

دلكي شعرك المبلل، اغسليه ثم اشطفيه. كرري العملية عند الحاجة.

Comment

As can be observed, the translator has opted for a translation by a more general word when dealing with the verb *'apply'*. The denotative meaning of the verb *'apply'* is wider and less specific than its counterpart in the TT دلّك *'to rub'*. In this regard, Baker (1992/2011: 25) holds that this strategy, translation by a more general word (superordinate), is used "to overcome a relative lack of specificity in the target language compared to the source language".

72 *Annotating local strategies*

To cast more light on the use of a general word to overcome a lack of a one-to-one equivalent, in particular in the area of propositional meaning, let us consider the following text quoted from Abdul-Sattār Nāṣir's story (2009: 21) ثلاث قصص ليست للنشر 'Three Stories Not for Publishing':

ST:

في الليل، صاح المتهم الجميل:
- نعم، أنا القاتل . . .
ثم كف الجلاد عن ضربه، وابتسم له:
- كان عليك أن تعترف منذ الشهر الماضي!

TT:
At night, the defendant shouted:
"Yes, I am the murderer".
So the torturer stopped lashing him, smiled at him and said:
"You should have confessed a month ago".

Annotation

(a) Checking the meaning of the ST word المتهم in a good bilingual dictionary, such as Al-Mawrid, one can suggest words like *'convicted'*, *'condemned'*, *'sentenced'*, *'pronounced guilty'*, *'found guilty'* and so forth. Taking into account that the English legal system makes a distinction among words like *'suspected'*, *'charged'* and *'accused'* according to his/her situation in the stages of the case, one may well opt for a general term to cover all these terms, as in *'defendant'*.

(b) The word جلاد derives from the verb جلد *'to whip, lash'* and so on. The word *'whip'*, for instance, as a noun offered by a bilingual dictionary like Al-Mawrid, does not function well in this context. Tracing its meaning in a monolingual dictionary, one can come up with (1) "a member of the U.S. Congress or the British Parliament who is responsible for making sure that members of their party attend and vote" and (2) "a written order sent to the U.S. Congress or the British Parliament telling them when and how to vote" (Longman Dictionary of Contemporary English 1987/1995: 1200). So it has nothing to do with lashing somebody being in prison for the purpose of extracting his/her confession. Translating it into *'guard'*, for instance, even though it makes sense and conveys the original writer's intention, in particular when it is followed by the phrase *'stopped lashing him'*, it suffers a lot of loss in its denotative meaning. As such, an attempt is made to opt for a generalizing translation in which the *'torturer'*, the hyperonymy of the Arabic word جلاد, is used.

Translation by a more neutral/less expressive word

Translators, for different reasons, such as a lack of a one-to-one equivalent and the like, resort to more neutral expressive words. By way of explanation, let us

Annotating local strategies 73

consider the following authentic example quoted from Mahfouz's novel ثرثرة فوق النيل *'Adrift on The Nile'* (1966: 9) translated by Frances E. Liardet (1993: 2):

ST:

- سأجيب أنا عنك. إنك لم تر الصفحة لأنك مسطول! . . .
- يا سعادة ..
- دعنا من السعادة والتعاسة، حقق لي هذا الرجاء المتواضع وهو ألا تبلع في أثناء العمل ..

TT:

"I shall answer for you. You did not see what was on the page, because you were . . . drugged!"
"Sir!" . . .
"Enough sir-ing and demurring. Be so good as to comply with my humble request and leave your habit at home".

> **Comment**
>
> Here, in an attempt to inject his text with vividness on the one hand and let one of the in-text participants express his attitude to the listener on the other, the original writer employs some expressive lexical items, such as مسطول and تبلع. Although these words share the same core denotative meaning of يتناول الخمر/يشرب الخمر and مخمور/سكران, the speaker's implied attitude to the listener produces a different impact in each case. Thus, the translator has opted for a more neutral word in the first example *'drugged'* and for a more general word (superordinate) and less expressive in the second example *'habit'*.

Here is another example extracted from Haifā' Zangana's story مثوى *'Dwelling'* (2009: 53):

ST:

تصل ركنها وهي تسير ببطء. تشحط قدميها وحقيبتها وأكياسها. تشحط رأسها الثقيل المجيّم الجالس باستكانة على براغي العنق الغليظ، الحاط بدوره على كتفيها العريضين

TT:

She gets to her corner, walking slowly, dragging her legs, her suitcase and her bags. She also pulls along her heavy head, screwed with resignation onto her huge neck, set in its turn on her broad shoulders.

> **Annotation**
>
> The challenging word in this extract is the word مجيّم, which derives from the verb جيّم. Basically such a word is used colloquially in Iraq when we talk about a screw sticking to its place giving no movement, as it has been left for a long time without unscrewing, or it might be gotten wet due to water

74 *Annotating local strategies*

> and so on. In a similar vein, it is used figuratively to describe somebody or something sticking to its place, unwilling to leave. Also, it is used to describe somebody who has not had sexual intercourse for a long time. Thus, it follows from this discussion that (1) its denotative meaning can be elicited as *'unmovable'*, (2) the register of the extract in which such a word is used is informal and (3) it is used figuratively. To minimize the loss and benefit from condensation mechanism, the word *'screw'* has been utilized as a verb in its past participle form to stand for the ST word مجيَّم.

Translation by cultural substitution

Translation by cultural substitution is a local strategy resorted to by translators when the TL does not have an equivalent that has the same meaning but is likely to have something that has "a similar impact on the target reader, for instance by evoking a similar context in the target culture" (Baker 1992/2011: 29). By way of explanation, let us consider the following example (quoted from NIDO PLUS; emphasis in the original):

ST:

NIDO ® 1 PLUS is not a breast-milk substitute but a milk specially suited to healthy young children from 1 to 3 years.

TT:

نيدو واحد بلس، ليس بديلا لحليب الأم، بل تركيبة حليب مناسبة للأطفال الأصحاء من عمر 1–3 سنوات.

> **Comment**
>
> As can be observed, the translator, in an attempt to have a similar impact on the TL reader, has replaced the word *'breast'* with أم *'mother'*. This can be considered as an example of translation by cultural substitution, to use Baker's (1992/2011: 29) terminology. Baker (Ibid.) holds that the translator's decision to adopt this strategy and exclude others depends, among other factors, on "the norms of translation prevailing in a given community".

Translation using a loan word or loan word plus explanation

This local strategy is employed by translators when they come across culture-specific terms and expressions. By way of illustration, let us consider the following example extracted from Samīra al-Mānī''s (1997: 7) novella القامعون *'Oppressors'* translated by Paul Starkey (2008: 1):

ST:

في ليلة من ليالي شتاء بغداد، أثناء ما تكون السماء ملتصقة بالأرض من شدة العتمة، سُمع صياح وضوضاء خارجاً من إحدى غرف داخلي طالبات كلية الآداب. هرعت ست ماري، مديرة الداخلي منفزعة، مهيئة نفسها لمعاقبة العابثات المزعجات.

TT:

One Baghdad winter's night, – a night so dark that the sky seemed to merge into the earth, – a great commotion could be heard coming from a room in the Faculty of Language girls' boarding house. Satt* Marie, the House Principal, hurried out in alarm, preparing herself to punish the girls who were to blame. * Satt indicates title of Miss

---

Comment

As can be seen, the translator has used *'Satt'* for the Arabic word ست followed by an explanation in the form of a footnote. This is an example of 'translation using a loan word plus explanation' (Baker 1992/2011: 33). Baker states that it is of paramount importance that the loaned word is to be followed by an explanation, in particular when it is "repeated several times in the text" (Ibid.). In general, borrowings are divided into two categories: cultural borrowings and core borrowings. Cultural borrowings are defined by Myers-Scotton (2005: 331) as "words that fill gaps in the recipient language's store of words because they stand for objects or concepts new to the language's culture". Core borrowings, on the other hand, are words that duplicate elements that the recipient language already has in its word store. When two languages are spoken in the same community, the other language becomes the recipient language in borrowing and will even replace its own words with words from the dominant language. So the core borrowings duplicate already existing words in the recipient culture's language and only seem to appear after long or intensive contact (Ibid.). This is quite similar to what happens in English and Arabic, where many English words in the field of fast-food advertisements invade the Arabic texts.

Translation by paraphrase using a related word

This local strategy is normally opted for when a concept is lexicalized in both languages differently, but "the frequency with which a certain form is used in the source text is significantly higher than would be natural in the target language" (Baker 1992/2011: 36). Following is an example in which the translator has resorted to translation by paraphrase using a related word (Sultan 2007: 4, 22):

ST:
Torture is a process: a limited dialectic between torturer and prisoner and dialectic between a torturing regime and its internal enemies. It is a limited dialectic between a torturer and tortured because the prisoner is unable to exercise reflexivity, is denied the possibility of agency in the torture context.

TT:
والتعذيب يكون على مراحل فهو : جدلية واضحة بين من يمارس التعذيب وبين الشخص الذي يتم تعذيبه وهو أيضا عملية جدلية بين نظام حكم يمارس التعذيب وأعداءه (.sic) الداخليين. إنها عملية جدلية محدودة [بين] من يمارس التعذيب وبين من يتم تعذيبه لأن السجين لا يستطيع ممارسة رد الفعل ومحروم من إمكانية التصرف ضمن سياق عملية التعذيب.

76 *Annotating local strategies*

> **Comment**
>
> Here, it seems that the translator, having taken into account that translating lexical items such as *'torturer'*, *'prisoner'* and *'torturing'* literally would strike the TL reader as unusual and nonidiomatic, has opted for translation by paraphrase as in نظام حكم يمارس and الشخص الذي يتم تعذيبه, من يمارس التعذيب التعذيب, respectively. Such a strategy has led to Catford's (1965) 'unit shift' in which nouns, such as *'torturer'*, *'prisoner'* and *'torturing'*, have been translated into phrases.

Translation by paraphrase using unrelated words

This is another local strategy used by translators when a concept is lexicalized in one language or when it is lexicalized in both languages but used differently in different contexts. By way of illustration, let us consider the following example taken from Samhat (2014: 9):

ST:

Debates over the nature of future warfare drive much of U.S. defense planning, from decisions on force structure to resource allocation, modernization, joint doctrine, transformation, and the use of force. And these debates are powerfully influenced by interpretations of recent combat experience – both our own, and others'.

TT:

تحدد النقاشات حول طبيعة مستقبل التفكير الحربي وجهة معظم التخطيط الدفاعي الأمريكي، بدءاً من القرارات بشأن هيكل القوة وصولاً إلى تخصيص الموارد والتجديد والعقيدة المشتركة والتحوّل واستخدام القوة. تتأثر هذه النقاشات بشكل كبير بتفسيرات الخبرة القتالية الحديثة – من جانبنا ومن جانب الآخرين.

> **Comment**
>
> Here, the translator has opted for Baker's (1992/2011: 38) 'translation by paraphrase using unrelated words' where she has translated *'drive'* as تحدد . . . وجهة. It is worth noting that this is also an example of 'unit shift', to use Catford's (1965) terminology.

Translation by omission

At times, when the word or expression used in the ST is redundant, it provides the translator with a reasonable justification to omit it, as is in the following example quoted from Samhat (2014: 10):

ST:

A central issue in today's debate is the role of nonstate opponents in defense planning. It is widely believed that such enemies will be increasingly common in the future, and many now advocate sweeping change in U.S. military posture to prepare for this.

TT:

يشكّل دور الخصوم الفاعلين خارج إطار الدول نقطة أساسية في نقاش اليوم حول التخطيط الدفاعي. ويسود الاعتقاد بأن وجود هؤلاء الأعداء سيصبح أكثر شيوعاً في المستقبل، لذا ينادي العديد اليوم بإجراء تغيير جذري على الهيكلية العسكرية الأمريكية من أجل الجهوزية لهذا الأمر.

> **Comment**
>
> As can be seen, the translator, in an attempt to activate a desired level of naturalness, has resorted to Baker's (1992/2011: 42) 'translation by omission', where she has omitted the adverb *'widely'* and made up for the loss in using the lexical item يسود *'prevail'* in place of the formal correspondent يُعتقد *'it is believed'*. Such a local strategy has led to a combination of two types of shifts, namely 'structure shift' and 'unit shift'. She has translated *'it is believed'* expressed in a passive form in the ST into يسود الاعتقاد, which is active in the TT. Further, the verb *'believe'* has been translated into a noun اعتقاد, which is an example of 'class shift'.

Translation by illustration

At times, translators resort to translation by illustration for a variety of different reasons: to avoid confusion, to reflect a semiotic dimension, to meet the requirements of the TL genre, for the purpose of greater comprehensibility and so on. By way of explanation, let us consider the following example quoted from Orwell's (1960) novel *Animal Farm* cited in and translated by Al-Rubai'i (2005: 37):

ST:
Napoleon was a large, rather fierce-looking Berkshire boar, the only Berkshire on the farm, not much of a talker, but with a reputation for getting his own way.

TT:
كان نابليون خنزيراً شرس المظهر نوعاً ما، من سلالة بيركشر [التي تتميز بضخامتها، وغلبة اللون الأسود عليها، وتسلطها]. كان الوحيد من هذه السلالة في الحقل، لا يحسن الحديث، ولكنه عرف بأنه يفعل ما يريد.

> **Comment**
>
> Semiotically speaking, relying on the TL denotational equivalent of the ST expression *'Berkshire boar'* خنزير بيركشير without any sort of explication might seriously affect the intentionality of the ST sign; hence the importance of providing the reader with the missing information by either using square brackets or a footnote (for more details on semiotic aspects, see Chapter 8 in this book).

Further reading

Baker, M. (1992/2011). *In Other Words: A Coursebook on Translation*. London/New York: Routledge.
Catford, J. C. (1965). *A Linguistic Theory of Translation*. Oxford: Oxford University Press.
Chesterman, A. (1997/2000). *Memes of Translation: The Spread of Ideas in Translation Theory*. Amsterdam/Philadelphia: John Benjamins.
Dickins, J., Hervey, S., & Higgins, I. (2002). *Thinking Arabic Translation*. London/New York: Routledge.
Farghal, M., & Shunnaq, A. (1999/2011). *Translation with Reference to English and Arabic: A Practical Guide (1ST edition)*. Jordan: Dār al-Hilāl for Translation.
Malone, J. L. (1988). *The Science of Linguistics in the Art of Translation*. Albany: State University of New York Press.
Newmark, P. (1988). *A Textbook of Translation*. New York/London/Toronto/Sydney/Tokyo: Prentice Hall.
Taylor, C. (1998). *Language to Language: A Practical and Theoretical Guide for Italian/English Translators*. Cambridge: Cambridge University Press.
Vinay, J. P., & Darbelnet, J. (1958/1995). *Comparative Stylistics of French and English: A Methodology for Translation*. Translated into English by Juan Sager & M. J. Hamel. Amsterdam/Philadelphia: John Benjamins.

Companion website and online resources

http://cw.routledge.com/textbooks/translationstudies/
www.est-translationstudies.org/

Assignment 1: Discuss the local strategies that have been adopted by the translator of the text extracted from the Ministry of Information, Sultanate of Oman. Then outline the strategies you think appropriate or not (to read the whole text, pay a visit to their website: www.omaninfo.om/english/index.php):

ST:
تقع سلطنة عُمان في أقصى الجنوب الشرقي لشبه الجزيرة العربية بين خطي عرض 16° 40' و 20' °26 شمالاً وبين خطي طول 50' °51 و 40' 59° شرقاً، وتطل على ساحل يمتد إلى 3165 كيلومتراً يبدأ من أقصى الجنوب الشرقي حيث بحر العرب ومدخل المحيط الهندي، ممتداً إلى بحر عُمان حتى ينتهي عند مسندم شمالاً، ليطل على مضيق هرمز الاستراتيجي حيث مدخل الخليج العربي.

TT:
Sultanate of Oman is located in south-eastern part of the Arab semi-peninsula, between latitudes 16.40 and 26.30 and longitudes 51.50 and 59.40. Its shore extends from Hormoz in the north to Yemen republic in the south, so it is open to three seas: Arab Gulf, Oman Gulf and Arab sea. Bordered by UAE and Saudi Arabia in the west, Republic of Yemen in the south, Hormoz bay in the north, and Arab Sea in the eastern border. This location has given Oman its historical role in connecting Arab Gulf states with these countries . . .

Assignment 2: Select some articles from the Constitution of Jordan (http://cco.gov.jo/en-us/documentsofthecourt/jordanianconstitution.aspx) and comment on the translation of the text, paying special attention to the local strategies taken by you while translating.

Assignment 3: Select an English text from BBC (no more than 500 words) and translate it for publication in one of the local newspapers in your country. Before embarking on the actual act of translating the text, adopt the most appropriate global strategy. In no more than 300 words, tell us in your introduction why you have opted for this particular global strategy. Then annotate your local strategies that are to be consistent with your global strategy.

Assignment 4: *Instructors*: Discuss with your students the strengths and weaknesses of the annotations offered by an MA student with respect to local strategies adopted. In your discussion, you may touch on whether:

(i) there is an external coherence in the translator's annotation. In other words, does s/he link his/her annotation to others' studies?
(ii) there are other examples that need to be annotated.

ST:
It has also responded with new policies on financial reporting, better intelligence coordination, and a stronger police and military. The government plans to make laws that will weaken the protections against searches of mosques and legalize the ability to search outside databases in order to profile suspects. Although numerous such proposals have been discussed, little legislative action has actually been completed (Netherlands Report).

TT:
وقد استجابت الحكومة أيضًا بأحداث (1) سياسات جديدة تتعلق بتقديم التقارير المالية، وتنسيق الاستخبارات على نحو أفضل، وإيجاد (2) شرطة وجيش أكثر قوة. وتخطط الحكومة لسن القوانين التي من شأنها إضعاف الحماية ضد عمليات تفتيش المساجد وتشريع القدرة على البحث خارج قواعد البيانات من أجل تحديد سمات المشتبه بهم. وذكر تقرير هولندا أنه على الرغم من مناقشة عدة مقترحات كهذه، لم يستكمل سوى القليل من الإجراءات التشريعية بشكل فعل (3).

Annotation

1 أحداث 'making' is added using amplification procedure (Vinay and Darbelnet 1995, cited in Munday 2012: 89).
2 Another amplification procedure application is undertaken here with the verb إيجاد 'creating' added (Vinay and Darbelnet 1995, cited in Munday 2012: 89).
3 Modulation technique (Vinay and Darbelnet 1995 cited in Venuti 2000/2004: 89–90, 2012: 88) is used whereby the positive point of view *'little legislative action has actually been completed'* is changed into a negative one لم يستكمل سوى القليل من الإجراءات التشريعية بشكل فعلي. This is for the purpose of producing natural and clear TT. It is important to note that this shift in viewpoint does not change the contextual meaning of the ST because of the addition of سوى 'only'.

80 *Annotating local strategies*

Assignment 5: *Instructors*: Discuss with your students the strengths and weaknesses of the annotations offered by an MA student with respect to local strategies adopted. In your discussion, you may touch on whether:

(i) there is an external coherence in the translator's annotation. In other words, does s/he link his/her annotation to others' studies?
(ii) there are other examples that need to be annotated.

ST:
The duties of the First Minister and Deputy First Minister will include, inter alia, dealing with and co-ordinating the work of the Executive Committee and the response of the Northern Ireland administration to external relationships .

The Executive Committee will provide a forum for the discussion of, and agreement on, issues which cut across the responsibilities of two or more Ministers, for prioritising executive and legislative proposals and for recommending a common position where necessary (e.g. in dealing with external relationships).

TT:
ستشمل واجبات الوزير الأول ونائب الوزير الأول، من جملة أمور أخرى (1)، التعامل مع أعمال اللجنة التنفيذية ومع استجابة إدارة ايرلندا الشمالية للعلاقات الخارجية وتنسيقها.
ستعدّ اللجنة التنفيذية مُلتقى للنقاش والاتفاق على القضايا التي تتخلل مسؤوليات اثنين أو أكثر من الوزراء، وذلك من أجل إيلاء(2) الأولوية للاقتراحات التنفيذية والتشريعية ولتزكية موقف مشترك عند الضرورة (على سبيل المثال في التعامل مع العلاقات الخارجية (3)).

Annotation

1. According to *Faruqi's Law Dictionary* (1983), the phrase "inter alia" can be translated into بين أشياء أخرى، من ذلك، من عدة أشياء أخرى. However, I found that rendering it as من جملة أمور أخرى harmonises more with such context.
2. I preferred using the word إيلاء instead of using the word إعطاء since it makes the Arabic legal features more distinctive.
3. Hatim (1997b: 16) states that "A literal approach to the translation of legal texts necessitates that we preserve source text word order as far as possible". However, in this context, preserving the word order would not reflect a good Arabic structure. Therefore, changing the order of the verb "co-ordinating" with the repetition of the preposition مع helps in making the TT sentence more grammatical.

Assignment 6: *Students*: Select an English text (no more than 500 words) and translate it for publication in one of the local newspapers in your country. Before embarking on the actual act of translating the text, adopt the most appropriate global strategy. In no more than 300 words:

(i) tell us in your introduction why you have opted for this particular global strategy.
(ii) annotate any type of shift occurred while translating the text.

The Routledge Course in Translation Annotation website at www.routledge.com/cw/almanna contains:

- PowerPoint slides
- Further reading links
- Further assignments
- More research questions
- Further annotated texts

4 Annotating grammatical issues

> **In this chapter ...**
>
> The previous chapters have looked into translation strategies (be they global or local). In this chapter, special attention will be paid to how to annotate and comment on grammatical issues, in particular **number**, **passive voice**, **active voice**, **tense**, **aspect** and **modality**. To this end, ample authentic data drawn from existing translations or translated for the purposes of this study will be used to drive home relevant theoretical constructs.
>
> **Key issues**
>
> - Grammatical equivalence
> - Modality
> - Morphology versus syntax
> - Number
> - Passive voice versus active voice
> - Tense versus aspect

Grammatical equivalence

Grammatical equivalence refers to the diversity of grammatical categories across languages. Grammatical rules may vary across languages, and this may pose some problems in terms of finding a direct correspondence in the target language. Different grammatical structures in the source language and target language may cause remarkable changes in the way the information or message is carried across. These changes may require translators to intrinsically manage the ST by (1) adding some information to the ST, (2) omitting some information from the ST and/or (3) making some syntactic and textual adjustment.

Grammar has two main dimensions: 'morphology' and 'syntax' (cf. Crystal 1980; Baker 1992/2011; Baker and Hengeveld 2012). Morphology concerns the structure of single words, the way in which their form varies to indicate specific contrasts in the grammatical system (e.g., singular/dual/plural; past/present/future; passive/active; etc.). Syntax, on the other hand, deals with the grammatical structure of groups of words (clauses vs. sentences) and the linear sequence of classes of words (noun, verb, adverb, adjective, etc.). The syntactic structure imposes restrictions on the way messages can be organized in the text.

Choices in language can be expressed grammatically or lexically. Choices made from closed systems (singular/dual/plural; past/present/future; active voice/passive voice, etc.) are grammatical; those made from open-ended sets are lexical. Grammatical categories are not identical in all languages. Languages differ widely in the way they map various aspects of world experiences. In this regard, Baker (1992: 84) rightly comments:

> Languages which have morphological resources for expressing a certain category such as number, tense, or gender, have to express these categories regularly; those which do not have morphological resources for expressing the same categories do not have to express them except when they are felt to be relevant.

English, for example, has certain morphological resources to express aspects, such as perfective or progressive (see what follows). Therefore, to express a progressive aspect, for example, in English, the language user has to express it grammatically as in:

- *He is reading a novel.*
- *He has been reading a novel.*
- *He will be reading a novel.*

However, to translate the same aspect into Arabic, which has no grammatical category for a progressive aspect, translators can express it lexically by using lexical items, such ما يزال/لا يزال '*still*', الآن '*now*', في هذه الأثناء '*at this moment*', مُنكبّاً/منهمكاً '*busy with*' and so on, but they do not have to, because lexical choices are largely optional.

To show how not taking morphological asymmetries between the interfacing languages may lead to an inaccurate mental image, let us consider the translation offered by a translation trainee to the following text:

ST:
Standing in what is left of his burnt-out home this week, Jehad showed me a photo on his mobile phone. It was of a cheeky, chunky, round-faced little boy in denim dungarees, chuckling in a pushchair, dark-eyed with a fringe of fine brown hair pushed across his brow.

TT:
وعندما كان جهاد واقفا في ما تبقّى من بيته المحروق في هذا الأسبوع، أراني صورة في هاتفه المحمول. كانت لولد صغير ذي وجه مستدير، مكتنز، ممتلئ الخدين وكان يرتدي رداءا قطنيا وكان ضاحكا في عربة أطفال، وعيناه قاتمتان ذات أهداب بنية رقيقة تصل إلى حاجبيه.

84 *Annotating grammatical issues*

> **Comment**
>
> Apart from the accuracy of translation, the student translator has confused the two semantically related English words *'cheek'* and *'cheeky'* when rendering the word *'cheeky'* in the English ST. This confusion has skewed the coherence of the text. Checking up the meaning of the adjective *'cheeky'* in a number of monolingual dictionaries, one may well conclude that it has nothing to do with *'cheek'*. Rather, it simply means slightly rude or showing no respect, but often in a funny way.

Number

Number is a grammatical category of noun, pronoun, adjective and verb agreement that expresses count distinctions, and denote whether the writer/speaker is referring to 'one', 'two', 'three' or more. Languages are different in the way in which they treat count nouns in terms of number. English, for example, refers to one (singular) or more than one (plural): *'house > houses', 'man > men', 'car > cars'* and so on. Arabic, however, makes a distinction between one (singular), two (dual) and more than two (plural): ولد *'boy' >* ولدين/ولدان *'two boys' >* أولاد *'boys'*.

Arabic expresses these categories – singularity, duality and plurality – grammatically by using certain morphemes. English, on the other hand, expresses singularity and plurality grammatically but expresses duality lexically. Then where is the problem if languages have the potential resources to express these number categories whether grammatically as in Arabic, grammatically and lexically as in English and lexically as in Japanese or Chinese?

The question that springs to mind in this respect is that how translators deal with duality when translating a text from a language that has a grammatical category, say Arabic, to a language that lacks such a grammatical category, say English! Baker (1992: 88) rightly comments that translators have two main options: (1) omitting "the relevant information on number" or (2) encoding "this information lexically", for instance, by using lexical items that have the ability to express duality, such as *'two'* or *'both'*.

Baker (Ibid.) warns against exaggerating in reflecting these grammatical categories in the target language that has no specific grammatical category that could correspond to the grammatical category in the source language. Such exaggeration may make the translation "awkward and unnatural because it will not reflect normal ways of reporting experience in the target language" (90). However, it is worth noting that when we translate from a language that has no grammatical category for duality, say English, into a language that has a grammatical category for duality, say Arabic, and we come across a count noun that, for sure, refers to two of the entities (e.g., *the girl's eyes, the man's ears, the boy's hands,* etc.), then such duality needs to be reflected in the target text. Consider the following example quoted from Almanna and Almanna (2008: 40):

ST:

The doctor examined the patient's kidneys and discovered that the patient had been suffering from kidney failure for three months.

TT:

فحص الطبيب كليتي المريض واكتشف أنه كان يعاني فشلاً كلوياً منذ ثلاثة أشهر.

> **Comment**
>
> In translating from English to Arabic, Arabic requires the use of the dual form when referring to the patient's kidneys (something left implicit in English) in a contrastive structure as the one quoted.

However, do we need to annotate our translation on these issues? Annotation is needed by translators/annotators when translating a segment that leaves them with more than one option to follow. In this case, the translator starts a series of actions, including analyzing the ST, highlighting the elements that need to be reflected in the TT and prioritizing among the competing elements. Hence the need for annotation to persuade their readers that they are aware of other options but opted for this particular local strategy or a combination of many local strategies in rendering the text at hand. A translator working from a language that has no duality form, say English, into a language that has a number distinction, say Arabic, needs not to translate and then annotate duality-indicated lexical items, such as *'two'* or *'both'*. Consider the following example extracted from Rhonda Byrne's book *'The Secret Daily Teachings'* (Al-Ismail 2009: 53):

ST:

In every moment of your day, there are two paths before you. Take the path of goodness, for goodness' sake.

TT:

في كل لحظة من لحظات يومك ستجد أمامك طريقين، فاسلك طريق الخير لتنعم بالخير.

Closely related to number is the issue of countability as opposed to noncountability. Again, languages are different in how they treat nouns in terms of countability versus noncountability. A great number of nouns that are countable in one language are not in another. Words like معلومة > معلومات *'information'*, دليل > أدلة *'evidence'*, فاكهة > فواكه *'fruit'*, تشريع > تشريعات *'legislation'*, بحث > بحوث *'research'*, نصيحة > نصائح *'advice'* and مطر > أمطار *'rain'* are countable nouns in Arabic but noncountable in English. Consider the following example in which a countable noun in Arabic is translated into noncountable without any attempt to insert the missing information (Haroun 2013: 12–13):

ST:

هناك كتابات كثيرة عالجت هذا الموضوع لكنها لم تشبعه بحثاً، وحتى الآن، فإن الآراء لم تتفق حول المسائل الأساسية التي تتحكم في كل دراسة علمية والتي بدون الفصل فيها لا يمكن التوصل إلى حقيقة ما وقع في ذينك الاسبوعين الأول والثاني من شهر مايو (أيار) سنة 1945.

86 *Annotating grammatical issues*

TT:
There has been a great deal of research addressing this topic but it has not done it justice. In most historical studies, there are different academic perspectives on the crucial issues that arise; therefore it is impossible to discover what actually happened in the first and second weeks of May 1945 without resolving these issues.

> **Comment**
>
> As can be observed, the translator has translated كتابات 'lit. *writings*' into *'research'*, which is a noncountable noun in English. Semantically speaking, the denotative meaning of the word *'writing'* is wider and less specific than that of *'research'* as the latter is part of the former, which covers, in addition to research, essays, books, monographs and so on. From the context and co-text, it is clear that the original writer means a particular type of writing based on research as sharply indicated by لم يشبعه بحثًا. However, had the translator given full consideration to the issue of countability, he could have suggested a rendering like: *'pieces of research'*.

Active versus passive

Voice is a grammatical category of verbs that is related to what thing or person is acting (active) and what thing or person is being acted upon (passive; Crystal 1997). When a verb is used to describe what an entity (thing or person) is doing, it is active. However, when it is used to describe what is done to an entity (thing or person), it is passive (Swan 1995). According to Swan, not all verbs can be expressed in the passive voice. For example, *'die'*, *'go'*, *'arrive'* and *'have'* are all inherently active. This is related to whether a verb is transitive or intransitive.

Active and passive are two different forms grammatically, semantically and pragmatically. They have different meanings and perform different functions in language (cf. Ghazala 2011: 101). Most languages have a variety of potential resources for constructing 'agentless' clauses, and these "variations in structure of the clause are said to relate to different world views and to relay different ideological slants" (Hatim and Mason 1997: 225). These variations in structure can therefore pose various problems in translation, depending on

1 Are there similar structures in the target language?
2 Are these structures marked or unmarked in the target language?
3 Do these structures in the target language have meanings and perform functions similar to those performed by the source language?
4 What is the global strategy that should be adopted by the translator, taking into account the purpose of the translation, text type, translation function, the generic conventions and the target reader's expectations?

Wilson (1993) emphasizes that in English, some verbs (such as *'open'*, *'wash'*, *'read'*, *'translate'*, *'interpret'*, *'sell'*, *'cultivate'*, etc.), although they are in the active voice, can express a passive meaning. For example: *'these clothes wash well'* can have the meaning: *'these clothes are washed well'*. This type of sentence occurs in a number of languages, such as English and Chinese; hence it is named a 'national passive' or 'middle voice/passival' (for more details, see Oxford English Dictionary, entry for *passival*).

The term *middle voice* or *passival* is sometimes used to refer to verbs used without a passive construction but in a meaning in which the grammatical subject is understood as undergoing the action. The meaning may be reflexive as in: *'Fred shaved'*, meaning *'Fred shaved himself'*, but is not always:

- *These cakes sell well*: [we] sell these cakes [successfully]
- *The clothes are soaking*: [the water] is soaking the clothes.
- *The ticket is printing*: [the machine] is printing the ticket.

Another construction sometimes referred to as *passival* involves a wider class of verbs and was used in English until the 19th century. Sentences having this construction feature progressive aspect and resemble the active voice but with meaning like the passive. Examples of this would be:

- *The house is building* (modern English: The house is being built).
- *The meal is eating* (modern English: The meal is being eaten).

In Arabic, which is a Semitic language whose verbal system is morphologically rich, there are also two voices: passive and active. Like English, in Arabic, passive functions in the same way, that is, passive can be constructed only when a transitive verb is used. At times, passive is resorted to because of its brevity and conciseness, thus shifting the focus of attention toward the recipient and the action rather than the doer. Consider the following examples from the Holy Qur'an in which passivization is opted for:

- فَإِن لَّمْ تَجِدُوا فِيهَا أَحَدًا فَلَا تَدْخُلُوهَا حَتَّىٰ يُؤْذَنَ لَكُمْ وَإِن قِيلَ لَكُمُ ارْجِعُوا فَارْجِعُوا هُوَ أَزْكَىٰ لَكُمْ وَاللَّهُ بِمَا تَعْمَلُونَ عَلِيمٌ (النور، 28).
- هَذِهِ جَهَنَّمُ الَّتِي كُنتُمْ تُوعَدُونَ (يس، 63).
- قَالُوا مَا أَخْلَفْنَا مَوْعِدَكَ بِمَلْكِنَا وَلَٰكِنَّا حُمِّلْنَا أَوْزَارًا مِّن زِينَةِ الْقَوْمِ فَقَذَفْنَاهَا فَكَذَٰلِكَ أَلْقَى السَّامِرِيُّ (طه، 87).
- وَإِذَا قِيلَ لَهُمْ لَا تُفْسِدُوا فِي الْأَرْضِ قَالُوا إِنَّمَا نَحْنُ مُصْلِحُونَ (البقرة، 11).

In touching on the main reasons for using passivization in Arabic, Wright (1975: 50) holds that passive is used for four reasons. They are:

1 When God or a higher being is the doer of the action.
2 When the doer of the action is unknown or at least not known for sure.
3 When the text producer does not want to name the doer of the action for any reason.
4 When greater attention is placed on the entity affected by the action rather than on the doer of the action.

88 *Annotating grammatical issues*

In Arabic, however, some sentences can express both passive and active:

أصلحت سيارتي:

- *I repaired my car* (expressing an active meaning, i.e., I repaired it by myself).
- *I had my car repaired* (expressing a passive meaning, i.e., my car was repaired by a mechanic).

قص شعره.

- *He cut his hair* (expressing an active meaning, i.e., he cut his hair by himself).
- *He had his hair cut* (expressing a passive meaning, i.e., his hair was cut by a barber).

صبغ بيته.

- *He painted his house* (expressing an active meaning, i.e., he painted his house by himself).
- *He had his house painted* (expressing a passive meaning, i.e., his house was painted by somebody).

Again, when an issue under consideration is due to the mismatches between the interfacing languages, it loses its appeal in the practice of annotating – it does not require a host of annotation as in their actual practice of translating, translators are inherently required to intrinsically manage their translations to be in line with the TL linguistic and stylistic norms (cf. Farghal 2012: 85–176). By intrinsic managing, Farghal (2012: 89) states that it refers to

> the alterations effected in the TL text due to the mismatches existing between the TL and the SL. These mismatches range from the most micro- to the most macro-levels, including phonic, syntactic, semantic, pragmatic, textual, and cultural disparities. The appropriate managing of these disparities is a prerequisite in the process of translating, for leaving them unmanaged would produce unintelligible and/or awkward translations, which, in many cases, cause communication breakdowns in the TL.

Consider the following example quoted from Abdulrahman Al-Rubai'i's story ذلك الأنين *'Groaning'* (for more details on the author and the story, see Chapter 1 in this book) that exhibits that passive and active voices in transitivity choices are not identical and have different functions and effects and reflect different points of view and ideologies among languages:

ST:

ثم سقطت في إحداها، لم أعد قادرا على الخروج، قوة ساعدي لم تسعفني، وعندما أفلحت أحاط بي رجال ملثمون يتبادلون كلمات مبهمة ويستحثون بعضهم عليّ،

TT:

Then, I fell into one of them; I was unable to get out. My arm was not strong enough to help me get out. When I did have some luck, some hooded men surrounded me exchanging strange words, urging one another to attack me.

Annotation

Here, the actors of the material processes in the fifth, sixth and seventh clauses in the above example, i.e. ..... أحاط بي رجال ملثمون. is sharply determined by the original writer, viz. رجال ملثمون, i.e. *'hooded men'*. The TT, English, offers two options: active *'hooded men surrounded me'* and passive *'I was surrounded by hooded men'* on the one hand, and English stylistically accepts the active form in such a context without injecting the structure with markedness on the other. Further the active voice in such a text type and context is not inconsistent with the global strategy that the translator may well adopt. As such, there is no need to change it into a passive form.

Here is another example of translation extracted from Cultural and Scientific Cooperation between the government of the Hashemite Kingdom of Jordan and the government of the Sultanate of Oman for the Years 2002–2003–2004:

ST:
يخصص الجانب العُماني عددا من المنح الدراسية للطلبة الأردنيين في مؤسسات التعليم العالي بالسلطنة معفية من الرسوم الدراسية ويخصص الجانب الأردني عددا مساوياً من المنح الدراسية للطلبة العمانيين في مؤسسات التعليم العالي الرسمية في الأردن على أن يتفق على الأعداد والتخصصات سنويا وفق إمكانيات كل طرف وذلك بالطرق الدبلوماسية.

TT:
The Omani Party shall allocate a number of scholarships free from tuition fees for Jordanian students at institutions of higher education in the Sultanate, and the Jordanian Party shall allocate an equal number of scholarships for Omani students at public institutions of higher education in Jordan, providing that the Parties hereto agree upon numbers and specializations annually according to the potentials of each Party and through diplomatic channels.

Annotation

To respond to the marked use of the verbalized structure in the passive form in the original text, i.e. على أن يتفق or شريطة الاتفاق, instead of على أن يتم الاتفاق, an attempt has been made, here, to reflect such markedness by opting for the active voice *'provided that Parties hereto agree upon . . .'* despite the availability of the passive voice.

Tense versus aspect

Aspect is often confused with the closely related concept of tense because they both convey information about time. While the tense locates an action, activity or state in time, the aspect conveys other temporal information, such as completion, noncompletion, frequency, continuity and so forth (cf. Radwan 1975; Aziz 1989; Baker 1992; Khalil 1999; Gadalla 2006, among others). To put this differently, the tense refers to *'temporally when'*, while aspect refers to *'temporally how'*. For example, consider the following sentences: *'I drink'*, *'I am drinking'*, *'I have drunk'* and *'I have been drinking'*. All are in the present tense, as they describe the present situation, yet each conveys different information, or points of view, as to how the action pertains to the present. As such, they differ in aspect. In other words, the verb form tells us two types of information:

1 The tense – time reference or time relation – may indicate whether an action, activity or state is in past, present or future.
2 The aspect, the temporal distribution of an event, covers the semantic ranges of continuity, frequency, regularity, completion, noncompletion, momentariness and so on. (cf. Radwan 1975: 30; Baker 1992: 98; Gadalla 2006: 52–53).

According to Celce-Murcia and Larsen-Freeman (1999: 110), there are four types of aspects in English, namely "simple (sometimes called zero aspect), perfect, progressive, and their combination perfect progressive". Jarvie (1993: 39) states that these four aspects can be reduced to only two marked aspects: "progressive aspect and perfect (or perfective) aspect". While the former refers to an action "in progress, or ongoing or continuous at the point of time", the latter indicates that "the action is retrospective or has been completed". By way of explanation, let us consider the following example (Ghazala 2012: 10):

ST:
No one is sure whether, from Israel's current perceived position of strength, he genuinely wants a lasting peace that would give the Palestinians a proper state. He leaves room for maneuver. He is flexible to a point of opportunism.

TT:
وفي ظل سطوة الموقف الإسرائيلي في الوقت الراهن، فلا أحد يعرف بشكل قاطع ما إذا كان حقاً يريد سلاماً دائماً يمنح بموجبه الفلسطينين دولةً حقيقيةً أم لا. إذ إنه عادة ما يترك باب المناورة مفتوحاً فهو مرن إلى حدّ الانتهازية.

> **Annotation**
>
> Here, it is felt that the addition of the phrase عادة ما *'usually'* is needed in Arabic to make the text read smoothly on the one hand, and lay emphasis on the regularity and frequency of the action as a matter of routine on the other. It is worth noting that unlike English that has to express the regularity and frequency of an action grammatically, Arabic can express them lexically

Annotating grammatical issues 91

when they are relevant (cf. Baker 1992). Languages differ widely in the way they map various aspects of world experiences. In this regard, Baker (Ibid.: 84) rightly comments:

> Languages which have morphological resources for expressing a certain category such as number, tense, or gender, have to express these categories regularly; those which do not have morphological resources for expressing the same categories do not have to express them except when they are felt to be relevant.

> Actually, it is the aspectual rather than temporal reference that causes problems in translating from Arabic to English. In this regard, Shamaa (1978: 36–37) states: "To render the original meaning as faithfully as possible, it is therefore essential to determine whether a given action is completed or in progress, instantaneous or enduring, momentary or habitual, etc.".

To demonstrate the aspectual rather than temporal reference that needs to be given full consideration in the process of translating between Arabic and English, let us discuss the following example (Almanna 2014: 50):

ST:
People start smoking for a variety of different reasons. Some think it looks cool. Others start because their family members or friends smoke. Statistics show that about 9 out of 10 tobacco users start before they're 18 years old.

TT:
يبدأ الناس عادة التدخين لأسباب عديدة، فبعضهم يظن أنه أمر رائع، وآخرون يبدأونه متأثرين بأحد أفراد عائلته أو أصدقائه الذين يدخنون. أظهرت الإحصائيات أن 9 أشخاص من أصل 10 يبدأون التدخين قبل سن الثامنة عشر.

> **Annotation**
>
> Here, attention is paid to verb aspects. In the ST, the original writer uses a simple present tense expressed by *'start', 'think', 'smoke', 'show'*, etc. However, the emphasis in the third sentence *'statistics show . . .'* is on the completion of the action, rather than on its continuity or frequency; hence the possibility of opting for a simple past tense in Arabic as in:
>
> أظهرت الإحصائيات أن 9 أشخاص من أصل 10 يبدأون التدخين قبل سن الثامنة عشر.
>
> Opting for a simple past tense despite the availability of a formal correspondent, i.e. the simple present tense, will lead to what is labelled by Catford (1965) as 'intra-system shifts'. According to Catford (80), intra-system shifts occur where the SL and TL possess systems which approximately correspond formally as to their constitution, but translators for a particular reason resorts to selecting a non-corresponding term in the TL system.

92 *Annotating grammatical issues*

To further cast light on the importance of determining whether a given action is completed or in progress, instantaneous or enduring momentary or habitual and so on, let us consider the following example extracted from Yāsīn's story بصمة مواطن *A Citizen's Fingerprint* (n.d.):

ST:

و(هناك) قام أحدهم بنزع القيود التي كانت على حواسه . . . فتح عينيه ليجد نفسه في مكتب فاخر يشغله ضابط . . . تتشاجر الشرائط على كتفه لتجد مكانا كافيا لها . . . وهنالك من هو مثله انتزعت قيوده قبل صاحبنا بدقائق فقط . . .

TT:

And 'there' one of them removed the restraints which had covered his senses. He opened his eyes to find himself in a luxurious office occupied by an officer whose stripes were fighting to find a place for themselves on his shoulder. And 'there' was someone else like him whose restraints had been removed just minutes before our friend's.

Annotation

Extra attention is paid to verb aspect as the emphasis in some parts of the ST is placed on the sequence of events, not on the completion of these actions, as in:

1 التي كانت على حواسه . . . (i.e. first the restraints had covered his senses, and then somebody removed the restraints)
2 انتزعت قيوده . . . (i.e. first the restraints of someone else had been removed, and then the restraints of the main character was removed).

It is worth noting that giving no consideration to verb aspect can produce a change in time reference, thus affecting the pragmatic communicative effect. As such, one would not hesitate to avoid the use of simple past tenses in the TT, and instead, s/he may use past perfect tenses, viz. *'. . . had covered'* and *'had been removed'*.

Further, in the first clause و(هناك) قام أحدهم بنزع القيود, a 'weak verb', namely قام is used. It is worth noting that in Arabic, there are a number of verbs, such as صار, راح, قام, among others which are sometimes used, in addition to stylistic reasons, to emphasize an aspectual reference. It is clear from the context and/or co-text that the emphasis in the above example is placed on the completion of the action rather than its continuity or frequency, hence the use of the past simple tense expressed by *'one of them removed the restraints'*.

To cast more light on the importance of determining the aspectual reference in the nexus of translation, let us reconsider the following extract discussed earlier from a different perspective (Alqunayir 2014: 10–11):

ST:

Derrida was referring to the suppression of the Islamic element in the history of the Mediterranean and, by extension, of Europe.

TT:
أخذ دريدا يشير إلى قمع العنصر الإسلامي في تاريخ منطقة حوض البحر المتوسط، بل توسع ليشمل أوروبا في وصفه أيضًا.

> **Comment**
>
> Here, the original writer, in an attempt to lay emphasis on the continuity of the action 'referring' in a particular period in the past, opts for the continuous past tense, expressed by *'was referring'*. To reflect such an aspectual reference into Arabic, which has no grammatical category for a progressive aspect, the translator has resorted to the use of the lexical item أخذ *'lit. to take'*. Like the verb كان *'was/were'*, one of the functions of the verb أخذ in Arabic is to emphasize the continuity of an action in the past; hence the possibility of rendering the extract into كان يشير إلى .... or أخذ يشير إلى ....

Modality

Modality has been investigated from various perspectives by a great number of scholars, yielding numerous definitions of modality. It is defined by the *Oxford Concise Dictionary of Linguistics* by P. H. Matthews (2005: 228) as "category covering either of a kind of speech act or the degree of certainty with which something is said". According to Quirk and colleagues (1985: 219), "modality may be defined as the manner in which the meaning of a clause is qualified so as to reflect the speaker's judgment of the likelihood of the preposition it expressed being true". In a similar vein, Halliday (1970: 349) holds that modality is "external to the content, being part of the attitude taken up by the speaker". It refers to "the speaker's assessment of probability and predictability" (349). It is "a form of participation by the speaker in the speech event. Through modality the speaker associates with the thesis an indication of its status and validity in his own judgment, he intrudes and takes up a position" (335).

Modality is the soul of the sentence/clause. There is no utterance without modality. Modality is a blurred concept that centres on such notions as obligation, necessity, lack of necessity, prohibition, expectation, advisability, possibility, ability, request, permission, preference, lost opportunities and habitual past (for more details and examples, see Almanna and Almanna 2008: 61–86).

Cast in less technical terms, modality, for example in English, normally expressed by modal verbs (such as *'can'*, *'may'*, *'shall'*, *'must'*, etc.), adverbs (such as *'possibly'*, *'probably'*, etc.), phrases (such as *'be going to'*, *'be used to'*, *'be supposed to'*, etc.) or clauses (such as *'it is possible that'*, *'it is likely that'*, *'it is probably that'*, etc.) is used by language users (be they speakers or writers) to express their attitudes, opinions or moods in terms of degrees of certainty and obligation and so forth towards what happens or what exists in the outside world. The speaker/writer's choice of modal verbs or expressions signals both the degree and type of involvement s/he has in superimposing certain directionality on the message *per se* to be in line with his/her mood and/or attitude (cf. Quirk *et al.* 1985: 219). Language users are in need of expressing such notions because "such notions are conceptually grounded in the fact that human beings often think and behave as though things might be, or might have been, other than they actually are, or were" (Perkins 1983: 6). In a similar vein, Palmer (1986: 58) states that "by uttering a modal, a speaker may actually give permission (may, can), and make a promise or threat (shall) or lay an obligation (must)".

English modals have received a remarkably extensive investigation during a prolonged period of time. However, due to the fact that Arabic does not have a well-defined class of modals perfectly corresponding to English modal verbs and expressions (Aziz 1989; Khalil 1999; Farghal and Shunnaq 1999; Abdel-Fattah 2005; Al-Qinai 2008), modality has not received a fair share of that extensive body of research in the field of contrastive studies between Arabic and English. The "only valid arguments for comparison are [...] the semantic-pragmatic ones" (Al-Qinai 2008: 30). This is "because of the extent to which languages differ in their mapping of the relevant semantic content onto linguistic form" (Bybee and Fleischman 1995: 3). Further, modality is usually associated with issues such as 'contextuality', 'ambiguity' and 'indeterminacy'; hence its difficulty in transferring from one language to another adequately (Coates 1983; Perkins 1983; Abdel-Fattah 2005; Jarjour 2006, among others).

Modality in language falls into two main categories (Halliday 1970; Lyons 1977; Hoye 1997; Farghal and Shunnaq 1999; Jarjour 2006; Al-Qinai 2008, among others):

    a)   *deontic modality*

The term *'deontic'* comes from Greek, where the word *'deon'* means 'duty', 'necessity', 'obligation' and the like. It is normally used to affect the situation; it is obligation/necessity-oriented. In other words, it describes how things ought to be. However, some scholars (cf. Downing and Locke 1992; Farghal and Shunnaq 1999; Jarjour 2006) state that deontic modality is also concerned with the concept of 'permission'.

    e.g., You **have to** visit your family. (obligation/necessity)
    e.g., You **may** go. (permission)

    b)   *epistemic modality*

The word *'epistemic'* comes from Greek, where the word *'epistemikos'* means 'to understand' or 'to have knowledge'. Epistemic modality is concerned with the degree of the language user's commitment to the truth of the proposition (cf. Downing and Locke 1992; Farghal and Shunnaq 1999; Jarjour 2006).

    e.g., He's studied well; he **should** pass the exam (*'should'* here refers to expectation).

Further, there are two subtypes of modality in language. These are: 'dynamic modality' and 'root modality' (cf. Jarjour 2006).

Annotating grammatical issues 95

c) *dynamic modality*

The dynamic modality centres on the concept of 'ability'. So it has nothing to do with the language user's opinion, attitude or mood.

*e.g., He **can** speak English fluently.*

Here, the speaker is describing a factual situation about the doer of the action, the actor. So the modal verb *'can'* in this sentence can be replaced with the modalized phrase *'be able to'*.

d) *root modality*

The root modality is characterized by ambiguity, as it combines 'dynamic modality' and 'deontic modality'.

*e.g., Tom **can** go to the party.*

Here, the modal verb *'can'* can be replaced with the modalized phrase *'be able to'* as in: *'Tom is able to go to the party'*, that is, 'dynamic modality' or can be understood as: *'Tom is permitted to go to the party'*, that is, 'deontic modality'.

Arabic, for its turn, does not have a closet, well-defined class of modals to express such notions as obligation, necessity, lack of necessity, prohibition, possibility, advisability, ability, permission, request, expectation and so on. However, it still has the potential resources to express the speaker/writer's attitude, opinion or mood toward what happens or what exists in the outside world (Almanna and Almanna 2008: 61–87). In this study, modality in Arabic is classified into four groups:

1	Modalized particles	قد, لعل, سوف, سـ, ــ, etc.
2	Modalized verbs	يستطيع, يُحتمل, يُستحسن, يُرجّح, يتوجّب, ينبغي, يتعيّن, يجب, يفترض, يُستبعد, يُحبّذ, يفضّل, etc.
3	Modalized prepositions	على, لـ, etc.
4	Modalized prepositional phrases	من الواجب, من المفروض, من الجائز, من الممكن, من المرجّح, من المستحسن, من المحبّذ, من المستبعد, من المفضّل, من المتعيّن, etc.

In legal, particularly in legislative texts, a fifth group can be added, that of the simple present tense, as it has the ability to express obligation, thus reflecting the illocutionary force of an order. Consider the following example quoted from The Law of Income Tax on Companies of 1981 along with its official translation:

ST:

المادة 1
1 – يسمى هذا القانون ضريبة الدخل على الشركات لعام 1981.
2 – يسري مفعول هذا القانون على كافة أنحاء سلطنة عمان . . .

96 *Annotating grammatical issues*

TT:
Article 1

1   *This Law shall be called The Law of Income Tax on Companies of 1981.*
2   *This Law shall be effective in all parts of the Sultanate of Oman* . . .

As such, translating from English into Arabic, the legal *'shall'* lends itself to a simple present tense, as in the following example extracted from the agreement between the government of Ireland and the government of the United Kingdom of Great Britain and Northern Ireland, which was reached on April 10, 1998, in the multiparty talks (Al-Hinai 2009: 12–13):

ST:

1   *This Agreement shall replace the Agreement between the British and Irish Governments done at Hillsborough on 15th November 1985 which shall cease to have effect on entry into force of this Agreement.*
2   *The Intergovernmental Conference established by Article 2 of the aforementioned Agreement done on 15th November 1985 shall cease to exist on entry into force of this Agreement.*

TT:

1   يحل هذا الاتفاق محل الاتفاق المنعقد بين الحكومتين البريطانية والايرلندية في هيلسيروه بتاريخ 15 نوفمبر/تشرين الثاني 1985 والذي ينتهي سريان مفعوله عند دخول هذا الاتفاق حيز التنفيذ.
2   يكون المؤتمر الحكومي الدولي المنشأ بموجب المادة ٢ من الاتفاق المذكور أعلاه والمبرم بتاريخ 15 نوفمبر/تشرين الثاني 1985 لاغياً عند دخول هذا الاتفاق حيز التنفيذ.

Comment

Here, the modal *'shall'* has nothing to do with 'futurity'; rather, it is treated as "an inseparable part of the verbal elements in which it occurs" (Hatim 1997b: 30). In Arabic legal, however, to express the parties' obligation, the simple present tense is preferably used. Being aware of the conventions of the legal language in both languages, the translator has resorted to a simple present tense expressed by يحل and يكون as an equivalent to *'shall'* plus the verb *'cease'*.

The difficulty of rendering modality between English and Arabic lies, first, in that Arabic does not have a well-defined class of modals precisely corresponding to English modal verbs and expressions and, second, in that modality in general is characterized by ambiguity, contextuality and indeterminacy (cf. Bybee and Fleischman 1995; Abdel-Fattah 2005). As such, special attention needs to be paid to the identification of the function of the modal in question. By way of explanation, let us consider the following example extracted from Greene's *The Bomb*

Annotating grammatical issues 97

Party (1980: 9–10) and translated into Arabic by a number of translation students at their final year of the BA programme:

ST:
I think that I used to detest Doctor Fischer more than any other man I have known just as I loved his daughter more than any other woman.

TT 1:
لم أبغض في حياتي أكثر من شخص الدكتور فشر ولم أعشق امرأةً أكثر من أبنته في ذات الوقت.

TT 2:
أعتقد بأني بدأت امقت الدكتور فيشر أكثر من أي رجل اعرفه وذلك بمجرد ما إن تعرفت بابنته التي عشقتها أكثر من أي امرأة أخرى.

TT 3:
أظن إنني اعتدت على كرهي للدكتور فشر أكثر من أي رجل عرفته وكان مقدار هذا الكره كمقدار حبي لابنته التي أحببتها أكثر من أي امرأة أخرى.

TT 4:
تماما كما أحببت إبنته اكثر من أي إمرأة أخرى أعتقد إني اعتدت على كره الدكتور "فيشر" أكثر من أي شخص عرفته.

TT 5:
إنني كنت أمقت الطبيب فيشر أكثر من أي رجل آخر عرفته، تماماً كما احببت ابنته أكثر من أي امرأة أخرى.

> **Comment**
>
> As can be observed, the students have failed to intrinsically manage the text – they have failed to deal with issues such as the ST parallelism and antonyms (*'detest'* vs. *'love'* and *'man'* vs. *'woman'*), not to mention grammatical and spelling errors. As far as modality is concerned, three students (1), (4) and (5) have changed a mere possibility expressed by *'I think'* in the ST into an absolute certainty. Further, three students (1), (2) and (4) have failed to deal with the modal *'used to'*, which is used in English to express habitual past. Having given full consideration to modality, they could have suggested something like:
>
> أعتقد أنني كنت أكره الدكتور فيشر أكثر من أي رجل آخر، تماما كما كنت أحب ابنته أكثر من أية امرأة أخرى.

Here is another example of translation from a different text type extracted from Rhonda Byrne's book *The Secret Daily Teachings* (Al-Ismail 2009: 5):

ST:
If you find fault with another, then you just brought others finding fault with you. If you judge another, then you just brought judgment to you. And if you appreciate others, you will bring appreciation to you. You have to make the quality dominant in you first, before you can attract it in your outside world.

TT:

إن كنت ممن يتصيد أخطاء الناس وينتقدهم فستجد منهم من يعاملك بالمثل، وإن كنت مقدرا لهم فستكسب تقديرهم. فما عليك إلا أن تجعل هذا النوع من التعامل هو الصفة المهيمنة على طباعك أولا، قبل أن تترجمها إلى تصرفاتٍ في عالمك الخارجي.

Comment

Here, three modal verbs, namely *'will'*, *'have to'* and *'can'*, are used by the original writer to express her attitudes, opinions or moods in terms of degrees of certainty and obligation, and so on towards what happens or what exists in the outside world. The first modality *'will'* lends itself to the modalized particle س, thus maintaining its function in the TT. As for the second modal *'have to'*, it is used deontically to describe how things ought to be, so it is obligation/necessity-oriented. The translator, having figured out its function, has opted for the modalized preposition على, thus reflecting its function in the TT. With respect to the third modal *'can'*, it has nothing to do with the language user's opinion, attitude or mood. Rather, it is used to describe a factual situation about the doer of the action. Had the translator given full consideration to the function performed by the modal *'can'* in the example, he could have suggested renderings like:

قبل أن تتمكن من أن تترجمها إلى تصرفاتٍ في عالمك الخارجي.
قبل أن يكون بمقدورك أن تترجمها إلى تصرفاتٍ في عالمك الخارجي.
قبل أن يكون باستطاعتك أن تترجمها إلى تصرفاتٍ في عالمك الخارجي.

To highlight the importance of determining the function of modality prior to embarking on the actual act of translating, let us consider the following example extracted from the monograph *'The 2006 Lebanon campaign and the future of warfare: Implications for army and defense policy'*, coauthored by Stephen Biddle and Jeffrey A. Friedman and translated by Samhat (2014: 10):

ST:

The 2006 conflict between Israel and Hezbollah in Lebanon could prove comparably influential today. A central issue in today's debate is the role of nonstate opponents in defense planning. It is widely believed that such enemies will be increasingly common in the future, and many now advocate sweeping change in U.S. military posture to prepare for this.

ST:

واليوم، قد تثبت حرب تموز 2006 بين إسرائيل وحزب الله في لبنان أنها على القدر نفسه من التأثير. يشكّل دور الخصوم الفاعلين خارج إطار الدول نقطة أساسية في نقاش اليوم حول التخطيط الدفاعي. ويسود الاعتقاد بأن وجود هؤلاء الأعداء سيصبح أكثر شيوعاً في المستقبل، لذا ينادي العديد اليوم بإجراء تغيير جذري على الهيكلية العسكرية الأمريكية من أجل الجهوزية لهذا الأمر.

> **Comment**
>
> In this example, the original writers, in order to express their commitment to the truth of the proposition, use two modal verbs, namely *'could'* and *'will'*. To begin with, the modal *'could'* in this example is used epistemically, indicating a possibility. Identifying the function of the modal verb *'could'* in this example, the translator has opted for the modalized particle قد *'may/might'*, thereby reflecting the possibility in the TT. As for the second modal *'will'*, it is used to refer to futurity, thus lending itself to the modalized particle سـ *'will/shall'* in the TT.

Further reading

Abdel-Fattah, M. M. (2005). "On the Translation of Modals from English into Arabic and Vice Versa: the Case of Deontic Modality," *Babel*, Vol. 51 (1), pp. 31–48.

Baker, M. (1992/2011). *In Other Words: A Coursebook on Translation*. London/New York: Routledge.

Bybee, J., & Fleischman, S. (1995). "Modality in Grammar and Discourse: An Introductory Essay." In J. Bybee & S. Fleischman (eds.), *Modality in Grammar and Discourse,* pp. 1–14. Amsterdam/Philadelphia: Benjamins, Amsterdam.

Farghal, M. (2012). *Advanced Issues in Arabic-English Translation Studies*. Kuwait: Kuwait University Press.

———, & Al-Shorafat, M. (1996). "The Translation of English Passives into Arabic: An Empirical Perspective," *Target*, Vol. 8 (1), pp. 97–118.

Gadalla, H. (2000). *Comparative Morphology of Standard and Egyptian Arabic.* Muenchen, Germany: Lincom Europa.

———. (2006). "Arabic Imperfect Verbs in Translation: A Corpus Study of English Renderings," *META: Journal des Traducteurs, Les Presses de l'Universite de Montreal,* Vol. 51, No. 1, pp. 51–71.

Hatim. B. (1997). *English-Arabic/Arabic-English Translation: A Practical Guide.* London: Saqi Books.

Hoye, L. (1997). *Adverbs and Modality in English*. London: Longman.

Shamaa, N. (1978). *A Linguistic Analysis of Some Problems of Arabic into English Translation*. Unpublished PhD thesis. Oxford: Oxford University Press.

Companion website and online resources

http://cw.routledge.com/textbooks/translationstudies/
www.est-translationstudies.org/

> **Assignment 1:** *Instructors*: Select an English or Arabic text (depending on your students' translation directionality – whether they translate out of Arabic or into Arabic) from BBC (no more than 500 words). Then ask them to translate the text to be published in one of the local newspapers, paying special attention to grammatical issues.

100 *Annotating grammatical issues*

Assignment 2: *Instructors*: Discuss with your students the strengths and weaknesses of the annotations offered by an MA student with respect to translating passive/active voices. In your discussion, you may touch on whether:

(i) there is an external coherence in the translator's annotation. In other words, does s/he link his/her annotation to others' studies?
(ii) there are other examples that need to be annotated.

ST:
Only 5 percent have advanced degrees, compared to 19 percent of the broader population. In France, 56 percent of those from majority Muslim countries have a secondary education or less, compared to 46 percent in the broader population. Higher degrees are more equally distributed in France.

TT:
ويملك 5 في المئة فقط شهادات عليا، مقارنة بنسبة 19 في المئة من السكان على نطاق أوسع. وفي فرنسا، يحصل 56 في المئة من أولئك الذين ينتمون للبلدان ذات الأغلبية الإسلامية على تعليم ثانوي أو أقل منه، مقارنة مع 46 في المئة من عدد السكان على نطاق أوسع. بينما يكون الحصول على الشهادات الأعلى، أكثر تكافئًا.

Annotation:

If the ST is translated into passive voice, the TT will be something like وتُوزَّع الشهادات الأعلى بصورة أكثر تكافئًا. However, this sounds like a literal translation which contradicts the aim of the translation approach. Therefore, I have decided to employ communicative translation (Newmark 1988: 46–48). In doing so, many changes have been made. These include بينما *'while'* is added at the beginning of the sentence. Moreover, the verb *'distributed'* is translated using its dynamic equivalent الحصول *'gaining'* (Nida 1964, cited in Venuti 2000/2004: 136–140).

Assignment 3: *Students*: Comment on the following translation offered by an MA student translator by paying special attention to grammatical issues, in particular modality and transposition:

ST:
To understand the power and the magic of gratitude, you have to experience it for yourself. So why not begin by deciding to find 100 things a day to be grateful for? If you practice gratitude every day it won't take long before gratitude is your natural state of being, and when that happens you will have unlocked one of the greatest secrets to life.

Annotating grammatical issues 101

TT:
عليك أن تعيش بنفسك التجربة مع الشكر لتدرك قوته وفاعليته. جرب ذلك بمحاولتك إيجاد عدد مئة من الأشياء التي أنت ممتن وشاكر لها كل يوم. فإن مارست عادة الشكر يوميا فستصير طبيعة فيك وبهذا ستكتشف واحدا من أعظم أسرار الحياة.

Assignment 4: *Students*: Select an English text (no more than 500 words) and translate it for publication in one of the local newspapers in your country. Before embarking on the actual act of translating the text, adopt the most appropriate global strategy. In no more than 300 words:

(i) tell us in your introduction why you have opted for this particular global strategy.
(ii) annotate any grammatical issues that you have faced while translating the text.

Assignment 5: *Students*: Select a legislative text (no more than 500 words) and translate it to a professional level. Before embarking on the actual act of translating the text, adopt the most appropriate global strategy. In no more than 300 words:

(i) tell us in your introduction why you have opted for this particular global strategy.
(ii) annotate any grammatical issues that you may face while translating the text.

Assignment 6: *Students*: translate the following text taken from the book titled *'State Crime: Governments, Violence and Corruption'* by Penny Green and Tony Ward (2004, cited in Sultan 2007: 18) by paying special attention to the grammatical differences between English and Arabic:

ST:
The crime of torture also creates victims well beyond the tortured person. The evidence accumulated by the torture treatment centres around the world reveals a powerful international legacy. Children of tortured parents, whether or not they themselves were tortured, are reported to suffer a range of reactive symptoms including psychological trauma, recurrent nightmares, recurrent states of anxiety, emotional, sleeping and eating disorders, development delays, problems with regulation of aggression and an inability to develop basic trust . . . in this sense torture can be understood as an act of cultural transformation, moulding and shaping societies within its frame work of, often arbitrary, cruelty, and creating in its wake dislocated, apathetic and fearful populations who withdraw from public life.

The Routledge Course in Translation Annotation website at www.routledge.com/cw/almanna contains:

- A video summary of the chapter
- PowerPoint slides
- Further reading links
- Further assignments
- More research questions
- Further annotated texts

5 Annotating lexical and phraseological choices

> **In this chapter . . .**
>
> The previous chapter has looked into how to annotate and comment on grammatical issues. In this chapter, special attention will be paid to language role–related issues, such as **lexical choices, denotation versus connotation, open choice principle versus idiom principle, metaphor, simile, idioms and collocations.** To this end, ample authentic data drawn from existing translations or translated for the purposes of this study will be used to drive home relevant theoretical constructs.
>
> **Key issues**
>
> - Collocation
> - Connotation
> - Denotation
> - Open choice principle
> - Idiom
> - Idiom principle
> - Metaphor
> - Simile

Lexical choice

Lexical items (words) are not confined to one single meaning. Most lexical items have multiple meanings, which are categorized as either denotative or connotative meanings. The denotation of a word is its explicit definition as listed in a dictionary. In this regard, Dickins and colleagues (2002: 66) state that "the meaning of a text comprises a number of different layers: referential content, emotional colouring, cultural association, social and personal connotations, and so on. The many-layered nature of meaning is something translators must never forget". For example يتسكّع، يتجوّل and يخوّر are synonyms or near-synonyms in terms of their

104 *Lexical and phraseological choices*

denotative meanings (i.e., they mean to go for a walk, to make a trip through an area or place, or to travel from one place to another), but they have different overtones. To begin with, يتجوّل is a neutral word used in many contexts in a positive way, whereas يخوّر and يتسكّع have negative, pejorative overtones. Further, يخوّر is different from يتسكّع in the sense that the former is a dialectal word used in some countries in their spoken language, while the latter is standard but can also be used in spoken language. Let us consider the word شلغم, which is used in some countries, such as Iraq and Kuwait. The denotative meaning of the word شلغم *'turnip'*, which is called in some Arab countries لفت (Egypt and Jordan), refers to a physical object in the real world, a root vegetable commonly grown in temperate climates worldwide for its white bulbous taproot (*Oxford Wordpower* 2010: 842). However, the word is also used in these dialects, particularly by young people to refer to somebody who does not want to leave a place, position or the like (connotation), thus creating a relationship between the denotative meaning and the connotative one, 'interpretant' that works as a sign according to Peircean terminology.

Another interesting example is the word جامد/گامد used in Egypt, which means *'strong'*, *'handsome'*, *'beautiful'*, *'nice'* and so on (connotation) in addition to its literal, straightforward meaning *'to be frozen'* (denotation; its denotative meaning is derived from the verb جَمَدَ *'jamada'*, which is pronounced in some areas of Egypt (such as Kafr El Sheikh, Al Dakahliya, Al Buhairah, Al Gharbiyah among others) گَمَدَ *'gamada'*, hence the adjective گامد *'gāmid'*). The connotative and denotative meanings of words are both correct, but a word's connotation determines when it is used in a particular context. By definition, synonyms have the same denotative meaning but almost always have different connotations, or shades of meaning. For example, the synonyms of *'boat'* include *'ship'*, *'yacht'*, *'dinghy'*, and *'ferry'*. All these words refer to the same thing in the real world, but each elicits a different association in the reader's mind. At times, translators opt for a particular lexical item, thus excluding others for stylistic reasons. Here is an example extracted from Greene's *The Bomb Party* (1980: 9):

ST:
I think that I used to detest Doctor Fischer more than any other man I have known just as I loved his daughter more than any other woman.

TT:
أعتقد أنني كنت أكره الدكتور فشر أكثر من أيّ رجل آخر عرفته، تماماً كما كنت أحبّ ابنته أكثر من أية امرأة أخرى.

> **Annotation:**
>
> Here, there is an example of parallelism: (I used to detest Doctor Fischer more than any other man / I loved his daughter more than any other woman) that needs to be reflected in the TT as in:
>
> أكره الدكتور فشر أكثر من أيّ رجل آخر . . .
> أحبّ ابنته أكثر من أية امرأة أخرى . . .

Lexical and phraseological choices 105

> Further, the original writer, Greene, introduces two antonyms, *'detest'* vs. *'love'* and *'man'* vs. *'woman'*, in a very short extract. Such antonyms fall in parallel structures, as explained above, thus having a stylistic feature that needs to be maintained in the TT, hence our rendering: أكره (i.e., *'I hate'*) vs. أحبّ (i.e., *'I love'*) and رجل (i.e., *'man'*) vs. امرأة (i.e., *'woman'*). It is also worth noting that the main reason for opting for the lexical item كره (i.e. *'hate'*) rather than بغض (i.e. *'hate'* + *'hostility'*) or مقت (i.e. *'hate'* + *'censure'*) is to make up for the alliteration utilized by the original writer, *detest Doctor*.

To cast more light on how not taking into account the deliberate and conscious selections made by the original writer may create a misleading mental image in the minds of the TL readers, let us consider the following excerpt quoted from 'Abdul-Raḥmān al-Rubai'ī story ذلك الأنين *'Groaning'* (2009: 165) and translated for the purposes of this study:

ST:

حلمان تداخلا مع حلمك في أن أحدا قد إغتالني وذهبت، سدد إلي إطلاقات مسدسه ونخرني نخرا، وكنت تصرخين لعل أحدا يأتي ولكن صراخك يتردد في واد لا رائحة فيه لآدمي.

TT:

Two dreams intervened in your dream – someone had murdered me, but you went away. He opened fire on me and filled me with holes. You were screaming perhaps someone would come, but your scream resounded through a valley where there was no trace of anyone.

> **Annotation:**
>
> (a) In the original text, the verb used is اغتال *'to assassinate/to murder'*. An attempt is made to avoid translating it into قتل *'to kill'*, as the verb قتل has a wider and less specific denotative meaning than that of the original اغتال — the meaning of the verb *'to kill'* includes *'to murder'* or *'to assassinate'* among other meanings, such as *'to slaughter'*. On the other hand, the English verb *'to assassinate'* has a political connotation that might invoke in the mind of the reader particular memories and/or images, whereas the verb *'to murder'* does not have any direct political associations. As such, the verb *'to murder'* renders more effectively and accurately the original verb اغتال and its shades of meaning.
>
> (b) Further, the writer, in an attempt to emphasize the act of نخر 'lit. *making holes'*, opts for المفعول المطلق *'absolute object'*, which reads well in Arabic. However, adhering to the ST and translating very close to it might strike the target reader as unusual. As such, one can map such a world experience cognitively yet idiomatically by focusing on the mental picture that might be conjured up in the mind of the target reader, as in *'he opened fire on me and filled me with holes'* or just *'he opened fire on me'*.

106 *Lexical and phraseological choices*

To see trainees' successes and failures while prioritizing the competing elements prior to finalizing their drafts, let us consider the following example given to a number of undergraduate translation students (fourth year, Dept. of Translation, College of Arts, University of Basra):

ST:
Jehad burst out of the editing suite screaming. He sprinted down the stairs, his head in his hands, his face ripped with anguish.

TT 1:
خرج جهاد من مكتب التحرير صارخا. وركض بأقصى سرعة إلى الطابق السفلي وكان منفزعا ووجهه حاملا علامات الألم.

TT 2:
اندفع جهاد من قسم التحرير منفجرا بالصراخ والعويل وراكضنا بأقصى سرعته إلى الطابق السفلي ويده على رأسه.

TT 3:
خرج جهاد من قسم التحرير بأقصى سرعته وهو يصرخ ويده على رأسه وبدت على وجه علامات الحزن.

Comment:

As can be observed, the three trainees have opted for different lexical items in dealing with words/phrases like *'burst out'*, *'sprint down'*, *'rip'* and *'anguish'*. To begin with, خرج *'to go out'* is different from اندفع *'to burst out'*, as the former does not indicate that the doer of the action *'Jehad'* has gone with top speed, while the latter does. The same holds true for نزل *'to go down'* and ركض *'to run'*. As for the expression *'his face ripped with anguish'* can be translated as:

بدت على وجهه علامات الألم / ارتسمت على وجهه علامات الألم / تعلو وجهه علامات الألم / وعليه علامات الألم / ووجهه يُعبِّر عن ألم / خيَّمت على وجهه علامات الألم

Although all these renderings cognitively conjure up in the mind of the reader almost one picture that 'pain appears on his face', they differ in terms of their degree of pain. It starts with بدت على وجهه علامات الألم 'lit. *signs of pain began on his face*' and then grows stronger and stronger in ارتسمت على وجهه علامات الألم 'lit. *pain made signs on his face*', تعلو وجهه علامات الألم 'lit. *his face is covered with signs of pain*' or وجهه يُعبِّر عن الألم 'lit. *his face shows pain*', and in خيَّمت على وجهه علامات الألم 'lit. *signs of pain prevailed on his face*'. However, taking into account the metaphorical use of the original expression, one can suggest something like: يعتصر وجهه الألم '*his face is squeezed/contorted with pain*', as in:

اندفع جهاد من جناح التحرير وهو يصرخ، فنزل إلى الطابق السفلي بأقصى سرعته – كانت يداه على رأسه .. كان يعتصره الألم.

Lexical and phraseological choices 107

To show how being content with one side of the coin without giving full consideration to the context in which the sign occurs may well lead to a different syntagm, thereby affecting the overall meaning of the text. Let us consider the following example quoted from *Human Rights Watch* (2014, August; their own official translation):

ST:

في يناير/كانون الثاني 2011 خرج المصريون إلى الشوارع احتجاجاً على وحشية الشرطة وللمطالبة بالعيش والحرية والعدالة الاجتماعية.

TT:

In January 2011, Egyptians took to the streets protesting police brutality and demanding bread, freedom, and social justice. (p. 25)

Comment:

Here, the sign that needs special attention is العيش 'lit. *living*'. In Egypt, this word is used to refer to خبز '*bread*' with slight modification in its pronunciation in terms of vowels as in العِيْش '*bread*' in contrast with العَيَش '*living*'. To test the significance of each sign and the difference between them, one can rely on the sign's paradigmatic and syntagmatic axes. Approached from this perspective, mentioning micro signs such as:

خرج – المصريون – إلى – الشوارع – احتجاجا على – وحشية – الشرطة – و – المطالبة بـ – . . . . – والحرية – والعدالة الاجتماعية.

invokes in the mind of the translator the sign العيش in the sense of '*living*' rather than العيش in the sense of '*bread*'. However, taken into consideration that the word العيش '*bread*' is used in Egypt as a symbol for '*living*', the translator has opted for العيش in the sense of '*bread*'. This clearly illustrates why Anne Alexander and Mostafa Bassioiuny have resorted to '*bread*' in the title of their newly published book *Bread, Freedom and Social Justice: Workers and the Egyptian Revolution* (2014).

The following example, quoted from Ghazala (2012: 10) and translated for the purposes of this study, shows the importance of giving full consideration to the demands of text typologies and generic conventions on the one hand and living up to the TL readers' expectations on the other:

ST:

Mr Netanyahu, not Mr Obama, is the real enigma. His record suggests a reluctance to make the compromises that could bring a deal.

TT:

تكمن المعضلة الحقيقية في السيد نتنياهو وليس في السيد أوباما، إذ يُظهر سجله الخاص عدم رغبته في تقديم تنازلات من شأنها أن تُرسي قواعد السلام في المنطقة.

108 *Lexical and phraseological choices*

> **Annotation:**
>
> (a) The noun *'enigma'* can be translated as مُعَمّى، طِلَسْم، مُشْكِلَة، لُغْز، أُلْقِيّة، أُحْجِيّة etc. However, in an attempt to reflect the ST emphasis which is placed on *'Mr Netanyahu'* by thematizing it, it is felt that a verbal sentence containing a structure that is able to maintain such a characteristic is needed as in:
>
> ... تكمن المعضلة الحقيقية في السيد نيتنايهو وليس السيد أوباما
>
> Here, the verb تكمن in Arabic collocates well with the noun معضلة; hence the use of معضلة instead of the other possible options, such as لغز or مشكلة etc.
>
> (b) The verb *'suggest'* lends itself to يُظهر in the TT.
> (c) Translating the word *'deal'* into صفقة will strike the TL reader as unusual in such a context, and translating it into تسوية, which is fine and makes sense in such a context, will create a lexical repetition; hence its translation into سلام *'peace'*. Such a semantic adjustment requires us to have a verb that collocates well with the noun سلام, such as يُرسي قواعد السلام or يبسط السلام, on the one hand, and motivates us to add the phrase في المنطقة *'in the region'* on the other.

To demonstrate how not paying special attention to the deliberate and conscious selections made by the original writer may create a different mental image in the minds of the TL readers, let us consider the following excerpt given to a number of undergraduate translation students (fourth year, Dept. of Translation, College of Arts, University of Basra):

ST:
Earlier, two men extradited from the UK with Abu Hamza also appeared in court. Khaled al-Fawwaz and Adel Abdul Bary are charged with participating in the bombings of embassies in Tanzania and Kenya in August 1998.

TT 1
وقد ظهر في المحكمة اثنان من المتهمين تم ترحيلهما في وقت سابق من المملكة المتحدة مع أبي حمزة. وهما خالد الفواز وعادل عبدالباري اللذين اتهما بالمشاركة في تفجيرات السفارتين في تنزانيا وكينيا في شهر آب عام 1998.

TT 2
وفي وقت سابق ظهر أيضا شخصان في المحكمة تم استلامهما من المملكة المتحدة مع أبي حمزة، وهما خالد الفواز وعادل عبدالباري المتهمان بمشاركتهما بضرب السفارتين في تنزانيا وكينيا بالقنابل في شهر آب من عام 1998.

TT 3
وفي وقت يسبق ذلك، ظهر أيضا رجلان في المحكمة قامت بتسليمهما المملكة المتحدة مع أبي حمزة هما خالد الفواز وعادل عبدالباري المتهمان بالمشاركة في تفجيرات السفارتين في تنزانيا وكينيا في شهر أغسطس عام 1998.

Lexical and phraseological choices 109

Comment:

(a) As can be seen, the student translators have opted for different lexical items in dealing with words like *'extradite'*, *'appear'*, *'participate'* and *'bombing'*. To begin with, the two words سلّم *'to surrender'* and استلم *'to receive'* are completely different. In the TT2, the trainee has opted for changing the actor of the process of doing along with the process itself (*'extradite'* into استلم, *'receive'*), thus changing the form of the message, but without changing the mental image. This is an example of 'optional modulation' to borrow the term from Vinay and Darbelnet (1958/1995) and 'structure shift' to use Catford's (1965) term.

Further, in such a context the verb رحّل *'to expel (a person from a country)'* is different from سلّم *'to extradite'* in the sense that the latter indicates that an alleged fugitive or criminal is returned to another country where s/he has been accused of committing something illegal, while the former means that an alien is expelled from the country.

(b) Taking into account the demands of the text type and generic conventions of the TL, the verb *'appear'* lends itself to مثّل in place of the direct translation of the verb ظهر. The same holds true for the verb *'participate'* that lends itself to ضلوع, *'to involve'* + negativity.

(c) As for the translations suggested by the trainees for *'bombing'*, it is worth noting that تفجيرات *'bombings'* is slightly different from الضرب بالقنابل as the denotative meaning of the former is wider and less specific than the latter ضرب بالقنابل *'to attack with bombs'*.

Multiword Units

Semantically speaking, any language mainly consists of lexical features and phraseological features (cf. Sinclair 1991, 1998, 2008; Francis 1993; Farghal 2012). These two types of features cover both compositional meaning and unitary meaning. Therefore, in order to understand the meaning of a sentence/clause, one needs to be familiar with both features: lexical and phraseological features by relying on two principles: open choice principle (or terminological tendency) and idiom principle (or phraseological tendency). To begin with, a language user can sometimes elicit the meaning of the whole sentence/clause from its words and their arrangements – the syntax of any language can specify the slots into which memorized items can be inserted. This principle is also known as 'slot and filler', as it tells us the basic restrictions on the possible choices of lexical items that can be utilized by a language user to syntactically fill in every slot identified in any given text (Sinclair 1991: 109). For example, the meaning of the sentence:

e.g., My friend usually goes to school with his dad.

is compositionally driven by the meanings of its lexical items along with the function words used to form the sentence. Open choice principle for Sinclair (1991: 109) is

> a way of seeing language as the result of a very large number of complex choices. At each point where a unit is complete (a word or a phrase or a clause), a large range of choices opens up and the only restraint is grammaticalness.

The idiom principle, however, posits that a language user "has available to him or her a large number of semi-preconstructed phrases that constitute single choices, even though they might appear to be analysable into segments" (Sinclair 1991: 110). The rest of this section will show the validity of idiom principle in dealing with metaphor, simile, idioms and collocation.

Metaphor

On the traditional view of metaphor that goes back to Aristotle, metaphor is principally envisaged as a matter of a resemblance between two entities. Thus, metaphors like:

- *'Her eyes were fireflies'.*
- *'Life was a fashion show'.*
- *'Laughter is the music of the soul'.*
- *'The exam was a nightmare'.*

work because they assert a resemblance between *'her eyes'* and *'fireflies'*; *'life'* and *'a fashion show'*; *'laughter'* and *'the music of the soul'*; and *'the exam'* and *'a nightmare'* respectively. As such, understanding the meaning of the first metaphor, for instance, involves identifying things *'eyes'* and *'fireflies'* might hold in common.

Traditionally, metaphor is defined as a word or expression which has departed from its basic meaning to refer to other things, there are two levels of meaning in metaphor: surface meaning and deep meaning, which are not identical, in most cases. The idea of surface meaning in contrast to deep meaning is adapted, partly not entirely, from the American linguist Noam Chomsky's theory 'deep structure' (1957), in which he stresses that the underlying structures of language do not change; what changes, as he states, is only the surface structure; hence different forms for the same thought. Although Chomsky does not link his own theory to the question of translation, it influences translation scholars that followed him, in particular Eugene Nida, who first introduces the concept of 'kernel sentences' (1964: 66). By kernel sentences, he means that the minimal structures in a language "from which all other structures are developed by permutations, replacements, additions, and deletions" (Ibid.: 68).

> It is both scientifically and practically more efficient (1) to reduce the source text to its structurally simplest and most semantically evident kernels, (2) to transfer the meaning from source language to receptor language on a structurally simple level, and (3) to generate the stylistically and semantically equivalent expression in the receptor language.

On the conceptual metaphor view, metaphor is seen as a cognitive process that helps us phraseologize and idiomatize our sociocultural experiences by establishing correspondences between easily understood entities and hard-to-understand entities. On this understanding, Lakoff and Johnson (1980: 7–9) state that metaphor is a comparison of two entities. This comparison consists of two elements: the 'vehicle', the existing entity to which the other entity, the 'target', is compared to for the purpose of emphasis, freshness, eloquence and so on. Such a "metaphorical mapping allows knowledge about metaphor's vehicle domain to be applied to the target in a way that fundamentally determines or influences the conceptualization of the target" (Riemer 2010: 246). Thus, in the metaphor *'silence is gold'*, the vehicle is *'gold'* and the target is *'silence'*. Here, *'silence'* (the target) is compared to *'gold'* (the vehicle) to highlight the importance of silence (the ground). From the point of view of translation, priority needs to be given first to the ground of the comparison, then the target. Assume that there is not a functional equivalent to such a metaphorical expression in Arabic. In this case, the translators need to pinpoint first the ground of the comparison, which is *'the importance of being silent'*. Then they try to maintain the target, which is *'silence'*. If it is culturally acceptable, then they try to utilize the same vehicle, *'gold'*. To put this differently, *'silence is gold'* means silence is highly recommended or important. Thus, it is the translator's duty to transfer at least this underlying (deep) meaning. Of course, there will be some sort of loss in the stylistic effect, but better safe than sorry.

Let us now move on to nonstructural metaphor, in which the surface meaning is completely different from its underlying meaning and does not rely on comparison between things. For native English speakers, the expression *'to carry the can'* means *'to take the blame for something'*. As can be seen, its surface lexical items depart from their basic, straightforward, referential meaning to refer to something else, say somebody who, in a certain situation, takes the blame for something even though it is not his/her own mistake. Following is an illustrative example extracted from Yāsīn's story بصمة مواطن *A Citizen's Fingerprint* (n.d.):

ST:

يبتلعه المساء . . . فيوغل في أحشاء الصمت . . . ومن ذا الذي يستطيع فرارا إذا عسعس الألم داخل النفس . . . وتوغلت الأحزان في حنايا الفؤاد

TT:

The night swallows him so he delves ever deeper into the heart of silence. Who can, then, escape if the pain is densely settled inside the self and sadness penetrates the depths of the heart?

Annotation:

(a) In the above example, a personification is used whereby المساء *'evening'* is talked of in terms of having the power to swallow somebody. Such an image is created in a single verb يبتلع *'to swallow'*. An attempt is made to reflect such an image in the TT, hence the metaphorical use *'the night swallows him'*.

112 *Lexical and phraseological choices*

> (b) Further, another attempt is made to resist the temptation of opting for an unmarked collocation, viz. *'wall of silence'* or *'a vow of silence'* and so on in the rendering of the marked collocation in أحشاء الصمت *'the bowels of silence'*. This is exactly what Trotter (2000: 351) tries to lay emphasis on when he states: "Translation requires invariance in the markedness of collocates, rather than replacing abnormal usage in an original with normal usage in translation".
>
> (For more details on annotating this example, see annotating stylistic features in this book.)

Metaphor may be 'single', one word, or 'extended', a collocation, an idiom, a sentence, a proverb, an allegory, a complete imaginative text (Newmark 1988: 104). In this section, due to space limitations, the focus of attention will be shifted toward 'extended metaphor' only, namely 'similes', 'idioms' and 'collocations' (for more examples, see Annotating Stylistic Features in this book). For a fuller description of metaphor, see Dickins and associates (2002: 146–161).

Simile

Simile can be treated in much the same way as metaphor. Simile is a figurative expression used to describe something by comparing it with something else, using comparison markers, such as *'like'*, *'as'* and so forth. It has a quadripartite structure, consisting of:

1 'topic', the entity described by the simile, known in Arabic as *Mushabah*;
2 'vehicle', the entity to which the topic is compared, known in Arabic as *Mushabahun bihi*;
3 'similarity feature(s)', the properties shared by topic and vehicle, known in Arabic as *Wajhu ash-Shabah*;
4 'comparison marker', the article used to draw a comparison between the topic and vehicle, known in Arabic as *Adatu al-Tashbih*.

So, in an idiomatic simile like *'he is as brave as a lion'*, the topic is *'he'*, the vehicle is *'lion'*, the similarity feature is that they are both *'brave'* and the comparison marker is *'as . . . as'*. Such structural features will definitely help us identify the similes easily; however, it is not always as such. Simile is not used just to decorate text with rhetorical language or to show eloquence. It, however, performs a great number of functions inside text. At the forefront of them comes the function to communicate precisely and efficiently. Second, it is used to clarify the point in question, although it is not always easy to interpret a simile, because some of them are culturally bound.

In an attempt to investigate the problematic nature each type causes to translators, simile can be classified in this chapter into three types, namely *'conventional'*, *'encyclopedic'* and *'compressed'*. To start with, a conventional simile, sometimes labeled idiomatic simile, is a type of simile in which the vehicle is an entity representing conventionally certain characteristics to native speakers and is fixed in two common syntactic structures in English:

- topic + verb to be + as + comparison feature (adjective) + as + vehicle (noun/noun phrase), as in:

  I am as busy as a bee.
  The exam was as tough as a stone.
  The question was as difficult as algebra.

- topic + verb + like + vehicle (noun/noun phrase), as in:

  You change your style/your opinion like the weather.
  You eat like a pig.
  You laugh like a hyena.

When the writer/speaker opts for the use of a proper noun as a vehicle, there will be an encyclopedic simile, which can be expressed in the same syntactic structures used in the idiomatic simile. For Pierini (2007: 3), the proper noun in an encyclopedic simile represents a cultural allusion whose interpretation depends on one's knowledge of the world, as in these examples:

He is as happy as Larry.
She feels as pleased as Punch.
She is as rich as Croesus.

The third type of simile in English is the compressed simile, in which information is condensed into a two/three-word lexeme as in:

U-shaped movement
terrorist-type offence
native-like proficiency

Syntactically speaking, this type of simile is not as clear as conventional or encyclopedic similes. However, by studying its syntactic structure and the relations of its lexical items, one can distinguish its vehicle (U, terrorist, native) from its topic (movement, offence, proficiency).

Unlike Arabic, English is characterized by its highly productive process; it has the ability to create a great number of new words and expressions that are rarely found in dictionaries. The difficulty of translating such a simile lies, first, in its compressed structure. which is difficult to render in Arabic unless the translator, prior to embarking upon rendering it, unfolds its compressed structure. So a simile like *'it is a U-shaped movement'* is an alternative to a relative clause with its precedent, *'a movement which is like the letter U'*. By doing so, the process of translation will definitely become easier.

114 *Lexical and phraseological choices*

By way of explanation, let us consider the following lines from a poem titled أنشودة المطر *'Rain Song'* by the late Iraqi poet Al-Sayyāb (1971: 474) translated by Christopher Middleton and Lena Jayyusi (in S. K. Jayyusi 1987: 427):

ST:

عيناكِ غابتا نخيلٍ ساعةَ السحرِ،
أو شرفتانِ راحَ ينأى عنهُما القمرُ
عيناكِ حين تبسمانِ تُورقُ الكرومُ،
وترقصُ الأضواءُ .. كالأقمارِ في نهرٍ

TT:

> Your eyes are two palm tree forests in early light,
> Or two balconies from which the moonlight recedes
> When they smile, your eyes, the vines put forth their leaves,
> And lights dance . . . like moons in a river

Comment:

(a) As can be observed, a conventional simile, expressed by ترقص الأضواء .. كالأقمار في نهر, is used in which the vehicle الأقمار *'moons'* is an entity representing conventionally certain characteristics, such as beauty, to native speakers. In an attempt to reflect the same image in the mind of the TL reader, the translators have opted for maintaining the topic الأضواء *'lights'*, the vehicle الأقمار *'moons'*, the comparison marker كـ *'like'* and the similarity feature is that they are both *'beautiful'*, thus producing a conventional simile.

(b) Further, there are two examples of personification, عيناك حين تبسمان and ترقص الأضواء. In these two examples, العين *'eye'* and الضوء *'light'* are talked of in terms of having the ability to smile and dance, respectively. Having taken into account these metaphorical uses, the translators have opted for reflecting these two images in the TT.

(c) Also, an example of marked collocation غابة نخيل *'lit. palm trees forest'* is used by the original writer in place of the commonly used collocation بستان نخيل *'palm trees grove'*. Given full consideration to the markedness of this collocation, the translators have opted for a literal translation, thereby maintaining the degree of markedness (for more details on collocation, see what follows).

Idioms

An idiom, by dictionary definition, means "a phrase, construction or expression that is recognized as a unit in the usage of a given language and either differs from the usual syntactic patterns or has a meaning that differs from the literal meaning of its parts taken together" (*Webster's New World Dictionary* 1991: 670). This means that one cannot rely on the open choice principle, relying on the meaning

Lexical and phraseological choices 115

of its components, to figure out its meaning and significance; s/he has to resort to the idiom principle. Unlike collocations, which "are fairly flexible patterns of language which allow several variations in form", idioms allow no variation (Baker 1992/2011: 67). Thus, an idiom like *'to smell a rat'* allows no variation in form under normal circumstances.

In translating idioms, translators, prior to embarking on selecting the appropriate local strategy in rendering the ST idiomatic expression, are required to analyze the text in terms of

1   its macro factors, such as genre, readership, context of use and rhetorical effect;
2   its micro factors, such as type, syntactic structure and function of the idiomatic expression; and
3   its relevant to the message and the writer's intention.

It is not always easy to find an appropriate local strategy that goes in line with the global strategy adopted by the translator, in particular when one deals with an idiomatic expression. It is a misleading technique to decide the strategy once one comes across an idiomatic expression. However, the ST (more specifically the segment of the text) at hand needs to be translated first intralingually, analyzing its surface meaning in order to pinpoint its underlying/deep meaning. Then the underlying/deep meaning is transferred literally into the TL. At this stage, the translator decides on the appropriate local strategy in rendering the idiomatic expression.

By and large, local strategies, such as cultural translation, paraphrasing, omission, addition and the like (see Baker 1992: 72–78; Dickins *et al.* 2002; also see Chapter 3 in this book) lead to one of the three types of equivalence: formal versus functional versus ideational equivalence (Farghal 2012: 45–48). When the form of the SL idiomatic expression, the image that is conjured up in the mind of the SL reader, is given full consideration by the translator, the result is a formal equivalent. Here is an example from the Holy Qur'an translated by M. H. Shakir (1995):

ST:

فرجعناك إلى أمك كي تقر عينها ولا تحزن.

TT:

So We brought you back to your mother, that her eye might be cooled and should not grieve.

Comment:

In the original text, there is a body-related idiom, تقر عينها. Unlike universal idioms, which can be easily understood and transferred to another language/ culture, this Quranic idiom is culture specific, and its meaning is far-fetched to the non-Arab readers. Etymologically speaking, the verb قر is derived

116 *Lexical and phraseological choices*

> from the noun القر, which means البرد, 'coldness', and from القرور, which means الماء البارد, 'cold water' (cf. Tawfik 2011: 89). Being aware of its significance and etymology, the translator has adopted a literal approach, thus producing a formal equivalent.

However, when special attention is paid to the function of the SL idiomatic expression, independently of the form and its image conjured up in the mind of the SL reader, it is a functional equivalent. At times, the interfacing languages conceptualize the world experience linguistically in a similar way, "giving rise to optimal equivalence" in which both formal and functional equivalents coincide (see Baker 1992: 72; Farghal 2012: 47). By way of explanation, let us consider the following example (Haroun 2013: 34–35):

ST:
يجب علينا اتخاذ الإجراءات الملائمة لإيقاف الحركة، ولكي تعلم الجماهير أننا غير مستعدين لغض الطرف. ولقد علمنا من جهات مختلفة أن عملية ما، يجري تنظيمها بمناسبة انتهاء الحرب، وسوف تكون عامة. أما مناطقها الحساسة فكثيرة ومنها: سطيف، تبسة، بسكرة، الأوراس، الجزائر، تلمسان، وهران، ومعسكر.

TT:
We have to take the appropriate actions to stop the movement, so the masses know that we are not turning a blind eye. We were informed through various sources that an operation was being organised to take place at the end of the war. This operation will be nationwide and it comprises many sensitive regions such as: Setif, Tebessa, Biskra, Aures, Alger, Tlemcen, Oran and Mascara.

> **Comment:**
>
> Here, it so happens that Arabic and English lexicalize, phraseologize and idiomatize the sociocultural experience غض الطرف and *'to turn a blind eye'* in a similar way, thus giving rise to full or optimal equivalence in which formal equivalence (focusing on the image conjured up in the mind of the reader), ideational equivalence (focusing on the idea) and functional equivalence (focusing on the function and effect of the expression) coincide (cf. Farghal 2012: 47).

When a formal equivalent is unworkable or not a priority and a functional equivalent is not reachable, then the focus is shifted toward the sense, the idea of the SL idiomatic expression, independently of the form and function. By way of explanation, let us consider the following legislative text taken from the agreement between the government of Ireland and the government of the United Kingdom

Lexical and phraseological choices 117

of Great Britain and Northern Ireland, which was reached on 10 April 1998 in the multiparty talks (Al-Hinai 2009: 9–10):

ST:
If in the future, the people of the island of Ireland exercise their right of self-determination on the basis set out in sections (i) and (ii) above to bring about a united Ireland, it will be a binding obligation on both Governments to introduce and support in their respective Parliaments' legislation to give effect to that wish.

TT:
إذا، في المستقبل، مارس شعب جزيرة إيرلندا حقه في تقرير المصير على الأساس الوارد في الفقرتين أعلاه لتحقيق وحدة إيرلندا، فإنه سيكون واجبا ملزما على كلا الحكومتين أن تضع تشريعات (i) و(ii) برلمانيهما موضع الاستعمال وتدعمهما لتنفيذ تلك الرغبة؛

Comment:

As can be observed, the translator has adopted a literal translation when handling the segments of the text. In translating legal documents, in particular legislative writing, priority is given to clarity, accuracy and all-inclusiveness at the expense of naturalness (Almanna 2005); hence the importance of adopting a literal approach (cf. Hatim 1997b; Farghal and Shunnaq 1999) to reflect such basic quality of legal writing. Here, the translator, for the sake of acceptability and readability, has opted for the idiomatic phrase تضع موضع الاستعمال as an equivalent to the verb *'introduce'*, thus deviating from his global strategy adopted earlier. In this regard, Hatim (1997b: 14) holds, "Unless there is a good reason to do otherwise, translators must adhere to the source text syntax (e.g. word order) and semantics (e.g. the succinct expression of what words denote)". It seems that acceptability and readability present themselves as a good reason principle; hence the use of an idiomatic phrase instead of resorting to the direct equivalent قدّم of the ST word *'introduce'*.

Collocation

Collocation, on the other hand, is defined by Crystal as "the habitual co-occurrence of individual lexical items" (cited in Newmark 1988: 212). Generally speaking, words, in any language, are drawn to certain words rather than to others. Such combinations are not governed by certain rules, but rather they arbitrarily co-occur. Collocation is what adds a natural flavor to the lexicon of language and what distinguishes native speakers' languages from others. Let us take the word *'rain'*, which collocates well with the adjective *'heavy'* in English and try our hand at tracing it out in a number of languages to see how differently languages treat this linguistic phenomenon, collocation:

- In Arabic, مطر غزير literally means *'abundant rain'*.
- In German, it is *schwere regen*, literally *'difficult rain'*.

118 *Lexical and phraseological choices*

- In French, it is *pluie battante*, literally *'beating rain'*.
- In Spanish, *mucha lluvia* literally means *'much rain'*, or *lluvia tensa* literally means *'strong rain'*.
- In Italian, *forte pioggia,* literally means *'strong rain'*, but if the adjective comes after the noun, it is *pioggia abbondante*, literally *'abundant rain'*, or *pioggia fitta*, literally *'heavy rain'*.

McCawley (1968: 135) states that the tendency of words toward certain words is determined by two types of lexical rules, namely 'strict subcategorization rules' and 'selectional restriction rules'. The former is highly predictable, purely semantic in nature, and the violation of it results in ungrammatical combinations. The latter, on the other hand, is language specific and less predictable, and its violation might lead to figurative language. By contrast, Palmer (1976: 79) talks of three kinds of collocational restrictions. The first is linked to the meaning of the lexical item as in unlikely *'green cow'*. The second restriction is related to "range – a word may be used with a whole set of words that have some semantic features in common", as in the unlikeliness of *'the rhododendron passed away'*. The third restrictions are concerned neither with meaning nor with range, but rather "collocational in the strictest senses" as *'addled'* with *'eggs'* and *'brains'*. Such restrictions are what prevent a word from being placed with other words that its synonyms can collocate with. For example, there is no difference in English to say 'abnormal or exceptional weather', but 'an exceptional child is not an abnormal child'. The former implies 'defect' while the latter refers to 'a great ability' (Palmer 1976: 77). In other words, although collocation is an arbitrary combination, which is widely predicted by the meaning of its collocated terms, it is sometimes considered "to be idiosyncrasy of individual lexical items" (Belhaaj 1998: 50). Such an idiosyncrasy justifies why we say *'sour milk'* not *'rancid milk'*.

Translating collocations poses problems for translation trainees and sometimes for professionals. This is because "firstly, they are mostly lexicalised differently between any two languages and secondly, they hardly lend themselves to acceptable paraphrase in the TL" (Farghal 2012: 120). He states that "the only guarantee to handle collocations in translation activity is the translator's possession of a good bank of them in the language pair" (Ibid.). However, it is important for translators, while rendering collocation, to pay special attention to the degree of predictability of lexical co-occurrence, the degree of its markedness, as opposed to unmarkedness. Certain combinations are labeled unmarked when they strike native speakers as being basic and natural combination – mentioning one conjures up the other. Whereas marked collocation is the type of combination in which the collocated words are foreign from each other – they are deliberately used by the speaker/writer to create new images (Baker 1992: 51). By way of explanation, let us consider the following two excerpts from (Alqunayir 2014: 10–11):

ST:
Derrida was referring to the suppression of the Islamic element in the history of the Mediterranean and, by extension, of Europe. While the Greek, the Jew, and

the Arab are considered the three prototypes that have shaped the history of the Mediterranean, only a Euro-Christian memory, Derrida argued, has reached the modern period.

TT:

أخذ دريدا يشير إلى قمع العنصر الإسلامي في تاريخ منطقة حوض البحر المتوسط، بل توسع ليشمل أوروبا في وصفه أيضًا. فيقول دريدا وإذا كانت النماذج اليونانية، واليهودية، والعربية هي النماذج الثلاثة التي سطّرت تاريخ منطقة البحر الأبيض المتوسط، فإن الذكرى الأوروبية المسيحية هي الوحيدة التي عاشت حتى العصر الحديث.

> **Comment:**
>
> Here, the translator has opted for an unmarked collocation, سطّر التاريخ 'lit. *to line the history*' when translating the original unmarked collocation '*to shape a history*'. Translating it formally شكّل التاريخ '*to shape the history*' will definitely strike the TL reader as unusual and nonidiomatic, thus affecting the TT acceptability, readability and communicative value. In this regard, Trotter draws attention to the importance of markedness and unmarkedness of collocation to translation. He (2000: 351) emphasizes that translation "requires invariance in the markedness of collocates, rather than replacing abnormal usage in an original with normal usage in translation".

Here is another example:

ST:

There is a long history of debate over moral particularism versus moral universalism. Those who deride multiculturalism and define Islamic values as incompatible with those of the West claim that Muslims are unable to integrate into host societies where they are minorities.

TT:

إن تاريخ الجدل حول الانصرافية الأخلاقية وما يقابلها من الشمولية الأخلاقية تاريخ حافل، إذ يزعم أولئك الذين يسخرون من التعددية الثقافية وينظرون للقيم الإسلامية على أنها غير متوافقة مع القيم الغربية أن المسلمين غير قادرين على الاندماج في المجتمعات المستضيفة لهم حيث يشكلون الأقليات فيها.

> **Comment:**
>
> As can be observed, the translator has adopted a reader-oriented translation when handling the segments of the text, in particular the unmarked collocation '*long history*'. She has paid extra attention to the TL readers and their expectations. Instead of lingering within the bounds of literalness, the translator has opted for تاريخ حافل '*crowded history*' instead of opting for its formal equivalent to borrow terms from Nida (1964).

120 Lexical and phraseological choices

To further demonstrate the importance of identifying the collocations and their degree of markedness, let us consider the following extract taken from 'Abdul-Raḥmān al-Rubaiʿī story ذلك الأنين *Dhālik al-Anīn 'Groaning'* (2009: 165):

ST:

ثم إشتعلت نار في موقد يتوسط الغرفة وتعالى لهبها وعندما تسرب الدفء الى المكان أخذت الأفاعي تتحرك ثم إنسابت على أرضية الغرفة. كل واحدة مضت الى جهة، وتحت سريري دخل بعضها . . .

TT:
Then, a fire was lit in a hearth situated in the middle of the room – its flames flaring. When the warmth spread throughout the place, the snakes started to move and slithered across the floor, each in a different direction. Some of them went under my bed.

> **Annotation:**
>
> Here, there is an example of unmarked collocation in the ST, تعالى لهبها. To reflect such an unmarked collocation in the TT on the one hand and to produce an idiomatic literary rendering on the other, one can opt for verbs, such as *'flare'* or *'leap'* as they collocate well with the noun *'flame'*.

Further reading

Abrams, M. H. (1988/1993). *A Glossary of Literary Terms*. New York: Holt, Rinehart and Winston.
Baker, M. (1992/2011). *In Other Words: A Coursebook on Translation*. London/New York: Routledge.
Crystal, D. (1980). *A Dictionary of Linguistics and Phonetics*. Cambridge: Basil Blackwell.
Dickins, J., Hervey, S., & Higgins, I. (2002). *Thinking Arabic Translation*. London/New York: Routledge.
Dagut, M. (1976). "Can metaphor be translated?" *Babel*, Vol. 32, pp. 21–33.
Farghal, M. (2012). *Advanced Issues in Arabic-English Translation Studies*. Kuwait: Kuwait University Press.
Mandelblit, N. (1995). "The Cognitive View of Metaphor and Its Implications for Translation Theory," *Translation and Meaning*. Part 3. Maastricht: Universitaire Press.
Mason, K. (1982). "Metaphor and Translation," *Babel*, Vol. 28, pp. 140–149.
Newmark, P. (1988). *Approaches to Translation*. New York: Prentice Hall.

Companion website and online resources

http://cw.routledge.com/textbooks/translationstudies/
www.est-translationstudies.org/

Assignment 1: *Instructors*: Select an English or Arabic text (depending on your students' translation directionality whether they translate out of Arabic or into Arabic) from BBC (no more than 500 words). Then ask them to translate the text to be published in one of the local newspapers, paying special attention to lexical choices and phraseological choices.

Lexical and phraseological choices 121

Assignment 2: *Instructors*: Discuss with your students the strengths and weaknesses of the annotations offered by an MA student with respect to translating idioms (highlighted for you). In your discussion, you may touch on whether:

(i) there is an external coherence in the translator's annotation. In other words, does s/he link his/her annotation to others' studies?
(ii) there are other examples of idiomatic expressions that need to be annotated.

ST:
As if echoing Derrida's concerns on a different level, Charles Taylor has argued that the current debate about multiculturalism in Western countries has become a debate about Islam and Muslims. Taylor claims that multiculturalism has become suspect and inextricably linked up with Islam because "almost every reason for toleration's apparent fall into disrepute concerns Islam." Taylor's remark that the debate about Islam and Muslims in Western societies is turning into a crisis of multiculturalism is alarming to say the least. By and large, Islam has become part of a public debate to determine how far multiculturalism will go.

TT:

وكما لو أنه كان ترجيعًا لصدى مخاوف دريدا على مستوى مختلف، فقد ناقش تشارلز تايلور أن الجدل الراهن بشأن التعددية الثقافية في الدول الغربية قد أصبح جدلًا حول الإسلام والمسلمين. إذ يزعم تايلور أن التعددية الثقافية قد أصبحت مشبوهة **وارتبطت ارتباطًا وثيقًا بالإسلام** لأنه «تقريبًا كل سبب يقف وراء فقدان السمعة الحسنة لمبدأ التسامح متعلقٌ بالإسلام.» إن **أقل ما يقال** عن ملحوظة تايلور المتعلقة بتحول النقاش حول الإسلام والمسلمين في المجتمعات الغربية إلى أزمة تعددية ثقافية هو أنها مدعاة للقلق. حيث أصبح الإسلام إلى حد كبير جزءًا من نقاش عام لتحديد المدى الذي سوف تصل إليه التعددية الثقافية.

> **Annotation:**
>
> (a) The idiom 'to say the least' is fronted for better composition. Moreover, in this instance I decided to translate the idiom into an idiom of a similar form and meaning أقل ما يقال.
> (b) Toleration in the sentence is not specified e.g. political or religious toleration. However, the contextual meaning refers to any type of toleration i.e. the idea or principle of it. Thus, I added the word بمبدأ 'principle' (Dickins et al. 2002: 24).

Assignment 3: *Instructors*: discuss with your students the strengths and weaknesses of the annotations offered by an MA student with respect to translating collocations and lexical choices (highlighted for you). In your discussion, you may touch on whether:

(i) there is an external coherence in the translator's annotation. In other words, does s/he link his/her annotation to others' studies?
(ii) there are other examples of collocations and lexical choices that need to be annotated.

122 Lexical and phraseological choices

ST:

The principles of the law of attraction are a powerful tool to summon the healing power within us, and can be used as an aid in total harmony with all of the wonderful medical procedures that are available today. Remember that if there were no healing power within us, nothing could be healed.

If you ask for something but really deep down don't believe that it can be manifested immediately because it is so big, then you are the one who is bringing time into your creation. You are creating the time it will take based on your perception of the size of the thing you have asked for. But there is no size or time in the Universe. Everything exists now in the mind of the Universe!

TT:

تعتبر مبادئ قانون الجذب أداة فاعلة لاستجماع قوى الشفاء في داخلنا فمن الممكن استخدامها كوسيلة مساعدة لتحقيق الانسجام التام مع كافة الإجراءات الطبية **المتطورة** في وقتنا الحاضر. ولا تنسَ اننا لا يمكن أن ننعم بالشفاء لو لم يكن له وجود قوي في أنفسنا.

إن كنت تطمح إلى الحصول على شيء كبير ولكنك في أعماقك لست متأكدا من الحصول عليه مباشرة بسبب هذا الاعتقاد تقحم عامل الوقت في إمكانية الحصول عليه بسرعة. أنت من يحدد القوت الذي ستستغرقه العملية بناءً على تقديراتك لحجم ما كنت طامحا إليه، غير أن الكون لا يعرف حجما أو وقتا، لأن كل شيء موجود **ضمنه**.

Annotation:

(a) I have translated "wonderful" in the ST as متطور because, in the Arabic context, the literal meaning of wonderful رائعة does not collocate with "medical procedures."

(b) I prefer to say "ضمنه" instead of "في ذهن الكون" in order to make the TT more realistic and natural for the target readership as they may consider the latter a fiction. Therefore, in translating this paragraph, I have made some adjustments in order to render the same message and effects. In this type of text, free translation is the ideal method to use in order to accomplish dynamic equivalence (see Nida 1964).

Assignment 4: *Instructors*: Discuss with your students the strengths and weaknesses of the annotations offered by an MA student with respect to lexical choices (highlighted for you). In your discussion, you may touch on whether:

(i) there is an external coherence in the translator's annotation. In other words, does s/he link his/her annotation to others' studies?

(ii) there are other examples of collocations and lexical choices that need to be annotated?

ST:

ونحن عندما نعود إلى تلك الفترة الزمنية نستنطقها، وإلى النصوص المعاصرة نحللها ونفحص المعلومات الواردة فيها، وحينما نتوقف عند الشهادات التي أدلى بها المسؤولون السياسيون الذين كانوا يصنعون الحدث

Lexical and phraseological choices 123

التاريخي في ذلك الوقت، وعندما نعيد قراءة الجرائد والمجلات التي عالجت الموضوع في وقته، فإننا لا نستطيع سوى الاعتراف بأن ما وقع في شهر مايو سنة خمس وأربعين وتسعمائة وألف إنما هو حركة ثورية أعدت لها قيادة حزب الشعب الجزائري التي كانت قد أخذت كل الاحتياطات لتكون النتيجة الحتمية هي إقامة الجمهورية الجزائرية وما يتبعها من مؤسسات وطنية.

TT:
*When we **review** that time period < Ø > and the contemporary texts, we examine and analyse the information contained therein. Also, when the testimonies **given** by political officials, who played an important role at the time, are **considered** and when newspapers and journals **dealing with** this subject are re-read, we can only admit that what happened in May 1945 was a revolutionary movement organised by the leadership of the Parti du Peuple Algérien (PPA), which had taken all measures to bring about the inevitable result; namely, the establishment of a democratic Algeria and consequent national institutions.*

Annotation:

(a) The literal translation of the word "نعود" is "return". The word "review" was opted for instead of the literal translation because it sounds better. Also, the writer indicates in the ST that the actual action of the word "نعود" concerns the analysing and examining of the information. Therefore, the word "review" was chosen in this context. Communicative translation (Newmark 1988).

(b) The word "نفحص" was omitted from the TT because it is a synonym of the word "نستنطقها". In this case, it would be considered a repetition in English. Translation by omission (Dickins *et al.* 2002).

(c) The word "give" was chosen instead of the literal translation "adduce or make" of the word "أدلى" because it collocates better with the word "testimony" (Rundell 2010).

(d) The word "نتوقف" in this context carries a different meaning than the literal equivalent "stop". This verb here implies focusing and paying close and careful attention to details of the testimonies. This word was translated as "considered" which renders the same meaning of the ST.

(e) The expression "عالجت هذا الموضوع" was translated as "dealing with this subject". However, this is a different translation from the same expression in the first paragraph which was translated as "addressing this topic". The reason is to provide an idiomatic translation by using different synonyms and being faithful to the original.

Assignment 5: *Students*: Select an English text (no more than 500 words) and translate it for publication in one of the local newspapers in your country. Before embarking on the actual act of translating the text, adopt the most appropriate global strategy. In no more than 300 words:

(i) tell us in your introduction why you have opted for this particular global strategy.
(ii) annotate any lexical or phraseological choices that you have made while translating the text.

124 *Lexical and phraseological choices*

Assignment 6: *Students*: Select a legislative text (no more than 500 words) and translate it to a professional level. Before embarking on the actual act of translating the text, adopt the most appropriate global strategy. In no more than 300 words:

(i) tell us in your introduction why you have opted for this particular global strategy,
(ii) annotate any lexical or phraseological choices that you have faced while translating the text.

Assignment 7: *Students*: Translate the following text taken from the book titled *State Crime: Governments, Violence and Corruption* by Penny Green and Tony Ward 2004 (cited in Sultan 2007: 18). Then annotate your own translation, paying special attention to the lexical and phraseological choices.

ST:
The crime of torture also creates victims well beyond the tortured person. The evidence accumulated by the torture treatment centres around the world reveals a powerful international legacy. Children of tortured parents, whether or not they themselves were tortured, are reported to suffer a range of reactive symptoms including psychological trauma, recurrent nightmares, recurrent states of anxiety, emotional, sleeping and eating disorders, development delays, problems with regulation of aggression and an inability to develop basic trust . . . in this sense torture can be understood as an act of cultural transformation, moulding and shaping societies within its frame work of, often arbitrary, cruelty, and creating in its wake dislocated, apathetic and fearful populations who withdraw from public life.

The Routledge Course in Translation Annotation website at www.routledge.com/cw/almanna contains:

- A video summary of the chapter
- PowerPoint slides;
- Further reading links
- Further assignments
- More research questions
- Further annotated texts

6 Annotating aspects of cohesion

In this chapter . . .

The previous chapters have looked into lexical and phraseological choices (such as denotation, connotation, metaphors, similes, idioms and collocations) and grammatical issues (morphology and syntax). It is worth noting that the semantic and syntactic aspects of the text (discussed in the previous chapters) are not sufficient tools in text analysis, as there are other invisible forces in the text that are communicated rather than actually observed at the semantic or syntactic levels. The translator/annotator needs to examine these visible and invisible forces. In this chapter, special attention will be paid to aspects of textuality: both cohesive (such as **reference, substitution, ellipsis, conjunction** and **lexical cohesion**) and structural (such as **thematic progression, parallel structures** and **continuity of tenses and aspects**). To this end, ample authentic data drawn from existing translations or translated for the purposes of this study will be used to drive home relevant theoretical constructs.

Key issues

- Coherence
- Cohesion
- Conjunction
- Continuity of tenses and aspects
- Ellipsis
- Lexical cohesion
- Parallel structures
- Reference
- Substitution
- Thematic progression

Cohesion versus coherence

Many attempts in the field of linguistics and translation studies have been made to touch on the terms 'cohesion' and 'coherence' for some time now (see, for example, Halliday and Hasan 1976; Brown and Yule 1983; Newmark 1988, 1991; Hatim and Mason 1990; Bell 1991; Hoey 1991; Baker 1992/2011; Eggins 1994; Thompson 1996; Fawcett 1997; Stillar 1998; Titscher *et al.* 2000; Munday 2001/2008/2012; Dickins *et al.* 2002; Farghal 2012; Almanna 2013).

de Beaugrande and Dressler (1981) point out that any text should include seven criteria. These criteria are cohesion, coherence, intentionality (achieving the author's goals), acceptability (the relevancy and importance of the text to the reader), informativity (the amount of new information the text contains), situationality (the relevancy of the text to its context of situation) and intertextuality (the relation and dependency of the text with and on other texts). The first two criteria (cohesion and coherence) might be defined as 'text internal', which make the passage hang together as a text, whereas the remaining criteria are 'text external' (cf. Tischer *et al.* 2000: 22). So when we say that stretches of language do not hang together as a text, we mean that the passage lacks texture (that is, cohesion and coherence). Hatim and Mason (1990: 192) define texture as "a property which ensures that a text hangs together, both linguistically and conceptually".

To begin with, cohesion is achieved in a number of ways within the text, both grammatically and lexically. Halliday and Hasan (1976) identify two major types of cohesion: *'grammatical cohesion'* and *'lexical cohesion'*. While grammatical cohesion is achieved through *'reference, substitution, ellipsis'* and *'conjunction'*, lexical cohesion is achieved through *'reiteration'*, repeating lexical items, synonyms, hyponyms, myronyms or antonyms, and *'collocation'*. However, there are a number of cohesive devices that do not fall under any of these headings, such as thematic progression, parallelism, continuity of tenses and aspects and the like (cf. Hall 2008: 171).

Despite the fact that cohesion and coherence share the function of "binding the text together by creating a sequence of meaning", they are different from each other in certain aspects (Bell 1991: 164). Unlike cohesion, which involves textual relations appearing on the surface of the text, coherence is in the "mind of the writer and hearer: it is a mental phenomenon" (Thompson 1996: 147), in the sense that the reader or the hearer cannot capture these relations without depending on some external factors, such as his/her knowledge of the world and the subject-matter, personal experience, logic and others. Coherence does not involve explicit relations but rather implicit ones. In other words, coherence is not linked directly to the text but is related to the relation of the text with some external factors. Stillar (1998: 16) points out that coherence is related to the relation that connects the text to its context or, as Eggins (1994: 87) indicates, to the relation that links the text to its context of situation (i.e., register) and context of culture (i.e., genre).

The divergent patterns of coherence between the interfacing languages have an influential role in activating the reordering strategy, to use Malone's (1988) term. Generally speaking, languages normally conceptualize and record their experiences of the world differently. So what is acceptable in one language cannot be taken for

Annotating aspects of cohesion 127

granted in another. At times, translators, for the sake of acceptability and readability, reorganize the textual materials in the TT. Here is an example of textual restructuring extracted from 'Abdul-Sattār Nāṣir's story (2009: 15) ثلاث قصص ليست للنشر *Three Stories not for Publishing*:

ST:

وما أن أرجع نصف أموال الخزينة ثانية، حتى أعلن عن (نصر) كبير غامض، مات فيه عشرات الجنود، لكنّ السعادة كانت قد غمرت أهل المدينة كلهم.. ذلك أن كل بيت فيها يردد سراً:
الحمد لله لم يمت أحد منا..

TT:
Once he had restored the half of the treasury's revenues, he announced a mysterious and great 'victory' in which tens of soldiers had died. All the townsfolk were filled with happiness, each household repeating secretly, "Thanks be to God, none of us was killed".

Annotation:

Adopting Halliday's model for register analysis (for more details, see Chapter 7 in this book), one can infer that the ST word السعادة *'happiness'* is used as an actor of the process of doing and أهل المدينة *'townsfolk'* is the goal of the process – this is not only acceptable but a finer style in Arabic as well. To record such an experience of the world in English, one can say *'people are filled with/ glow with/weep with happiness'* but not the other way round in which *'happiness'* is the actor of the process. To put this differently, textual restructuring, i.e. "the reorganising of chunks of textual material in the TT in order to make them read more cogently" is needed in the translation of the above example (Dickins *et al.* 2002: 137). Such textual restructuring has led to 'structure shift' (Catford 1965) and 'optional modulation' (Vinay and Darbelnet 1958/1995) whereby the form of the message is changed without changing its content.

Reference

The term 'reference', in the sense that Halliday and Hasan (1976) use the term, involves the use of pronouns, articles or adverbs to refer back or forward to an item, thus creating an anaphoric cohesive relation within the text. Halliday and Hasan (Ibid.: 33) state that there are two main types of reference: 'endophoric reference' (i.e., textual reference) and 'exophoric reference' (i.e., situational reference), as in these examples:

Exophoric reference: *How much is that?* (pointing to a pen, for instance).
Endophoric reference:

(i) Anaphoric reference: *Look at the man. He is very tall.*
(ii) Cataphoric coreference: *In addition to its being semantic relations, cohesion involves textual relations.*

128 *Annotating aspects of cohesion*

Halliday and Hasan (Ibid.: 37) designate three sets of referential devices that are potentially capable of achieving a referential function in discourse. These are:

(i) Personal reference: *I, me, mine, my, you, he, she, we, they, it*, etc.
(ii) Demonstrative reference: *this, these, that, those, here, there, now, then*, etc.
(iii) Comparative reference: *same, identical, similar, equal, different*, etc.

Apart from comparative referential devices, all other sets can be applied to Arabic. Halliday and Hasan (Ibid.: 77) recognize two types of comparative reference: *'general'* and *'particular'*. General comparison denotes 'likeliness' or 'unlikeliness' of objects. This type of comparison can be achieved through the use of words like *'similar'*, *'same'*, *'different'* and so on. Particular comparison, on the other hand, refers to that type of comparison in terms of 'quality' or 'quantity'. Thus one can be *'bigger'* or *'smaller'*, *'better'* or *'worse'* and so on than another. In Arabic, however, the only type of comparison that conforms to Halliday and Hasan's classification is particular comparative reference. The comparative form in Arabic typically rhymes with the word أفعل, followed by the preposition من, as in أكبر من . . . *'bigger/older than . . .'*, أطول من . . . *'taller/longer than . . .'*.

Although general comparative referential devices do not exist in Arabic, Arabic has the resources that can accommodate such a type – for example, words like نفس *'same'*, مطابق *'identical'*, مثل *'such'*, مشابه *'similar'*, آخر *'other'*, مختلف *'different'* and so forth. By way of explanation, let us consider this example along with its formal translation (quoted from an Agreement between the State of Kuwait and the Republic of Austria for the Encouragement and Reciprocal Protection of Investment):

ST:
عندما تتعرض استثمارات تمت من قبل مستثمرين تابعين لأي من الدولتين المتعاقدتين للضرر أو الخسارة بسبب حرب أو نزاع مسلح آخر أو حالة طوارىء وطنية أو ثورة أو عصيان مدني أو اضطرابات أو أعمال شغب أو أحداث أخرى مشابهة في إقليم الدولة المتعاقدة الأخرى . . . .

TT:
When investments made by investors of either Contracting State suffer damage or loss owing to war or other armed conflicts, a state of national emergency, revolt, civil disturbance, insurrection, riot other similar events in the territory of the other Contracting State. . ..

Substitution

Substitution is a replacement of one lexical item/expression with another. Halliday and Hasan (1976) classify substitution into three main categories: nominal, verbal and clausal substitution. In English, every kind is achieved, respectively, by certain substitutes, namely *'one'*, *'ones'* and *'same'*; *'do'*, *'does'* and *'did'*; and *'so'* and *'not'*.

Reviewing the literature of Arabic linguistics, we find that it is completely devoid of any reference to substitution in Halliday and Hasan's sense. Despite that, Arabic has the potential resources to accommodate most of the substitutes provided by Halliday and Hasan (1976). The substitute *'one'*, for instance, has the Arabic equivalent واحد, which can be used in a somewhat similar context. The Arabic word نفس *'same'*, which is considered an equivalent for the English nominal substitute *'same'*, does not function as a substitute but rather as an instance of a comparative reference. With respect to verbal substitution, it is argued that it involves categories not all languages have. Arabic, for instance, does not have auxiliary verbs, which can be used instead of main verbs. Despite that, it has the potential to show connectivity via the verbal substitute, which is in this case the verb فعل *'to do'*. Further, the demonstrative ذلك *'that'* can be used in certain contexts to be an equivalent to the English clausal substitute *'so'*.

When translating legislative texts from English into Arabic, translators most often come across archaic adverbials, such as *'herein'*, *'hereof'*, *'herewith'*, *'therein'*, *'thereof'*, *'thereby'*, and so on. These archaic adverbials are used in legislative texts as cohesive devices. Here is an example (Al-Hinai 2009: 22–23):

ST:

Any institution established by or under the Agreement may exercise the powers and functions thereby conferred on it in respect of all or any part of the island of Ireland notwithstanding any other provision of this Constitution conferring a like power or function on any person or any organ of State appointed under or created or established by or under this Constitution.

TT:

يجوز لأي مؤسسة تأسست بواسطة أو بموجب الاتفاق أن تمارس الصلاحيات والوظائف الممنوحة لها في هذا الاتفاق بالنسبة لجميع أو أي جزء من جزيرة ايرلندا بصرف النظر عن أي حكم آخر من هذا الدستور يمنح سلطة أو وظيفة مماثلة لأي شخص أو أي جهاز في الدولة تم تعيينه بموجب هذا الدستور أو إنشاؤه أو تقريره بواسطته أو بموجبه.

Comment:

One of the features of legislative writing is the use of archaic expressions, such as *'herein'*, *'hereof'*, *'hereon'*, *'thereupon'* and so on (cf. Crystal and Davy 1969). These adverbs of place *'here'* or *'there'* plus a preposition have, in addition to the formal nature that they add to the document in which they occur, a cohesive function. Once a phrase like, for instance, *'in this document'*, *'in this contract'*, *'in this law'* and the like has been mentioned, then it can be replaced by the adverbial expression *'herein'*, which is not used in any variety of language except legislative writing. Unlike Arabic, English has the potential to show connectivity via these substituted forms; therefore, the translator has resorted to repeating the lexical item اتفاق *'agreement'*.

Translating from Arabic into English sometimes encourages translators to avoid the repetition of the lexical items, thereby resorting to these legal cohesive devices. Consider the following examples adapted from the General Sales Text Law No. 11 of the year 1991 (Egypt):

ST:

المادة الخامسة
ينشر هذا القانون في الجريدة الرسمية ويعمل به من تاريخ نشره في الجريدة الرسمية ويصدر وزير المالية اللائحة التنفيذية لهذا القانون خلال شهر من تاريخ نشره. يبصم هذا القانون بخاتم الدولة وينفذ كقانون من قوانينها...

TT:

Article (5)
This Law shall be published in the Official Gazette and shall come into force from the date of its publication therein. The Minister of Finance shall issue the executive regulations hereof within one month of publication. This Law shall receive the seal of the State and shall be effective as one of the State Laws . . .

> **Annotation:**
>
> Here, in rendering the phrases في الجريدة الرسمية *'in the official gazette'* and لهذا القانون *'for this law'*, I have opted for the archaic adverbials *'therein'* and *'hereof'* respectively. Using these substituted forms helps the TT hang together as a cohesive text by creating an anaphoric cohesive relation, which connects the two sentences to each other within the text.

Ellipsis

Ellipsis is the process of "repeating a structure and its content but omitting some of the surface expression" (de Beaugrande and Dressler 1981: 49). As with substitution, we can distinguish three types of ellipsis: *'nominal ellipsis'*, *'verbal ellipsis'* and *'clausal ellipsis'*.

In the case of *nominal ellipsis*, there should be a head modified by certain elements such as a deictic, numerative or an epithet; and one of these modifying elements is upgraded to function as the head of the clause. Al-Jabr (1987) shows that when the nominal group in Arabic has a deictic or epithet functioning as the head of the whole clause, there will be nominal ellipsis. Here is an example quoted from Halliday and Hasan (1976: 148) and translated by Al-Jabr (1987: 89):

ST:

- *Which last longer, the curved rods or the straight rods?*
- *The straight are less likely to break.*

TT:

- أيُهما يدوم زمناً أطول، القضبان المنحنية أم القضبان المستقيمة؟
- المستقيمة لا تنكسر بسهولة

However, unlike in English, a deictic is unlikely to function as a head in an Arabic phrase. Instead, the elliptical noun should be repeated in Arabic, as in the following concocted example:

ST:

I have lost my pen. Can I use yours?

TT:

لقد فقدت قلمي. هل ليّ أن استعمل قلمك؟

To understand what is meant by verbal ellipsis, recourse should again be made to Halliday and Hasan (1976: 170). They classify verbal ellipsis into two types: 'lexical ellipsis' and 'operator ellipsis'. Lexical ellipsis is a kind of ellipsis in which the lexical verb ('lexical verb', in most cases, if not all, means the main verb) is left out; it is ellipsis 'from the right'. Operator ellipsis involves the omission of the subject plus the 'operator ('operator verb' includes auxiliary verbs such as *can, have, will* and so on and semi-auxiliary verbs like *is/are/am going to, am/is about to, is/are to*, etc.): the lexical verb always remains intact', that is, it is ellipsis 'from the left', (p. 174). Consider this illustrative example:

John published an article, but Mary < Ø > a book. (lexical ellipsis)

Since Arabic has no auxiliaries in its linguistic system, we expect that there would not be operator ellipsis at all, as in the translated version of this example:

ST:
Ten people were killed today in Iraq and more than twenty < Ø > injured. (operator ellipsis)

TT:

قتل اليوم في العراق عشرة أشخاص وأصيب عشرون آخرون.

Remains another kind of ellipsis called clausal ellipsis; it is classified by Halliday and Hasan (1976: 197) into two types: 'modal ellipsis' and 'propositional ellipsis'. Therefore, any omission in modal elements (subject and operator verb) can be considered modal ellipsis; otherwise, when the deletion occurs in the propositional elements (lexical verb and complement or adjunct), there will be propositional ellipsis. To ascertain whether these sorts of ellipsis work in Arabic, let us consider these two concocted examples:

ST:
What was the teacher going to do? < Ø > Distribute [he] the prizes. (modal ellipsis)

TT:

ماذا كان ينوي المدرّس أن يفعل؟ يوزّع الجوائز.

ST:
Who was going to distribute the prizes? < Ø > the teacher [was]. (propositional ellipsis)

TT:

مَن كان ينوي أن يوزّع الجوائز؟ المدرّس.

In the first example, there is modal ellipsis in both English and Arabic, since the subject and operator are excluded. Here, in this example, for the purposes of the current study, كان ينوي is considered an operator, since it performs a function

132 *Annotating aspects of cohesion*

similar to that achieved by its English counterpart *'was going to'*. However, in the second example, there is propositional ellipsis in English only. This is because propositional ellipsis, which requires the omission of the main verb and complement or adjunct only and keeps the subject and operator *'the teacher was'* intact, is entirely unacceptable in Arabic.

The following authentic example extracted from the Holy Qur'an (Surah Yūsuf 12: 82) and translated by Yusuf Ali (1934/2006):

ST:

وَسْئَلِ الْقَرْيَةَ الَّتِي كُنَّا فِيهَا وَالْعِيرَ الَّتِي أَقْبَلْنَا فِيهَا وَإِنَّا لَصَادِقُونَ.

TT:

Ask at the town where we have been and the caravan in which we returned, and (you will find) we are indeed telling the truth.

> **Comment:**
>
> In this verse, there are two examples of ellipsis, such as أهل *'inhabitants'* in واسأل أهل القرية التي كنا فيها and أصحاب *'owners'* in وأصحاب العير التي أقبلنا فيها. Such ellipsis contributes to establishing cohesive links within the text on the one hand and attempts to physically get the reader involved in the text. The translator has opted for the reflection of the first ellipsis *'ask the town'* but opted for a collective noun in the second example, *'the caravan'*.

To observe how translators deal with ellipsis in another text type, let us consider the following text taken from an edited book titled *Islamophobia: The Challenge of Pluralism in the 21st Century* by Esposito and Kalın (Alqunayir 2014: 31–32):

ST:

Abdullah bin Bayyah, one of the foremost authorities of Sunni Islam, rejects moral relativism and affirms the existence of universal values that transcend cultural specificities. Basing his reasoning on a broad notion of "common sense", bin Bayyah believes that "shared values do exist. The best proofs for this are the human faculties of reason . . . and of language. Every rational mind recognizes justice and every language has a word for it . . . the same can be said for 'truth', 'liberty', 'tolerance', 'integrity' and many other concepts. These are praised by all cultures and expressed positively in all languages.

TT:

وفي هذا السياق، يرفض فضيلة الشيخ عبد الله بن بيّه، أحد أبرز علماء السنة، أي وجود للنسبية الأخلاقية ويؤكد على وجود قيم عالمية تتخطى حدود الخصوصيات الثقافية. واستنادًا على فكرة شمولية من «المنطق العام»، يرى الشيخ بن بيّه أن «القيم المشتركة موجودة حقًا، وإن أفضل أدلة على وجودها هي الاستدلالات الإنسانية على المنطق . . . وكذلك على اللغة. فكل عقل منطقي يُدرك العدالة، وتُحدد كل لغة مسمّى خاص بها . . . ويمكن أن يقال نفس الشيء عن (الحقيقة) و(التحرر) و(التسامح) و(الاستقامة)، بالإضافة إلى العديد من المفاهيم الأخرى. إذ تحتفي جميع الثقافات بهذه العبارات كلها وتعبّر عنها جميع اللغات بإيجابية».

> **Comment:**
>
> As can be observed, the original writer opts for the use of three dots twice to get his reader physically involved in the interpretation of the text on the one hand and to make his text hang together as a cohesive text. Being aware of this, the translator has tried her hand at reflecting such ellipsis.

Conjunction

Conjunction is a cohesive device that makes segments of a given text hang together as a cohesive text. Conjunction can be explicit or implicit. It is explicit and the relationship is marked when a conjunct is used; otherwise, it is implicit and the relationship is unmarked when no conjunct is used. Traditional grammarians classify conjuncts into two main types:

- Coordinating conjuncts: they are used to join individual words, phrases and independent clauses, as in these examples:

    She bought a car and a house last year.
    The house was neither large nor small.
    You could have your breakfast either in the dining room or in the garden.

- Subordinating conjuncts: they are used to join dependent clauses that cannot stand on their own to give a complete sense, as in the following examples:

    She sat down by a fallen tree trunk in order that she could smoke her pipe.
    As he was walking on the shore, he met his friend.

Subordinating conjuncts are known by modern grammarians as 'conjunctive adverbs'. These conjunctive adverbs can be (adapted from Collins Cobuild English Grammar 1990: 342–62):

• Adverbial clauses of reason, begin with:	*'as', 'since', 'because'*, etc.
• Adverbial clauses of purpose, begin with:	*'so that', 'in order that', 'lest'*, etc.
• Adverbial clauses of result, begin with:	*'so that', 'so'*, etc.
• Adverbial clauses of time, begin with:	*'before', 'after', 'as', 'while', 'since', 'as soon as', 'whenever', 'till', 'until'*, etc.
• Adverbial clauses of concession, begin with:	*'although', 'though', 'even though', 'however', 'whenever'*, etc.
• Adverbial clauses of place, begin with:	*'where', 'wherever'*, etc.
• Adverbial clauses of comparison, begin with:	*'as . . . as', 'not as (so) . . . as'*, etc.
• Adverbial clauses of condition, begin with:	*'if', 'unless', 'whether . . . not'*, etc.
• Adverbial clauses of manner, begin with:	*'as', 'as if', 'as though', 'like'*, etc.

134 *Annotating aspects of cohesion*

The same adverbial conjunct can sometimes be an indicator of the logical relationship between two separated sentences. In this case, it is called a 'logical connector' (Quirk *et al.* 1972: 661). Consider these examples:

She invited all her friends to her birthday party. However, nobody came.
You enrolled in the university late. However, you are still entitled to a student ID card.
He has a bad fever. Nevertheless, he refuses to call a doctor.

Arabic does have the potential resources for accommodating all English connectives shown to indicate the different relationships between discourse units. Consulting an English–Arabic dictionary, for example 'Al-Mawrid', one can easily find their equivalents in Arabic. However, it is worth noting that decontextualizing the ST conjunctive element and translating it literally by relying on its dictionary meaning may distort the relationship itself between the two chunks of information, shift viewpoint via changing the line of argumentation and strike the TL reader as unusual. By way of explanation, let us consider the following example in which *'but'* and *'or'* might be translated counter to their direct, literal meanings (Ghazala 2012: 10):

ST:
Mr Netanyahu, not Mr Obama, is the real enigma. His record suggests a reluctance to make the compromises that could bring a deal. But neither his American nor his Palestinian nor even his Israeli interlocutors find him easy to interpret.

TT:
تكمن المعضلة الحقيقية في السيد نتنياهو وليس في السيد أوباما، إذ يُظهر سجله الخاص عدم رغبته في تقديم تنازلات من شأنها أن تُرسي قواعد السلام في المنطقة، فلا مفاوضوه الأمريكان ولا الفلسطينيون ولا حتى الإسرائيليون أنفسهم يمكنهم أن يفسروا مواقفه هذه بسهولة.

> **Annotation:**
>
> (a) Here, the conjunctive elements in the ST *'but'* and *'or'* lend themselves to ف and و respectively. It is worth mentioning that the presence of any connective does not necessarily entail that it signal the same relation as that marked by its counterpart in the interfacing language. To illustrate this, some Arabic connectives perform more functions than some of their English counterparts and *vice versa*. For instance the connective ف "can be a marker of temporal sequence, logical sequence, purpose, result or concession" (Holes 1984: 234). As such, giving full consideration to the context and co-text, it is felt that translating but literally into لكن or إن بيد /إن غير/ إن إلا and *'or'* into أو by relying on their dictionary meanings will influence the flow of Arabic discourse, thus affecting its readability, acceptability and naturalness.
>
> (b) Further, in an attempt to naturalize and smooth the flow of the Arabic discourse, the suppressed cause-result relation in the original text is brought to the surface by employing the conjunction إذ i.e. *'because'*.

To shed some light on the translator's inability to cope with the textual mismatch between the interfacing languages, let us consider the following example quoted from Karīm 'Abid's story (غرام السيدة (ع)) 'The Passion of Lady A', cited in and translated by Eric Winkel (2010: 64–65):

ST:

عندما عادت الفتاتان إلى البيت لم تكن الأنسة (ع) تعرف ما حدث للرجل. كانت وهي تغيّر ثيابها وحيدةً تفكّر بطلبة قسم اللغة الفرنسية، فهي لم تجد فيهم من يثير إهتمامها على عكس ما كانت تتوقع قبيل دخول الجامعة.

TT:

The two ladies returned to the house. Miss A did not know what happened with the man. She changed her clothes and concentrated on thinking about the male students in the French Department. She hadn't found any of them who could rouse her interest, which was the opposite of how she felt before she went to the university.

Comment:

Here, in an attempt to take into account the stylistic norms of the TL, the translator has opted to disconnect the action processes by using two separate sentences. As a result, the pace of events is slowed down. The original subordinate sentence ... عادت عندما ... لم تكن is represented as two independent sentences in the TT, thereby generating a feeling that there is probably a time gap between the two events. In this regard, Shen (1987: 185) writes that the way "in which the syntactic units are connected (say, whether subordinated (one to another) or coordinated (with or without punctuation in between))" plays a vital role in determining the pace of the processes involved. However, unlike English discourse, which "is considerably asyndetic and hypotactic", Arabic discourse "is well-known for its explicit paratactic nature, with a heavy use of conjunction" (Farghal 2012: 141; see also Baker 1992; Hatim 1997a; Al-Khafaji 2011). In a similar vein, the change in aspect from a continuous past tense, expressed by كانت وهي تغيّر in the ST, to a simple past tense in the TT, does produce a change in time reference, affecting the pragmatic communicative effect, in that the emphasis in the ST is on the continuity of the action in a specific period of time, whereas in the TT, the emphasis is put on its completion. Further, opting for the connector *'and'* to connect the two events, as in *'she changed her clothes and concentrated on . . . '* does slow down their pace, thus generating a time gap between the two events.

To demonstrate how translators need to take utmost care about any textual asymmetry between the interfacing languages, let us consider the following journalistic text, which appeared along with its translation in Pragnell (2003: 62–63):

ST:

اجراءات لدول السوق الاوروبية تهدف إلى إنهاء الركود الاقتصادي والتخفيف من معدلات البطالة

كوبنهاغن – كونا- أيدت المجموعة الاوربية بقوة خططا لمضاعفة موارد الأقراض في صندوق النقد الدولي لحل ازمة ديون عالمية. وقالت إنه يجب مضاعفة أموالها الخاصة بالاستثمارات.
وقال زعماء المجموعة في بيان اختتموا به مؤتمر لهم هنا إنهم مستعدون للعمل على زيادة حصص الصندوق بشكل كبير وإنهم مصممون على اتخاذ قرار مبكر بهذا الشأن.
وكان أعضاء الصندوق الغربيين قد بحثوا في الأسبوع الماضي في باريس اقتراحات بزيادة موارد الصندوق إلى حوالي 60 بليون دولار وهناك خطط لمحاولة الحصول على موافقة سريعة للزيادة في اجتماع مبكر خاص للجنة المؤقتة التابعة للصندوق في الشهر المقبل بدلا من شهر نيسان (ابريل) من العام المقبل.

TT:

Common market measures aiming to end economic stagnation and lower levels of unemployment

Copenhagen CUNA – The European Community vigorously endorsed plans to double borrowing facilities in the IMF to solve the international debt crisis. It said that it was necessary to double its funds for investments.

In a communiqué conducting their summit conference here, Community leaders said that they were ready to work significantly to increase the quotes of the Fund and that they were determined to adopt an early resolution in this matter.

In Paris last week Western members of the Fund had discussed proposals for increasing the resources of the Fund to about 60 billion dollars. There are plans to try to obtain speedy agreement for the increase in an early private meeting of the Fund's interim committee next month, instead of in January next year.

Comment:

As can be observed, the ST invests cohesion through the employment of five instances of the connector و 'and':

وقالت إنه يجب ...
وقال زعماء ...
وإنهم مصممون ...
وكأن أعضاء ...
وهناك خطط ...

Several relations can be expressed by the same connective in different contexts: for instance, the connective و 'lit. *and*' "can mark temporal sequence, simultaneous action, semantic contrast and semantic equivalence, amongst other things" (Holes 1984: 234). Further, it is sometimes used for demarcating the boundaries of the sentences/clauses as another comma or a full stop (Ibid.) or to enhance naturalness at expense of accuracy (Baker 1992: 196). Thus, not all the intersentential instances of و should be treated as a real cohesive device. Having taken into account the textual asymmetries between the interfacing languages on the one hand, paying attention to text type demands and being aware of generic conventions on the other, the translator has intrinsically managed the text to be in line with the linguistic and stylistic norms of the TL, thus deleting the additive connector و 'lit. *and*' and breaking down the third paragraph into smaller sentences in the TT. Without doing so, the translation would most likely be awkward and lacking in naturalness, thereby striking the TL readers as unusual. As far as conjunction is concerned, it is worth mentioning that unlike English, which is basically implicative, Arabic is largely explicative (cf. Baker 1992; Hatim 1997a; Al-Khafaji 2011; Farghal 2012; Almanna 2013, among others).

Lexical cohesion

Lexical cohesion falls into two main categories, reiteration and collocation (Halliday and Hasan 1976). Reiteration is the most common device for holding stretches of language together as a cohesive text. It does not mean only the repetition of the same lexical items, but it covers certain relations that hold between lexical items, such as synonymy (as in *'big'* and *'large'*), antonymy (as in *'happy'* and *'sad'*), hypernomy-hyponymy (as in *'lawyer'* and *'solicitor'*) and general words (as in *'burger'* and *'hamburger'*). Collocation, on the other hand, refers to the tendency of some lexical items to collocate well with others, thus generating cohesive ties within the text (for more details on collocation, see Chapter 4 in this book). Contrastive studies (Al-Jabr 1987; Emery 1989; Abdulla 2001, Farghal 2012, among others) show that there is a tendency in Arabic toward the use of lexical repetition rather than lexical variation. By way of explanation, let us consider the following example taken from a book titled *Oman* describing all aspects of Oman translated and published by the Ministry of Information, Sultanate of Oman (2008/2009: 235/202–203):

ST:

يعتبر قطاع الثروة الحيوانية من القطاعات المهمة حيث يعمل في هذا القطاع شريحة كبيرة من المجتمع العماني في مختلف محافظات ومناطق السلطنة.
وتشير الإحصائيات إلى أن قطاع الثروة الحيوانية في تنامٍ مستمر، وقُدِّر الإنتاج المحلي من اللحوم الحمراء بحوالي 12400 طن في عام 2006 و172 مليون بيضة من بيض المائدة أما بالنسبة للحليب فقد بلغ الإنتاج 46700 طن كما بلغ إنتاج لحوم الدواجن 22200 طن.

TT:

Livestock is an important and growing sector that employs a large section of the Omani population. In 2006, domestic production totaled around 12,400 tonnes of red meat; 127 million eggs; 46,700 tonnes of milk and 22,200 tonnes of poultry.

138 *Annotating aspects of cohesion*

> **Comment:**
>
> As can be seen, the translator has opted for a number of local strategies in rendering lexical repetition in the example. The words قطاع *'sector'* and بيض *'egg'* are repeated many times in the ST; however, the translator, having taken into account the textual preferences and been aware of demands of genre and text type, has opted for restructuring the propositions in an attempt to avoid such lexical repetition. However, he could not avoid the three cases of recurrence طن *'tonnes'*, thus opting for lexical repetition.

Now let us see how translators deal with lexical cohesion in legislative texts (Almanna 2005: 31):

ST:

تقرر محكمة التحكيم التي يتم إنشاؤها بموجب هذه المادة، المسائل المتعلقة بالنزاع. . . . إن قرارات التحكيم . . . تكون ملزمة ونهائية لكل من طرفي النزاع. وتقوم كل من الدولتين المتعاقدتين بتنفيذ أي حكم مثل هذا دون تأخير، وتقوم بإتخاذ الإجراءات اللازمة للتنفيذ الفعلي لتلك الأحكام في إقليمها.

TT:

An arbitral tribunal established under this article shall decide the issues in dispute . . . . The awards of arbitration . . . shall be final and binding on the parties to the dispute. Each Contracting State shall carry out without delay any award and shall make provision for effective enforcement in its territory of such award.

> **Comments:**
>
> As can be observed, in the original text, there is partial repetition that contributes to text connectivity. Such partial repetition comes from the lexical items أحكام, حكم, حكيم, محكمة, and أحكام, whose morphological root is حَكَمَ. Such density of lexical repetition cannot be reflected in English due to the lack of such root repetition.

Thematic progression

Reviewing the literature on theme-rheme notion, we find two recognized approaches: the Hallidayan approach and the Prague School approach. Halliday and Matthiessen (2004: 64) point out that any clause comprises two parts: (1) the 'theme' of the clause (what the clause is concerned with) and (2) the 'rheme' of the clause (what is said about the theme), "whatever is chosen as a theme is put first'. He uses this gloss '*I'll tell about. . .*" to identify the function of theme. Consider the following example:

(i) *Tom asked the teacher a question.*
(ii) *A question was asked of the teacher by Tom.*

So in the example (i), the theme is *'Tom'* (*I'll tell you about Tom*), but in (ii), the theme is *'A question'* (*I'll tell you about the question*). This indicates that although the two examples convey the same meaning, there are two different points of departure – two different themes. Although Halliday and Hasan (1976) preclude the thematic progression within text as a cohesive device, they recognize its role in organization of the text. "The organisation of each segment of a discourse in terms of its information structure, thematic patterns and the like is also part of its structure [. . .] no less important than the continuity from one segment to another" (Halliday and Hasan 1976: 299). Stillar (1998: 17) argues that theme-rheme relations play a significant role in building cohesion within a text. "The thematic progression in a text – what its themes are, how they stay the same, how they change and so on over the course of the text – is a part of how it creates cohesion . . .". Despite the easiness of the Hallidayan approach in identifying the theme and rheme of the clause or the sentence, it cannot be applied to all languages, for example, languages with free word order like Arabic.

Linguists belonging to the Prague School look at the theme-rheme notion from a different perspective. They hold that theme-rheme relation relies on the notion of 'functional sentence perspective'. Functional sentence perspective is concerned with the degree of communicative dynamism over the elements of the clause or sentence. According to the Prague School's linguists, what has a lower degree of communicative dynamism in the clause or sentence is theme, and conversely what has a higher degree is rheme (Al-Jabr 1987; Baker 1992/2011).

Baker (1992/2011) discusses the theme-rheme notion in detail and classifies theme in terms of markedness into two types: marked theme (i.e., unusual or atypical) and unmarked theme (i.e., most usual or typical). Marked theme can be subdivided into three types (Ibid.):

- fronted theme, thematizing any constituent of a clause or sentence, which is atypical to occur initially, as in:
  In China the book received a great deal of publicity. (132)
- predicated theme, using 'cleft structure' (*It*-structure) in which *It* is 'an empty subject', while the theme occurs after the verb to be, as in:
  It was the book that received a great deal of publicity. (135)
- identifying theme using 'pseudo-cleft structure' (*Wh*-structure). Here is an example:
  What the book received in China was a great deal of publicity. (139)

However, she does not mention thematic patterns and sentences with more than one theme in her book. By contrast, Bloor and Bloor (1995) identify four types of thematic patterns: constant theme pattern (the theme of each sentence or clause is the same), linear theme pattern (the rheme of a sentence or clause becomes the theme of the following clause or sentence), split rheme pattern (the rheme of a clause or a sentence has two or more parts; each part becomes the theme of the following clause or sentence) and derived theme (the theme derives from a 'hypertheme').

140 *Annotating aspects of cohesion*

Unlike English, Arabic is a free-word-order language; therefore, the Hallidayan approach is inadequate to identify the theme in an Arabic clause or sentence. Beeston (in Al-Jabr 1987: 207) points out that the 'logical theme' of a verbal sentence in Arabic is the noun phrase, which follows the verb, while the theme of a nominal sentence always occupies an initial position. He adds that particles like إنّ and لعلّ, which are placed at the beginning of the sentence, are used just to draw the attention toward the theme following them and to assign an 'object status' to it. In fact, although Beeston's definition of the theme in Arabic avoids the intricate functional sentence perspective notion adopted by Prague School's linguists and fills in the gap that the Hallidayan approach falls in, it is still inadequate since it covers only the unmarked theme. Therefore, in order to fit the purpose of the current study, Beeston's definition needs to be enlarged to include the marked theme mentioned by many researchers (Baker 1992/2011; Halliday 1994; Eggins 1994, among others). Consider the following example quoted from an Agreement between the State of Kuwait and the Republic of Austria for the Encouragement and Reciprocal Protection of Investment:

ST:

1- يعني مصطلح "إستثمار" كافة أنواع الأصول، التي يمتلكها أو يهيمن عليها مباشرة أو غير مباشرة. . . .

2- يعني مصطلح "مستثمر":

(أ) بالنسبة لجمهورية النمسا: (1) شخص طبيعي يحمل تبعية جمهورية النمسا؛ . . .

(ب) بالنسبة لدولة الكويت (1) شخص طبيعي يحمل جنسية دولة الكويت

(ج) بالنسبة "لدولة ثالثة" شخص طبيعي أو كيان قانوني أو تنظيم آخر

3- يشمل مصطلح "يمتلك" أو "يهيمن" أيضا الملكية أو الهيمنة التي تتم مزاولتها من خلال شركات فرعية أو زميلة أينما كان مقر ها.

4- يعني مصطلح "عائدات" المبالغ التي يحققها إستثمار، بغض النظر عن الشكل الذي تدفع به. . . .

TT:

1   The term 'investment' shall mean every kind of asset, owned or controlled directly or indirectly.

2   The term 'investor' shall mean:

   (a) with respect to the Republic of Austria 1) a natural person holding the citizenship of the Republic of Austria. . . .

   (b) with respect to the State of Kuwait 1) a natural person holding the nationality of the State of Kuwait. . . .

   (c) with respect to a 'third state', a natural person, a legal entity or other. . . .

3   The term 'own' or 'control' includes also ownership or control exercised through subsidiaries or affiliates wherever located.

4   The term 'returns' shall mean amounts yielded by an investment, irrespective of the form in which they are paid. . . .

Comment:

In the ST, the thematic pattern is a constant thematic pattern. This is because the logical theme of each sentence مصطلح *'term'* remains the same. This holds true for the TT. The translator has succeeded in keeping the thematic pattern used in the ST intact. It is worth mentioning here that Baker (1992: 127), in analyzing a verbal sentence in Arabic, does not take Beeston's logical theme into consideration – she argues that what gives the verbal sentence "its sense of continuity is the frequent thematization of process" as expressed in verbs like يشمل, يعني , and the like.

Eggins (1994: 267) argues that there are "three different types of clause structure that can get to be Theme: topical (or experiential) elements, interpersonal elements, and textual elements". To put this differently, a clause or a sentence might have more than one theme, namely topical theme, textual theme and interpersonal theme. Here is an example quoted from the Law of Income Tax on Companies of 1981 (the Sultanate of Oman):

ST:

مع مراعاة الفقرتين (3) و(4) على كل شركة اعداد حساباتها لفترة محاسبية مطابقة لسنة ضريبية. . . .

وعلى ضوء هذه الحسابات وما يرى المدير اجراءه من تعديلات فيها يتم احتساب الضريبة

يجوز لأية شركة، بشرط أن تفعل ذلك بانتظام واستمرار ان تعد حساباتها الختامية. . . ،

وعندما تعد شركة حساباتها لفترة محاسبية تنتهي في يوم غير الحادي والثلاثين من ديسمبر فان الدخل الخاضع للضريبة لتلك الشركة عن تلك الفترة المحاسبية المنتهية في ذلك اليوم الأخير يعتبر. . . انه الدخل الخاضع للضريبة عن السنة الضريبية. . .

للشركة في بداية انشائها أن تعد حساباتها لفترة محاسبية تقل عن اثني عشر شهرا. . . .

ST:

Without prejudice to Paragraph (3) and (4) all companies must prepare their accounts for an accounting period corresponding to a tax year.

Tax shall be calculated in the light of these accounts and whatever amendments the Director may see fit to make.

Any company may provided that it does this regularly and continually prepare its final accounts. . . .

When a company prepares its accounts for an accounting period ending on a day other than the 31st December *the income* chargeable to tax for such company for such accounting period ending on such other date shall be considered . . . to be the income chargeable to tax for the tax year. . . .

142 *Annotating aspects of cohesion*

Any company may at the commencement of its operations prepare its accounts for an accounting period of less than twelve months. . . .

Comment:

(a) In complex sentences as in sentence (4), theme-rheme relations can be analyzed in a completely different way: the subordinate clause (*when a company prepares its accounts . . .*) is the main theme, while the main clause (*the income chargeable to tax . . .*) is the main rheme. Further, each clause has its own theme and rheme (for more details, see Thompson 2004). Consider the following tables in which thematic structures are analyzed in the ST and TT, respectively:

Rheme 2	Theme 2	Rheme 1	Theme 1
	على كل شركة اعداد. . . .	مع مراعاة الفقرتين (3) و(4)
	يتم احتساب الضريبة	وعلى ضوء هذه الحسابات . . .
	يجوز لـ. . .، بشرط أن تفعل ذلك	أية شركة
انه الدخل الخاضع . . . يعتبر	(فان) الدخل الخاضع للضريبة. . .	تعد. . . حساباتها . . .	و/عندما (textual) شركة/theme (topical theme)
	لـ+في بداية انشائها. . .	الشركة

Theme 1	Rheme 1	Theme 2	Rheme 2
Without prejudice to . . .	all companies must. . . .		
Tax	shall be calculated. . . .		
Any company	may provided that it. . . .		
When (textual theme)/ a company (topical theme)	prepares its accounts . . .	the income . . .	shall be considered . . .
Any company	may at the commencement. . . .		

It is clear from the tables that the most recurrent thematic pattern is the constant theme pattern in both texts. The translator has managed to retain the method of development in terms of markedness and thematic pattern. The only exception occurs in sentence 2, in which the marked theme . . . وعلى ضوء هذه الحسابات in the ST becomes an unmarked theme tax in the TT, and the derived theme is switched to a split rheme pattern.

(b) It is worth noting that ف is an obligatory stylistic device in Arabic in some sentences. The apodosis (result clause) of the protasis (conditional clause) should be introduced by ف if it is a nominal sentence or an imperative sentence or if it starts with one of the following particles: ما, لن, قد, سوف (السين), كأنما, لام الناهية, لام الأمر.

Parallelism and continuity of tenses/aspects

Parallelism here refers to the occurrence of a particular syntactic structure more than once in juxtaposition, thereby creating connectivity and continuity of discourse. Consider this example adapted from de Beaugrande's book *Text, Discourse and Process* (1980: 161):

> *The King was in his counting house, counting his money;*
> *The queen was in the parlour, eating bread and honey;*
> *The maid was in the garden, hanging out the clothes;*
> *Along came a blackbird and pecked off her nose.*

In the above example, the first three structures are well balanced: the definite article *'the'* + verb to be *'was'* + prepositional phrase *'in his counting house/in the parlour/in the garden'* + gerund *'counting/eating/hanging out'* + object *'his money/bread and honey/the clothes'*. Placing such parallel structures in juxtaposition can, in addition to the aesthetic and persuasive purposes that they accomplish, significantly enhance the degree of inferences in the default of explicit relations (de Beaugrande). So in this example, the parallel structures indicate that places *'counting house/parlour/garden'* and the events *'counting/eating/hanging out'* are proximate in their location and time. Also, it can be inferred that the pecked-off nose is the maid's not the queen's. Syntactically speaking, the parallel structures are equally important to one another; not one outweighs the other. Consider the following example extracted from Barack Obama's inaugural address along with its published translation offered by Al-Jazeera (Salih 2013: 96):

ST:

For us, they packed up their few worldly possessions and traveled across oceans in search of a new life. For us, they toiled in sweatshops and settled the West, endured the lash of the whip and plowed the hard earth. For us, they fought and died in places [such as] Concord and Gettysburg; Normandy and Khe Sanh.

144 *Annotating aspects of cohesion*

TT 1:

من أجلنا جمعوا ممتلكاتهم القليلة وشقوا عباب المحيطات بحثا عن حياة جديدة. من أجلنا عملوا ساعات طويلة واستوطنوا الغرب وقاسوا السوط وحرثوا الأرض الوعرة. من أجلنا قاتلوا وماتوا في أماكن مثل كونكورد وغيتيزبرغ ونورماندي وخي سان.

> **Comment:**
>
> As can be seen, the original text employs three parallel structures as well as a series of simple past tenses expressed by *'packed up', 'traveled', 'toiled', 'settled', 'endured', 'plowed', 'fought'* and *'died'*. Placing such parallel structures along with the continuity of the same tense and aspect (past with an emphasis on the completion of the action) in juxtaposition contributes to text connectivity, not to mention the aesthetic and persuasive purposes that are achieved by such parallelism and consistency of using tenses and aspects.

To see how a translator can successfully handle parallelism in the ST, let us consider the following text quoted from Ali Al-Qaradaghi's book (n.y.: 130) نحن والآخر, which has been translated into English by Syed B. A. Kashmiri (2014: 105) into *We and the Other*:

لم يصدق الكثيرون أن الصراع الرأسمالي مع المعسكر الشيوعي (أو صراع الغرب الرأسمالي مع الشرق الشيوعي) ينتهي بهذه السرعة، وأن الحرب الباردة التي دامت بعد الحرب العالمية الثانية حوالي خمسين سنة أن تدفن آثارها بسرعة، وأن ينتهي الاتحاد السوفيتي في عام 1992 ويدخل هو ومعسكره في أحضان الغرب الرأسمالي وتتغيّر سوقه الاقتصادية من الاشتراكية، بل والشيوعية المتطرفة إلى اقتصاد السوق والاقتصاد الرأسمالي وتتحكم فيها العولمة ومنظمة الجات، ثم المنظمة الدولية للتجارة الحرة.

Not many would have believed that the clash of Capitalism with the Communist block would come to an end so swiftly, that the cold war which continued for about half a century after World War II would be buried along with its imprints so quickly, and that Soviet Union (USSR) will cease to exist in 1992 and that it would fall in the arms of capitalist West; no one would have imagined that the socialist economy and extremist Communism would give way to capitalistic free market economy and that globalization, G8 and WTO would hold sway.

> **Comment:**
>
> As can be seen, the original writer, in addition to utilizing a number of cohesive devices, such as referential items, conjunction and lexical cohesion, introduces his sentences/clauses in parallel fashion, as in:
>
> لم يصدق الكثيرون أن الصراع الرأسمالي مع المعسكر الشيوعي . . . ينتهي بهذه السرعة . . .
> وأن الحرب الباردة . . . تدفن آثارها بسرعة . . .
> وأن ينتهي الاتحاد السوفيتي . . .
> ويدخل هو ومعسكره في أحضان الغرب الرأسمالي . . .
> وتتغيّر سوقه الاقتصادية . . .

Parallelism, according to Al-Jabr (1987: 173), "involves the use of particular syntactic and semantic configuration more than once, in rapid succession". Actually, placing these parallel structures in juxtaposition is not determined arbitrarily, but rather it is a result of choice. This accords well with Shen's (1987: 213) comments that in the actual act of translating, "one needs to bear in mind that deviant syntactic sequence, particularly in a well-formed text, may be associated with desirable literary effects. And if such is the case, the deviation should be preserved rather than 'normalized'". Such parallel structures need to be reflected in the TT, provided that such a reflection would not distort the TL linguistic and stylistic norms. It seems that the translator has felt that an addition is needed to reflect such parallel structures, thus adding 'no one would have imagined that . . .' to be in parallel fashion with 'not many would have believed that. . . '.

Following is another example quoted from Muḥsin Al-Ramlī's story البحث عن قلب حيّ *Search for a Live Heart* (2009: 31):

ST:

صمتٌ إلا من ثغاء بعض المجانين . . . صمتٌ إلا من نشرات الأخبار . . . صمتٌ حين نطلب منه شيئاً.. صمت إلا من حفيف المنافقين . . .

TT:

The silence is broken only by the bleating of some insane people. . . . The silence is broken only by news bulletins. . . . There is but silence when we ask for something, a silence that is broken only by the rustling of hypocrites . . .

Annotation:

Analyzing the ST syntactically, one can easily figure out its parallel structure صمت إلا من

> صمتٌ إلا من ثغاء بعض المجانين . . .
> صمتٌ إلا من نشرات الأخبار . . .
> صمتٌ حين نطلب منه شيئاً . . .
> صمتٌ إلا من حفيف المنافقين . . .

which has been repeated three times. It is an example of cumulative parallelism, i.e. incomplete parallelism, as there is a break to the whole parallel structure صمتٌ حين نطلب منه شيئاً '(there is but) silence when we ask for something'. Actually, placing these parallel structures in juxtaposition establishes their surface connectivity (i.e. cohesion) through the repetition of صمت إلا من followed by *idafa*-construction نشرات, ثغاء بعض المجانين الأخبار, and حفيف المنافقين. As such, an attempt is made to reflect such parallelism in the TT.

Now let us consider the following text along with its translation from (Al-Ismail 2009: 18–19):

ST:

If you don't have what you want, you are seeing the effect of your use of the law. If you don't have what you want, then you are creating not having what you want. You are still creating and the law is still responding to you.

TT:

إن لم تحصل على ما تريد، فهذا بسبب طريقة استخدامك للقانون. وإن لم تحصل على ما تريد، فذلك لأنك تستبعد من أفكارك الأشياء التي ترغب بها. وبهذا ستظل مكونا لتلك المفاهيم وبالمقابل وسيستمر القانون لأفكارك.

Comment:

As can be observed, the original writer employs parallelism (repeated twice in a very short passage) characterized by, first, a combination of present simple tenses (expressed by *'not have'*, *'want'*, *'not have'* and *'want'*) and present progressive tenses (expressed by *'are seeing'*, *'are creating'*, *'are creating'*, *'is responding'*) and, second, lexical repetition, as in *'if'*, *'you'*, *'don't'*, *'have'*, *'what'*, *'want'*, *'law'*, *'create'* and *'still'*. As stated, such structures in the ST is not piled up arbitrarily, but rather it is a result of choice. Taking into account such characteristics on the one hand and paying extra attention to the TL readers' expectations on the other, the translator has decided to reflect these parallel structures in the TT as in: إن لم تحصل على ما تريد, ف.

However, given full consideration to verb aspects, expressed by *'are creating'* and *'is responding'* as well as the repetition of the lexical item *'still'* in the last sentence – *'You are still creating and the law is still responding to you'* – he could have suggested something like وبهذا تبقى تشكّل مفاهيمك, ويبقى القانون يستجيب لها, in which the emphasis of the verb aspect is similarly placed on the continuity of the action (for more details on verb aspects and tenses, see Chapter 5 in this book).

Further reading

Baker, M. (1992/2011). *In Other Words: A Coursebook on Translation*. London/New York: Routledge.

Beaugrande, R. de, & Dressler, W. (1981). *Introduction to Text Linguistics*. London: Longman.

Bloor, T., & Bloor, M. (1995). *The Functional Analysis of English: A Hallidayan Approach*. London: Arnold.

Dickins, J., Hervey, S., & Higgins, I. (2002). *Thinking Arabic Translation*. London/New York: Routledge.

Eggins, S. (1994). *An Introduction to Systematic Functional Linguistics*. London/New York: Continuum.

Farghal, M. (2012). *Advanced Issues in Arabic and English Translation*. Kuwait: Kuwait University Press.

Annotating aspects of cohesion 147

Companion website and online resources

http://cw.routledge.com/textbooks/translationstudies/
www.est-translationstudies.org/

Assignment 1: *Instructors:* select an English or Arabic text (depending on your students' translation directionality whether they translate out of Arabic or into Arabic) from BBC (no more than 500 words). Then ask them to translate the text to be published in one of the local newspapers, paying special attention to textual choices.

Assignment 2: *Students:* In no more than 400 words, comment on:

(i) textual choices made by the translator, giving full consideration to parallelism.
(ii) any examples of textual shifts occurring through the nexus of translation.

ST:

(يرفع ذراعيه داعياً) أعده يا من تعيد الشمس والمطر.. أعده يا من أعدتَ يوسف إلى أبيه.. أعده يا من تعيد الصفاء إلى وجه السماء.. أعد الصفاء إلى سماوات نفوسنا يا ربّ.. يا ربّ: لِمَ لا تكترث بنا.. الحياة ونحن الذين نحيطها بكل هذا الاهتمام؟ هو الذي كان يهمه أمر كل شيء.. كل شيء وكأنه المسؤول عن هذا الكون. . . .

TT:

He lifts his arms to beseech God, 'Oh, my Lord, who can make the sun rise and the rain fall, please bring him back to us. Oh, my Lord, who brought Joseph back to his father, please bring him back. Oh, my Lord, who can make the sky clear again, please bring him back. Please bring light to the heavens of our souls. Oh, my Lord, why doesn't life care for us while we give every single bit of attention to it? He was the sort of man who cared for every single, tiny thing as if he had been responsible for the whole universe'.

Assignment 3: *Instructors:* discuss with your students the strengths and weaknesses of the annotations offered by an MA student with respect to translating cohesive devices (highlighted for you). In your discussion, you may touch on:

(i) Is there an external coherence in the translator's annotation? In other words, does s/he link his/her annotation to others' studies?
(ii) Are there other examples of cohesive devices that need to be annotated?

ST:
The declared purpose of torture is to force the enemy, the outsider, the insurgent, the criminal to talk – to reveal secrets and information which are

perceived in some way to threaten the state. In this way it is argued that torture is a justifiable practice employed only to protect the lives and integrity of legitimate citizens.

TT:

وإن الغرض المعلن للتعذيب هو إجبار كلٍّ من العدو والدخيل والمتمرد والمجرم على الكلام ـ ليكشفوا عن أسرار ومعلومات ينظر إليها على أنها تهدد الدولة بشكل ما. وهكذا يقال إن التعذيب هو ممارسة مبررة يقام بها لحماية حياة المواطنين الشرعيين وسلامتهم.

Annotation:

Cohesion is "the transparent linking of sentences" (Dickins *et al.* 2002: 128). English achieves cohesion implicitly. In other words, a reader of an English text is expected to figure out the relationship between sentences on his/her own just by understanding the context. Arabic, on the other hand, connects sentences rather explicitly through the use of connectors. According to Baker (1992: 196), translators attempt to "strike a balance between accuracy and naturalness. At the level of cohesion, naturalness is enhanced by using typical Arabic conjunctions such as wa and fa". The ST interconnects the two ST sentences with the expression 'in this way'. If this expression is literally translated as بهذه الطريقة, the two TT sentences will not read as smoothly as they do in the ST. In order to achieve the same level of cohesion as the ST, I used the Arabic word وهكذا which literally means *'thus'*.

Assignment 4: *Students:* select an English text (no more than 500 words) and translate it to be published in one of the local newspapers in your country. Before embarking on the actual act of translating the text, adopt the most appropriate global strategy. In no more than 300 words:

(i) tell us in your introduction why you have opted for this particular global strategy.

(ii) annotate any textual choices that you have made while translating the text.

Assignment 5: *Students:* select a legislative text (no more than 500 words) and translate it professionally. Before embarking on the actual act of translating the text, adopt the most appropriate global strategy. In no more than 300 words:

(i) tell us in your introduction why you have opted for this particular global strategy.

(ii) annotate any textual choices that you have faced while translating the text.

The Routledge Course in Translation Annotation website at www.routledge.com/cw/almanna contains:

- A video summary of the chapter
- PowerPoint slides
- Further reading links
- Further assignments
- More research questions
- Further annotated texts

7 Annotating register

In this chapter . . .

The previous chapter has discussed how to annotate issues such as cohesive devices, thematic progression and parallelism. In this chapter, special attention will be paid to the **field**, **mode** and **tenor** of discourse. Further, issues such as **formality**, **informality**, **personalization**, **impersonality**, **accessibility**, **inaccessibility**, **social status** and **standing** will be given full consideration. To this end, ample authentic data drawn from existing translations or translated for the purposes of this study will be used to drive home relevant theoretical constructs.

Key issues

- Accessibility versus inaccessibility
- Field of discourse
- Formality versus informality
- Mode of discourse
- Personalization versus impersonalization
- Register
- Social distance
- Standing
- Tenor of discourse
- Transitivity

The term *'register'* was first used by the linguist Thomas Bertram Reid in 1956. However, it was introduced to the linguistic studies in the 1960s by a group of linguists who tried their hand at distinguishing among user-based variations and use-based variations. In linguistics, register is defined as a variety of a language used for a particular purpose or in a particular social setting (cf. Halliday 1964; Halliday and Hasan 1976; Zwicky and Zwicky 1982; Gregory 1988, among others). In a formal setting, for example when communicating with other people, an English native speaker may well opt for formal lexical items (such as *'father'* instead of *'dad'*), formal syntactic structures and so on. The term 'register' is "used in so many different ways that it can be positively misleading" (Dickins *et al.* 2002: 162). Halliday (1978: 23) defines register as "the set of meanings, the configuration of semantic patterns, that are typically drawn upon under the specific conditions, along with the words and structures that are used in the realization of these meanings". To cast it in less technical terms, register can be defined as a semantic configuration that is associated with a particular situation type and characterized on the basis of three variables: *'field'*, *'tenor'* and *'mode'*. Although register analysis characterization in translation-oriented analysis cannot account for all contextual factors, it "still emerges as a powerful analytical tool and a necessary one, too, for communicative acts hinge upon the context of situation in which they occur" (Borrillo 2000: 1). In this regard, Borrillo (Ibid.) is of a view that register characterization plays a relevant part in the translation-oriented analysis of texts, as "it offers an initial interpretative hypothesis which then has to be substantiated against the textual evidence provided by linguistic structures and refined or modified by reference to the broader context of culture". In register analysis, special attention needs to be paid to the three variables – *'field'*, *'tenor'* and *'mode'* – via tracing the types of processes and their participants' roles (field of discourse); the degree of technicality, addressing terms, mitigating devices and euphemizers (tenor of discourse); and the interplay between grammatical complexity and lexical density as markers of oral and written language (mode of discourse).

Field of discourse

In analyzing discourse and register, Halliday provides a model based on studying systemic grammar. He spent many years working on his model. After various attempts, Halliday (1994) suggested a comprehensive model for register analysis. In contrast with the traditional grammarians, who view the concept of transitivity as a reference to verbs that take objects, Halliday (1976: 199) defines transitivity from a functional point of view as "the set of options relating to cognitive content, the linguistic representation of extralinguistic experience, whether of the phenomena of the external world or of feelings, thoughts and perceptions". In the sense that Halliday uses the term, 'transitivity' generally refers to the way in which the meaning is encoded and presented in the clause. So in transitivity, a number of processes can be identified as to whether they represent an action, behaviours saying, state of mind, state of being or state of existing, inter alia, process of doing, process of behaving, process of sensing, process of being and process of existing, respectively. There are three main components of the process of transitivity: (1) the process, (2) the participants and (3) the circumstance.

The process

(a) Material process (process of doing);

The teacher sent an email.
[Actor + process of doing + goal]

152 *Annotating register*

The girl sings.
[Actor + process of doing + no goal]

There are two types of material processes, namely 'event processes' in which the actor is inanimate and 'action processes' in which the actor is animate. Further, action processes are subdivided into two main types: 'intention processes' in which the action is done voluntarily and 'supervention processes' in which the action just happens, as in:

The teacher asked the students. (intention process)
The students laughed happily. (supervention process)

(b) Mental process (i.e., process of sensing);

He understood what you mean.
[Sensor + process of sensing + phenomenon]

(c) Behavioural process (i.e., process of behaving);

My son laughed at what she said.
[Behaver + process of behaving + phenomenon]

(d) Verbal process (i.e., process of saying);

My mother said that she would travel to London the following week.
[Sayer + process of saying + verbiage]

(e) Relational process (i.e., process of being);

My father is a doctor.
[Identified + process of identifying/being + identifier]

She has a lot of friends.
[Carrier + process of attributive/owning + attribute]

(f) Existential process (i.e., process of existing).

There are many cars in the street.
[Existent + process of existing + circumstance]

Participants

a.	Actor/goal	doing process
b.	Senser/phenomenon	sensing process
c.	Carrier/attribute vs. identified/identifier	relational process
d.	Behaver	behaving process

| e. | Sayer/verbiage/receiver | saying process |
| f. | Existent | existing process |

Circumstances

The circumstantials of time, place, manner and so on are normally expressed by prepositional phrases, adverbial phrases or adjuncts, as in the following examples:

> She ran **five kilometers.** (Circumstance of extent: spatial)
> We had an exam **two days ago.** (Circumstance of location: temporal)
> He expressed his opinion **with self-confidence.** (Circumstance of manner: quality)
> My father could not go to work yesterday **because he felt tired.** (Circumstance of cause: reason)
> I went to the shopping centre **to buy a new smart phone.** (Circumstance of cause: purpose)

By way of illustration, let us consider the following two examples quoted from Lubna Maḥmūd Yāsīn's (n.d.) story بصمة مواطن '*A Citizen's Fingerprint*':

ST:
يبتلعه المساء . . . فيوغل في أحشاء الصمت . . . ومن ذا الذي يستطيع فرارا إذا عسعس الألم داخل النفس . . . وتوغلت الأحزان في حنايا الفؤاد . . . يتآكل قلبه . . . تتساقط أشلاؤه . . . يتمزق صوته على حدود الزمان ولا من مجيب . . .

TT:
The night swallows him so he delves ever deeper into the heart of silence. Who can, then, escape if the pain is densely settled inside the self and sadness penetrates the depths of the heart?

Annotation:

In order to express the mental picture that she has of the world around her, the original writer opts for certain processes and participants, and determines, in advance, which participants will act and which one will be acted upon:

1- يبتلعه المساء

- material process, (actor + process of doing + goal), lends itself to a material process with a goal, as in: '*The night swallows him*'.

2- يوغل في أحشاء الصمت

- material process: (actor + process of doing + no goal), lends itself to a material process without goal, as in: '*he delves ever deeper into the heart of silence*'.

3- ومن ذا الذي يستطيع فرارا

- material process in the form of a rhetorical question lends itself to a material process + modality, i.e. '*can*', as in: '*Who can, then, escape . . .*' to maintain the rhetorical question.

4- عسعس الألم داخل النفس

154 *Annotating register*

- material process: (actor + process of doing + circumstance) lends itself to a material process as in: *'the pain is densely settled inside the self'*.
5- توغلت الأحزان في حنايا النفس
- material process: (actor + process of doing + circumstance) lends itself to a material process as in: *'sadness penetrates the depths of the heart'*.

The number of clauses is not an issue, but what is of greater importance in studying the transitivity choices is to maintain an accurate mental picture of the world around us through opting for "syntactic correspondence which maps synonymous or quasi-synonymous meaning across cultural boundaries" (Al-Rubai'i 1996: 103).

ST:
أين الملاذ؟؟ يريد أن يفتح جناحيه ويهرب من ظمئه .. ومن حدود مشاعره ..من عري أوجاعه يريد أن يحلق حيث لا أحد . . . لا أحد . . . أبدا . . .

TT:
Where to go?? He wants to spread his wings and escape from his thirst, from the boundaries of his feelings, from the rawness of his pains. He wants to soar where nobody is, nobody at all.

Annotation

In the above example, the ST shows a circumstantial element of location in space in the form of an adverbial clause حيث لا أحد. The adverbial clause حيث لا أحد refers to an assumed location that invokes different memories and/or imaginations in the mind of the reader. To reflect such an invitation achieved by the adverbial clause, one can resort to something like *'where nobody is'*.

To witness how (not) giving full consideration to text register may affect the quality of the TT, let us consider the following example quoted from Muḥammed Khuḍayyir's story حكايات يوسف *'Joseph's Tales'* (2011: 30):

ST:
قطعت أرض الصالة المصنوعة من لدائن زجاجية صلبة، وسرت بحذائي المطاطي إلى أحد المصاعد. كانت المقاعد البلاستيكية الملونة في أرض الصالة فارغة في مثل هذا الوقت، تنسكب عليها أضواء مصابيح مدفونة في السقف.

TT:
I crossed the hall floor made of solid vitreous plastic and walked in my rubber shoes to one of the lifts. The coloured plastic seats in the hall were empty at that time, and light from the bulbs recessed into the ceiling streamed down on them.

Annotation

In rendering the sentence كانت المقاعد البلاستيكية الملونة في أرض الصالة فارغة في مثل هذا الوقت, an attempt is made to avoid fronting the time adverbial في مثل هذا الوقت 'at this time . . .'. Actually, the original writer opts for certain processes and participants, and determines which participants will act and which one will be acted upon. In this sentence, he uses a relational process, i.e. process of being: identified: المقاعد (البلاستيكية الملونة في أرض الصالة) + process of being: كانت + identifier: فارغة, thus laying extra emphasis on the identified, i.e. 'seats', rather than the time adverbial. Syntactic choices play vital roles in offering various degrees of importance to the different parts of the message (cf. Shen 1987: 195). As such, the time adverbial *at this time* obtains more importance than its counterpart in the original when it is foregrounded. In this regard, Baker (1992: 129–130; emphasis hers) rightly comments:

> Meaning is closely associated with choice, so that the more obligatory an element is, the less marked it will be and the weaker will be its meaning. [. . .] putting a time or place adverbial, such as *today* or *on the shelf*, say, at the beginning of the clause, carries more meaning because it is the result of choice: there are other positions in which it can occur.

To further demonstrate how in not giving full consideration to the field of discourse and its processes, participants and circumstances may seriously affect the accuracy of translation, let us discuss the following two translations offered by two trainee translators:

ST:
Abu Hamza denies US terror charges.

TT:

أبو حمزة المصري ينفي تهمة الارهاب الموجه إليه في الولايات المتحدة.

Comment:

As can be observed, the trainee translator has failed to decipher the participants and their exact roles in the process, thus creating a misleading as well as inaccurate mental picture. She, in addition to adding unnecessary word المصري 'Egyptian', has changed one of the participants into a circumstantial of place, في الولايات المتحدة 'in the US', leaving the TL reader to wonder who has brought the charge of terror against Abu Hamza.

ST:
District Judge Katherine Forrest set a date of 26 August 2013 for Abu Hamza's trial, at which he will also face charges of abducting tourists in Yemen.

TT:

وحددت قاضي المحكمة العليا كاثرين فورست تاريخ 26 أغسطس 2013 موعدا لمحاكمةِ أبي حمزة، الذي سيواجهُ في ذلك الموعد أيضاً اتهاماتٍ بشأن خطف سيّاحٍ في اليمن.

Comment:

Here, the original writer opts for certain processes and participants and determines which participants will act and which one will be acted upon.

1 Material process: *District Judge Katherine Forrest* (actor) *set* (a process of doing) *a date of 26 August 2013 for Abu Hamza's trial* (goal);
2 Material process: *he* (actor) *will also face* (process of doing) *charges of abducting tourists* (goal) *in Yemen* (circumstantial of place).

The trainee translator has deciphered the participants and their exact roles in the processes, thus creating an accurate mental image.

Below is another example extracted from Mahfouz's novel ثرثرة فوق النيل (1966) and translated by Frances Liardet (1993) as *Adrift on the Nile* (quoted in Al-Saeghi 2014a: 21):

ST:

فأجاب الساعي وهو يقف أمام مكتبه.
ستجده على مكتبك عندما ترجع من مقابلة سعادة المدير العام.

TT:

"You'll find it on your desk", the office boy replied, "when you come back from seeing the Director General".

Comment:

As can be observed, the original writer in the example employs a process of saying (the sayer is الساعي, the process of saying is أجاب and the verbiage is ستجده على مكتبك عندما ترجع من مقابلة سعادة المدير العام and a circumstance of manner وهو يقف أمام مكتبه). Although the translator has maintained the process of saying (the sayer is *'the office boy'*, the process of saying is *'replied'* and the verbiage is the clause *'You'll find it on your desk, when you come back from seeing the Director General'*), he has failed to reflect a similar mental image to that conjured up in the mind of the SL reader. This is because he has decided to delete the circumstance of manner وهو يقف أمام مكتبه. Had he paid special attention to the importance of the circumstance of manner, he could have suggested something like: *'while he was standing in front of his office'*.

Tenor of discourse

In systemic functional linguistics, the expression *'tenor of discourse'* is used to describe the relationship between the in-text participants. The language used by people when communicating with each other partially depends on their relationship. For instance, a wife can call her husband *'honey'*, *'baby'* and the like and can go for imperative sentences without mitigating devices (see what follows), but in normal cases, she cannot use these terms and structures to address her boss. As such, tenor of discourse regulates such issues as formality versus informality, personalization versus impersonalization, accessibility versus inaccessibility and social distance versus standing (Bell 1991: 186–188).

Formality versus informality

The text is judged formal when the text producer pays extra attention to the message structuring. In this regard, Bell (1991: 186) holds, "Greater attention leads to more care in writing and this marks the text as possessing a higher degree of formality and signals a more distant relationship between sender and receiver(s)". In examining tenor of discourse in terms of formality, as opposed to informality, one can trace the lexical items, syntactic structures (be they complex or simple), punctuation and so on. Texts are considered formal when they require the reader/listener to spend extra time and effort on their lexical items, structuring and punctuation to decode their intended meaning. However, they are informal when they are easy to understand.

Personalization versus impersonalization

Personalization, as opposed to impersonalization, is very much related to subjectivity; it signals the presence of both the text sender and text receiver. It can be achieved via many techniques, including:

(a) the use of the first-person pronoun *'I'* or the second-person pronoun *'you'* instead of the pronoun *'it'*;
(b) the pronoun *'we'*, referring to both the writer and the reader;
(c) the use of directives, for instance, *'see below'*, *'for more details, see chapter three'* and the like.
(d) the use of rhetorical questions in the mouth of the in-text participants;
(e) active structures instead of passive ones;
(f) the presence of contractions and elliptical clauses; or
(g) the simplicity of noun phrases.

Accessibility versus inaccessibility

When language users (be they writers or speakers) assume that some pieces of information are universal or hypothetically shared by their intended readers, they tend to provide their readers with less information. Their texts therefore become less accessible and need an extra effort to be decoded. However, by doing so, they get their readers physically involved in the interpretation of the text (Bell 1991: 188). As such, accessibility, as opposed to inaccessibility, "refers to the amount of information that is assumingly shared by the writer and the intended reader", and they very much related to explicitness versus implicitness respectively (Almanna 2014: 129).

Politeness: Social distance versus standing

In the actual act of communication, people normally try to show their awareness of the public self-image of another person when they want to communicate politely. If they are socially distant, the relationship between them is often described in terms of respect. However, if they are socially close, then the relationship is often described in terms of friendliness and solidarity (Yule 1996: 60). In translation-oriented analysis, the tenor of discourse can be studied either horizontally when measuring the social distance between the in-text participants or vertically when measuring "power relationship connected with status, seniority and authority", or standing (Bell 1991: 187).

To witness how changing the tenor may affect the translation accuracy, let us consider the following extract quoted along with its published translation from Air Wick: Oud العود product label:

ST:

Do not spray or place on painted or polished surfaces. Keep out of reach of children. Pressurised container: Protect from sunlight; do not expose to temperature exceeding 50 C.

TT:

لا يرش أو يوضع على الأسطح المطلية أو الملمعة. يحفظ بعيدا عن متناول الأطفال. تحفظ العبوة المضغوطة بعيدا عن أشعة الشمس ولا يجب أن تتعرض لدرجات حرارة تزيد عن (50) درجة مئوية.

Comment:

In discussing the reflection of the exact degree of personalization, as opposed to impersonalization, in the TT, one may cast doubt on the quality of this translation. At times, analyzing the ST in terms of its degree of personalization gives the translator some useful hints on the social distance between the text sender and the text receiver, among other issues. In the ST, the writer opts for the use of the second-person pronoun '*you*' implicitly in the form of a series of imperative sentences, thus creating a feeling of solidarity and/or intimacy between him/her and the targeted audience. By contrast, the translator has resorted to passive forms, such as تُحفظ, يُحفظ, يُرش in addition to يجب أن تتعرض, thereby impersonalizing the text. To reflect the tenor of the extract in terms of its degree of personalization, one may well suggest a rendering like:

لا ترشها أو تضعها على الأسطح المطلية أو الملمعة. واحفظها بعيدا عن متناول الأطفال. العبوة مضغوطة: احفظها بعيداً عن أشعة الشمس ولا تعرضها لدرجات حرارة تزيد عن (50) درجة مئوية.

Annotating register 159

To further demonstrate how (not) taking into account the tenor of the text may produce an (in)accurate rending in terms of the degree of personalization, as opposed to impersonalization, let us consider the following example, quoted along with its published translation from Axe: Deodorant Body Spray product label:

ST:

Shake well before use. Hold can upright and spray away from face and body. Note that the spray is released upwards from the top of the cap. Caution: Pressurised container, protect from sunlight and do not expose to temperature exceeding 50 C.

TT:

رجّ العبوة جيداً قبل الاستعمال. امسك العبوة بشكل عمودي وقم برش البخاخ بعيداً عن الوجه والجسم. يجب ملاحظة أن البخاخ ينطلق نحو الأعلى من قمة الغطاء. **تحذير:** عبوة مضغوطة تحفظ بعيدا عن أشعة الشمس ويجب عدم تعريضها إلى درجات حرارة فوق 50 مئوية.

> **Comment:**
>
> As can be observed, the translator has reflected the tenor of the first three sentences in terms of their degree of personalization when opting for the use of the second-person pronoun *'you'*. However, in the fourth sentence, '*Note that the spray is released upwards from the top of the cap'*, s/he has resorted to the employment of the modalized verb يجب followed by a noun ملاحظة, thus impersonalizing the text and affecting the tenor of the text. Had the translator given full consideration to the tenor of the extract, s/he could have suggested something like:
>
> رجّ العبوة جيداً قبل الاستعمال. امسك العبوة بشكل عمودي وقم برش البخاخ بعيداً عن الوجه والجسم. لاحظ أن البخاخ ينطلق نحو الأعلى من قمة الغطاء. **تحذير:** عبوة مضغوطة احفظها بعيدا عن أشعة الشمس ولا تعرضها إلى درجات حرارة فوق 50 مئوية.

Here is another example extracted from Ariel Laundry Detergent:

ST:

Rinse clothes and hands with water after use. Keep out of reach of children. Avoid contact with eyes. In case of contact with eyes, rinse immediately with water. Better use gloves while washing.

ST:

اغسلي يديك واشطفي الملابس بعد الغسيل. يحفظ بعيدا عن متناول الأطفال. تجنبي ملامسة المسحوق للعينين. وفي حالة حصول ذلك اشطفي العينين حالاً بالماء. يفضل استخدام القفازات أثناء الغسيل.

> **Comment:**
>
> Here, the translator has reflected the tenor of the first, third and fourth clauses in terms of its degree of personalization when opting for the use of the second person pronoun *'you'*. However, in the second clause يحفظ, s/he

has resorted to the employment of passivization, thus impersonalizing the text and affecting the tenor of the text. Had the translator paid extra attention to the tenor of the extract, s/he could have suggested something like:

اغسلي يديك واشطفي الملابس بعد الغسيل. احفظيه بعيدا عن متناول الأطفال. تجنبي ملامسة المسحوق للعينين. وفي حالة حصول ذلك اشطفي العينين حالاً بالماء. يفضل استخدام القفازات أثناء الغسيل.

Now let us compare that example with the following example taken from the label of Fairy Liquid:

ST:
Rinse and dry hands after use. Keep away from eyes. If product gets into eyes rinse thoroughly with water.

TT:
تغسل اليدين وتجفف بعد الاستخدام. يحفظ بعيدا عن الأعين. في حالة لمس العينين، تغسل فورا وجيدا بالماء.

Comment:

As can be observed, the translator has changed the tenor of the clauses in terms of its degree of personalization when opting for passivization, يحفظ, تجفف, and تغسل. By doing so, s/he has impersonalized the text, thereby affecting the tenor of the text. Had the translator given full consideration to the tenor of the extract, s/he could have suggested something like:

اغسلي يديك وجففيهما بعد الاستخدام. احفظيه (المنتج) بعيدا عن العينين. في حالة لمس العينين، اغسليهما فورا بالماء غسلا جيدا.

To further demonstrate how not giving the tenor of discourse full consideration in translation may change the register of the text and, accordingly, affect the accuracy of translation, let us examine the following two examples quoted from Lubna Maḥmūd Yāsīn's (n.d.) story بصمة مواطن 'A Citizen's Fingerprint':

ST:
وضعوا على عينيه منديلا احكموه جيدا لكي لا يرى . . . وقُيد معصماه . . . وألصق شريط عريض فوق فمه . . . و مضوا به إلى (هناك).

TT:
They covered his eyes with a handkerchief; they tied it so tight that he couldn't see anything. His wrists were shackled; his mouth was covered with a wide piece of tape. They took him 'there'.

Annotation

Here, an attempt is made by the original writer to invoke different imaginations and/or memories in the minds of her readers on the one hand and to adopt a neutral tone on the other. She uses actors in the third and fourth material processes, such as قُيد معصماه and اَلصق شريط عريض على فمه, that can refer to anybody. Such an attempt is further enhanced by the deictic word *'there'*. As a deictic word, *'there'* refers to an assumed location in the mind of the speaker/writer, which is different from *'there'* in the mind of hearer/reader on the one hand and invokes different memories and/or imaginations on the other. So it is an open invitation to every reader in every location on the earth to enliven this moment of there-ness. Cognitively speaking, passive and active voices in transitivity choices are not identical. Rather, they have different functions, effects and reflect different points of view and ideologies (Ghazala 2011: 168).

ST:

قال للضابط بتأدب مفتعل: عفوا يا سيدي . . . ألم تتطابق ذات البصمة مع المواطن الذي سبقني . . .

TT:

He said politely: "Pardon sir, isn't it the same fingerprint that you correspond to the previous citizen?"

Annotation

Here, the original writer tries to let one of her characters use one of the honorifics, i.e. سيد 'lit. *sir*' to show his awareness of the addressee's negative face. It is worth noting that the term is used vertically (see above), so it is an example of standing, rather than social distance. Further, the original writer tries to personalize it via the deliberate use of the possessive adjective ي in سيدي '*my sir*' as well as, later, the object pronoun ي in الذي سبقني '*who preceded me*'. As such, an attempt is made here to reflect the power relationship connected with status on the one hand and to also maintain the same degree of personalization that contributes to the degree of formality.

Mode of discourse

In register analysis, the channel used by the writer or speaker to carry their message is termed 'mode of discourse'. This channel can be

(i) written, as in written to be spoken, written to be spoken as if not written and written not necessarily spoken, or
(ii) spoken, as in to be read, to be read as if heard or as if overheard (cf. Gregory and Carroll 1978: 37–47; Bell 1991: 191; Al-Rubai'i 1996: 69; Almanna 2014: 133).

162 *Annotating register*

In an attempt to inject their texts with vividness and credibility, writers, in particular literary writers, at times resort to employing spoken modes in their written ones by:

(a) utilizing "dialectal features";
(b) utilizing the "features of spoken language, e.g. elisions, fillers and corrections";
(c) "indicating the character's way of speaking", e.g. *she said in a low voice*;
(d) using "graphological devices", such as italics, capitalization, dashes, dots, quotation marks and the like (Al-Rubai'i 1996: 68).

By way of explanation, let us consider the following example quoted from Mahfouz's novel ثرثرة فوق النيل (1966) and translated by Frances Liardet (1993) as *Adrift on the Nile* (quoted in Al-Saeghi 2014a: 22):

ST:

هل اتممت البيان المطلوب؟
فجأب بلسان متراخ:
- نعم ورفعته للمدير العام ....
فتوقفت يده عن الكتابة وغمغم:
(الله) فقال زميله الأيمن:
- يابختك بفراغ البال.

TT:
"Have you finished that report?" the Head of Department asked.
Anis Zaki replied indolently. "Yes," he said. "I've sent it to the Director General." ...
He paused, pen in hand, and muttered: "Wonderful!"
"Lucky you, with no worries," said a colleague on his right.

> **Comment:**
>
> In his written mode of discourse, Mahfouz tries to indicate the character's way of speaking as in بلسان متراخ *'indolently'* as well as utilizing dialectal features, such as الله *'wonderful'* and يابختك *'lucky you'*, thereby placing extra efforts on the translator.

Here is another example quoted from Abdulsattār Nāṣir's story ثلاث قصص ليست للنشر *'Three Stories Not for Publishing'* (2009: 19):

ST:

قال المحكوم بصوت يشبه موجة بحر غاضب: من يصدق بعد هذا العذاب الطويل بأنني لست القاتل؟ سأموت وأنا وحدي وأنت معي فقط من يعرف الحقيقة..

TT:
In a voice like that of the wave of an angry sea, the condemned man says:
"Who will believe, after all that endless torture, that I'm not the murderer; I shall die with just you and me knowing the truth."

Annotation

As can be observed, the original writer, in an attempt to indicate the character's way of speaking in his written mode of discourse, opts for the use of a circumstantial of manner بصوت يشبه موجة بحر غاضب *'a voice resembles a wave of an angry sea'*. Further, the circumstantial of manner is used figuratively in the form of a simile: the topic is صوت *'voice'*, the vehicle is موجة بحر غاضب *'a wave of an angry sea'*, the similarity feature is that they are both غاضب *'angry'* and the comparison marker is يشبه *'resemble'* (see Chapter 5 in this book for more details). So the underlying meaning is that *'he says in an angry voice'*. An attempt is made to reflect both the mode of discourse indicating the character's way of speaking and the simile.

Further reading

Almanna, A. (2014). *Translation Theories Exemplified from Cicero to Pierre Bourdieu*. München: Lincom Europa Academic Publishers.
Al-Rubai'i, A. (2005). *Translation Criticism*. Durham: Durham Modern Languages Series.
Baker, M. (1992/2011). *In Other Words: A Coursebook on Translation*. London/New York: Routledge.
Bell, R. T. (1991). *Translation and Translating: Theory and Practice*. London/New York: Longman.
Borrillo, J. M. (2000). "Register Analysis in Literary Translation," *Babel*, Vol. 46 (1), pp. 1–19.
Dickins, J., Hervey, S., & Higgins, I. (2002). *Thinking Arabic Translation*. London/New York: Routledge.
Halliday, M.A.K. (1964). "Comparison and Translation." In M.A.K. Halliday, M. McIntosh, & P. Strevens (eds.), *The Linguistic Sciences and Language Teaching*, pp. 111–134. London: Longman.
Halliday, M.A.K. (1978). *Language as Social Semiotic: The Social Interpretation of Language And Meaning*. London: Edward Arnold.
Zwicky, A., & Zwicky, A. (1982). "Register as a dimension of linguistic variation." In R. Kittredge & J. Lehrberger (eds.), *Sublanguage: Studies of Languages in Restricted Semantic Domains*, pp. 213–218. Berlin/New York: Walter de Gruyter.

Companion website and online resources

http://cw.routledge.com/textbooks/translationstudies/
www.est-translationstudies.org/

Assignment 1: *Instructors*: Select an English or Arabic text (depending on your students' translation directionality whether they translate out of Arabic or into Arabic) from the BBC (no more than 500 words). Then ask them to translate the text to be published in one of the local newspapers, paying special attention to the field, tenor and mode of discourse.

Assignment 2: *Instructors*: Discuss with your students the strengths and weaknesses of the comments offered by one of the MA students with respect to translating the processes, participants and circumstances. In your discussion, you may touch on whether:

(i) there is an external coherence in the translator's comment. In other words, does s/he link his/her comment to others' studies?

(ii) there are other examples that need to be commented on.

ST:

وسأله رئيس القلم:
لماذا تنظر إلى السقف يا أنيس أفندي؟. . . .
قال الرجل بحنق: اقرأ.

TT:
"Why are you looking at the ceiling, Mr. Zaki?" the Head of Department asked. . . .
"Read it!" the man said angrily.

Comment:

(a) In this example, the translator has transferred the role of the participants successfully through transferring the process of doing: the actor in the ST is أنيس, the process of doing is تنظر and the circumstance of location is إلى السقف, which is similar to the TT: the actor is *'Mr. Zaki'*, the process of doing is *'are looking'* and the circumstances of location is *'at the ceiling'*. Here, the relationship between the participants is formal in both texts. Translating أنيس أفندي to *'Mr. Zaki'* is a good choice made by the translator to reflect the tenor.

(b) As for the sentence قال الرجل بحنق: اقرأ, it can be interpreted as a process of saying. The sayer is الرجل, the process of saying is قال and the verbiage is اقرأ. Therefore, the translator has reflected the same mental picture that exists in the original text in her translation: the sayer is *'the man'*, the process of saying is *'said'* and the verbiage is *'read it'*. Here, the tenor and the mode of discourse are transferred successfully through conveying the role of the participant الرجل and also the mood بحنق to describe his way of speaking which has been translated into *'angrily'*.

Assignment 3: *Instructors*: Discuss with your students the strengths and weaknesses of the comments offered by one of the MA students with respect to translating the processes, participants and circumstances. In your discussion, you may touch on whether:

(i) there is an external coherence in the translator's comment. In other words, does s/he link his/her comment to others' studies?

(ii) there are other examples that need to be commented on.

ST:

فقال زميله الأيمن: يا بختك بفراغ البال . . .
قال المدير: أعطني قلمك الساحر! . . .

TT:

"Lucky you, with no worries", said a colleague on his right.
"Give me this magic pen of yours!" the director said. . . .

Comment:

In this example, there are two processes of saying. The first proves: the sayer is زميله الأيمن, the process of saying is قال and the verbiage is يا بختك بفراغ البال. The translator has reflected the same mental picture that exists in the original text in her translation, the sayer is *'a colleague'*, the process of saying is *'said'* and the verbiage is the sentence *'Lucky you, with no worries'*. Here, the tenor of discourse is transferred successfully. As for the second process of saying, the sayer is المدير, the process of saying is قال and the verbiage is أعطني قلمك الساحر. Further, in its verbiage, the original writer uses a process of doing. The actor is implicit, the process of doing is أعطى and there are two goals: goal (1) is قلمك الساحر, goal (2) is الياء. In the translated text, the translator has succeeded in transferring a similar field of discourse by using a process of saying (the sayer is *'the director'*, the process of saying is *'said'* and the verbiage is *'Give me this magic pen of yours!'*) and a process of doing (the actor is implicit, the process of doing is *'give'* and there are two goals: goal (1) is *'this magic pen'*, goal (2) is *'me'*). Here, the translator has been able to convey the same mental picture which occurs in the source text.

Assignment 4: *Students*: In no more than 500 words, comment on the ST and TT, paying special attention to the field of discourse (quoted from Fred Pragnell 2003: 62–63).

ST:

كوبنهاغن – كونا – أيدت المجموعة الاوربية بقوة خططا لمضاعفة موارد الأقراض في صندوق النقد الدولي لحل ازمة ديون عالمية. وقالت إنه يجب مضاعفة أموالها الخاصة بالاستثمارات.
وقال زعماء المجموعة في بيان اختتموا به مؤتمر لهم هنا إنهم مستعدون للعمل على زيادة حصص الصندوق بشكل كبير وإنهم مصممون على اتخاذ قرار مبكر بهذا الشأن.
وكان أعضاء الصندوق الغربيون قد بحثوا في الأسبوع الماضي في باريس اقتراحات بزيادة موارد الصندوق إلى حوالي 60 بليون دولار وهناك خطط لمحاولة الحصول على موافقة سريعة للزيادة في اجتماع مبكر خاص للجنة المؤقتة التابعة للصندوق في الشهر المقبل بدلا من شهر نيسان (ابريل) من العام المقبل.

TT:

Copenhagen CUNA – The European Community vigorously endorsed plans to double borrowing facilities in the IMF to solve the international debt crisis. It said that it was necessary to double its funds for investments.

In a communiqué conducting their summit conference here, Community leaders said that they were ready to work significantly to increase the quotes of the Fund and that they were determined to adopt an early resolution in this matter.

> In Paris last week Western members of the Fund had discussed proposals for increasing the resources of the Fund to about 60 billion dollars. There are plans to try to obtain speedy agreement for the increase in an early private meeting of the Fund's interim committee next month, instead of in January next year.

Assignment 5: *Students*: translate the following text taken from the book titled تاريخ الجزائر المعاصر: دراسة written by Muḥammad al-'Arabī Zubayrī (1999, cited in Haroun 2013: 136). Then annotate your own translation, paying special attention to the field, tenor and mode of discourse:

> **ST:**
> كانت عمليات القمع رهيبة. ونحن نعتقد، رغم كل ما نشر، أن نتائجها لم تضبط حتى الآن، ولا يمكن أن تحصر بصفة دقيقة ونهائية، لكن الذي لا يعتريه أدنى شك هو أنها تأتي في مقدمة جرائم الحرب المرتكبة ضد الإنسانية، قبل كل الجرائم التي تحظى اليوم بعناية المؤرخين ورعاية الدول العظمى والمنظمات الدولية وخاصة منها منظمة الأمم المتحدة. فالأفران المحرقة شغلت نواحي مدينة قالمة: وما زال الشعب يذكر، بألم وحسرة، كيف كانت تبتلع بهم مئات الجثث الطاهرة البريئة. غير أن العالم، اليوم، لا يتحدث إلا عن الأفران التي قد يكون الألمان استعملوها لحرق اليهود أثناء الحرب الامبريالية الثانية. كما أن وسائل الإعلام الدولية ترفض أن تتوقف عند الأفران الأولى التي أقامها الجيش الاستعماري في منطقة الضهرة ليحرق قبيلة أولاد رياح مع معظم حيواناتهم الأليفة.

Assignment 6: *Students*: In no more than 150 words, comment on the translation offered by an MA student, paying special attention to the field, tenor and mode of discourse.

> **ST:**
> Hezbollah's observed behaviour is consistent with a model in which a largely brute force pattern of operational art is designed to serve largely coercive strategic ends – a combination that falls short of the conventional extreme, but which is very common in great power warfare all the same.
>
> **TT:**
> إن سلوك حزب الله الملاحظ يتوافق مع نموذج يتم فيه تصميم نسق من القوة العمياء في الغالب وخاص بالفنون العملياتية بهدف خدمة أهداف إستراتيجية ذات طابع إكراهي إلى حد كبير؛ وهذا مزيجٌ لا يصل إلى حد الحرب التقليدية، ولكنه يُعتبر شائعاً جداً في حروب القوى العظمى.

Assignment 7: *Students*: Select an English text (no more than 500 words) and translate it for publication in one of the local newspapers in your country. Before embarking on the actual act of translating the text, adopt the most appropriate global strategy. In no more than 300 words:

(i) in your introduction, tell us why you have opted for this particular global strategy.
(ii) annotate the field, tenor and mode of discourse.

The Routledge Course in Translation Annotation website at www.routledge.com/cw/almanna contains:

- A video summary of the chapter
- PowerPoint slides
- Further reading links
- Further assignments
- More research questions
- Further annotated texts

8 Annotating pragmatic, semiotic and stylistic aspects

In this chapter...

The previous chapters have looked into different aspects of language, such as lexical choices, phraseological choices, grammatical issues, register, cohesion, thematic progression and parallelism. In this chapter, special attention will be paid to how to annotate and comment on aspects of **pragmatics**, **stylistics** and **semiotics**. To this end, ample authentic data drawn from existing translations or translated for the purposes of this study will be used to drive home relevant theoretical constructs.

Key issues

- Addressing terms
- Cooperative principle
- Illocutionary acts
- Implicature
- Interpretive semiotics
- Locutionary acts
- Paradigmatic versus syntagmatic axes
- Perlocutionary acts
- Politeness
- Pragmatics
- Schemes
- Semiotics
- Speech acts
- Structural semiotics
- Stylistics
- Tropes

Aspects of pragmatics

Both semantics and pragmatics study meaning. However, unlike semantics, which begs close attention to meaning encoded in a given language by relying on structural and linguistic meaning, pragmatics pays extra attention to what is not explicitly expressed and the role of the context in interpreting a given utterance. According to Crystal (1997: 301; emphasis his), pragmatics is

> the study of LANGUAGE from the point of view of the users, especially of the choices they make, the CONSTRAINTS they encounter in using language in social interaction, and the effects their use of language has on the other participants in an act of communication.

As such, pragmatics can be envisaged here as the study of the ways in which context contributes to meaning. An example of pragmatics is how the same word can have different meanings in different settings or how people react differently in different settings. Several studies on pragmatic problems (Levinson 1983; Leech 1983; Farghal and Shakir 1994; Farghal and Borini 1996, 1997; Emery 2004; Hall 2008; Farghal 2012) have shown that speech acts, co-operative principle and its supporting maxims, addressing terms, conversational implicature and politeness strategies are the main areas that put extra efforts on the translators, requiring them to make every effort "to encode and decode contextually based implicit information" (Farghal 2012: 132).

To begin with, speech acts (Austin 1962) such as requesting, ordering, threatening, warning, suggesting, permitting and the like are universal. However, each language has its own conventionalized ways to express such speech acts; hence their nonuniversal cross-cultural application (cf. Farghal and Borini 1996, 1997; Abdel-Hafiz 2003; Hall 2008; Farghal 2012). For instance, while English customarily employs conventionalized indirect speech acts to express orders or requests, Arabic tends to utilize religious expressions, as in: الله لا يعطيك العافية, بارك الله فيك, الله يحفظك, الله لا يصغرك, يهينك, and so on or mitigating devices, such as ما عليك أمر, إذا أمكن, بلا زحمة and so on.

The contemporary use of the term goes back to J. L. Austin (1962). In his investigation of the force of linguistic expressions, Austin distinguishes among three types of act that each utterance has. They are:

1 **Locutionary act,** referring to the actual act of uttering something;
2 **Illocutionary act,** referring to the act performed in uttering something, that is, the intended/pragmatic meaning;
3 **Perlocutionary act,** referring to the act of producing an effect in the audience by uttering something.

Giving full consideration to the contextual situation and the level of interactional collaboration presented in a particular conversational exchange, translators need to

170 *Pragmatic, semiotic, stylistic aspects*

make fundamental decisions with respect to the transfer of perceived illocutionary force and perlocutionary effect of the ST utterances. To this end, they need to intrinsically manage the ST utterances to have them reflect effectively the Cooperative Principle and its maxims. P. Grice (1975) states that when we communicate with people, we unconsciously assume that we and the people we are talking to will cooperate to achieve mutual conversational ends. According to Grice, such a conversational cooperation manifests itself in a number of conversational maxims:

1 **Maxim of Quality:**
   - Do not say anything you believe to be false.
   - Do not say that for which you lack adequate evidence.
2 **Maxim of Quantity:**
   - Make your contribution only as informative as is required for the current purposes of the exchange.
   - Do not make your contribution more informative than is required.
3 **Maxim of Relevance:**
   - Be relevant.
4 **Maxim of Manner:**
   - Avoid obscurity and ambiguity.
   - Be brief.
   - Be orderly.

By way of explanation, let us consider the following example quoted from Fu'ad al-Takarlī's خزين اللامرئيات '*A Hidden Treasure*' cited in and translated by Husni and Newman (2008: 234–235):

ST:

ثم جاءها النصيب أخيراً فتزوجت منذ خمس سنوات واستقرت بها الحياة هنا.

TT:

Finally, she got married five years ago. Now she's settled here.

Comment:

In this example, there is a semantic repetition, جاءها النصيب '*luck came to her*' and تزوجت '*she got married*'. According to Arab culture, one can express such a world experience directly as in تزوجت '*she got married*' or indirectly جاءها النصيب '*luck came to her*'. Approached from a pragmatic perspective, in the first sentence جاءها النصيب '*luck came to her*', the narrator, while talking of a girl and her marriage opportunity, uses a locutionary act جاءها النصيب that has the illocutionary force of 'she got married', thereby flouting Grice's (1975) Cooperative Principle and its maxims, in particular, the quality maxim, that is, to speak the truth. Further, opting to express the same sociocultural experience indirectly, the narrator flouts the quantity maxim, that is, to make your contribution only as informative as is required, and

Pragmatic, semiotic, stylistic aspects 171

> confirms the fact that she finally got married. The translators, being aware of this culture-specific segment, have resorted to deletion of an introductory sentence, as rendering it literally would be unidiomatic and, indeed, somewhat superfluous in English. However, from a stylistic perspective, the translators should have taken this fatalistic shade of meaning into account, offering something like *'her luck changed and she got married'* or *'life smiled on her and she got married'*.

To further demonstrate how (not) taking the pragmatic aspects into account may seriously affect the quality of the TT, let us consider the following example quoted from Mahfuz's (1959/1986: 150) novel أولاد حارتنا *Children of the Alley* and translated by Theroux (1996: 122):

ST:

اسم الله على أمك وليالیها الملاح عند حمام السلطان.

TT:
"Not as much as your mother, with her famous nights at the Sultan Baths!"

> **Comment:**
>
> Here, the speaker in the original extract flouts the maxim of quality, to speak the truth, by opting for a metaphorical expression اسم الله على أمك *'the name of God/Allah on your mother'* in order to communicate and emphasize his message, thus giving rise to a conversational implicature. Being aware that relying on the locutionary act of the utterance without taking into account its illocutionary force would seriously affect the intentionality of the ST and alter the text type focus, the translator has intrinsically managed the text to be in line with the TL norms. The idiomatic expression *'not as much as your mother'* effectively reflects what is meant by the original writer.

Among many attempts to classify illocutionary acts, Searle (1969) has set up the following classification:

1 **Assertive verbs** or **representatives.** They are speech acts that commit a speaker to the truth of the expressed proposition, such as statements of events, facts, descriptions and so on;
2 **Directive verbs.** They are speech acts that are to cause the addressee to take a particular action, such as requesting, commanding, demanding, advising and so on.
3 **Commissive verbs.** They are speech acts that commit a speaker to some future actions, such as promising, threatening and so on;

172 *Pragmatic, semiotic, stylistic aspects*

4   **Expressive verbs.** They are speech acts that express the speaker's attitudes and emotions towards the proposition, such as congratulating, excusing, thanking, expressing states of joy, sorrow and so on;
5   **Declarative verbs.** They are speech acts that change the reality to be in line with the proposition of the declaration, such as baptisms, pronouncing someone guilty or pronouncing someone husband and wife.

The short piece of dialogue that follows offers examples of fictional speech acts. It is taken from Mahfuz's (1959/1986: 134) novel أولاد حارتنا *Children of the Alley* translated by Theroux (1996: 117). It takes place just after Zaqlut has announced to the Effendi, Hudaa and Gebel that Hamdaan's people have killed their strongman, Qidra.

ST:

وبدا أن الأفندي لم يفاجأه الخبر إذ قال:
- بلغتني أنباء عن اختفائه، ولكن هل يئستم حقا من العثور عليه؟
قال زقلط وكان نور الضحى الذي يقتحم باب البهو يؤكد سماجة ملامحه:
- لن يعثر عليه وأنا خبير بهذه المكائد.

TT:

Somehow the news did not come as a surprise to Effendi. "I have heard reports of his disappearance. Have you really given up hope of finding him?"

The morning light pouring through the door of the hall redoubled the hideousness of Zaqlut's face as he said, "He will not be found. I am an expert in these little schemes".

Comment:

In the ST, the Effendi's speech act بلغتني أنباء عن اختفائه offers a direct speech act of acknowledgement that the news Zaqlut has delivered does not come as a surprise, but the interrogative that follows هل يئستم حقا من العثور عليه offers an indirect speech act of confirmation: it is used to get confirmation of the news to convince all parties, especially Gebel. In this regard, Yule (1996: 54–55) states that "whenever there is a direct relationship between a structure and a function, we have a direct speech act. Whenever there is an indirect relationship between a structure and a function, we have an indirect speech act". As for the second part of the dialogue, Zaqlut's speech لن يعثر عليه وأنا خبير بهذه المكائد offers two speech acts of assertion, one supporting the other. Giving full consideration to these speech acts of acknowledgement, confirmation and assertion, the translator has tried his hand at reflecting them, thus performing effective representative illocutionary acts in the TT.

To cast light on the importance of paying extra attention to speech acts while translating, let us have a look at two BBC news items on the same topic (one in English and the other in Arabic, November 30, 2014):

Pragmatic, semiotic, stylistic aspects 173

ST:

Correspondents say rampant corruption in the Iraqi army is seen as one of the reasons why it has struggled to contain Islamic State militants.

TT:

ويقول مراسلون إنه يُنظر إلى تفشي الفساد في الجيش العراقي على أنه أحد الأسباب التي تجعله غير قادر على احتواء خطر مسلحي تنظيم "الدولة الإسلامية".

Comment:

As can be observed, the news reporter uses direct speech act of assertion *'say'*. Leech (1983: 224) is of a view that assertive verbs can be 'informative' (to announce or report an event) and 'argumentative' (to express the relation between the current truth claim and other truth claims made by the speaker or the addressee). It is clear that this direct speech act of assertion is informative. Further, it is followed by another speech act of assertion in the passive form *'is seen'*. Taking into account the function of such speech acts of assertion, the translator has accurately rendered them into two speech acts of assertion/informative يقول and ينظر.

The other pragmatic issue that might place extra pressure on translators is politeness. Politeness is defined herein as a means utilized by participants to show their awareness of others' face, whether negative or positive. Showing awareness of the public self-image of another person who is "socially distant is often described in terms of respect or deference", whereas showing awareness of the face of another person who is "socially close is often described in terms of friendliness, camaraderie, or solidarity" (Yule 1996: 60). Politeness in a given text can be detected by tracing certain markers: (1) addressing terms, (2) mitigating features, (3) euphemism and (4) norms of politeness. To show how the degree of severity of the face-threatening mode of action is different between languages, let us consider the following example quoted from Muḥsin Al-Ramlī's story البحث عن قلب حيّ *'Search for a Live Heart'* (2009: 39):

ST:

(يرفع ذراعيه داعياً) أعده يا من تعيد الشمس والمطر.. أعده يا من أعدتَ يوسف إلى أبيه.. أعده يا من تعيد الصفاء إلى وجه السماء.. أعد الصفاء إلى سماوات نفوسنا

TT:

He lifts his arms to beseech God, 'Oh, my Lord, who can make the sun rise and the rain fall, please bring him back to us. Oh, my Lord, who brought Joseph back to his father, please bring him back. Oh, my Lord, who can make the sky clear again, please bring him back. Please bring light to the heavens of our souls'.

174 *Pragmatic, semiotic, stylistic aspects*

> **Annotation:**
>
> In the ST, the speaker uses a direct speech act in addressing God, i.e. he opts for 'bald on record' strategy in which the imperative form, which is "the most face-threatening mode of action", is used (Cutting 2002: 64). Although politeness is a "universal characteristic across cultures that speakers should respect each others' expectations regarding self-image, take account of their feelings, and avoid face threatening acts", the way people follow in showing their awareness of others' faces when interacting with each other is different from one culture into another (Ibid.: 45). Thus, what is considered acceptable and polite in one culture cannot be taken for granted in another. The degree of severity of the face-threatening mode of action achieved by imperative forms is more forceful in English than that in Arabic, hence the need for 'mitigating devices', such as *'please'*, *'Could you. . . ?'*, *'Would you . . . ?'*, etc. to soften such severity (Yule 1996: 63).

Closely related to politeness strategies is the issue of addressing terms and their different pragmatic functions. In the following example, which is quoted from Mahfuz's (1959/1986: 219) novel أولاد حارتنا *Children of the Alley* and translated by Theroux (1996: 180), the translator, due to the cultural-pragmatic constraints imposed on them by the use of such an addressing term as ياعم *'Oh uncle'*, has taken into account the pragmatic function of the term in such a context as well as the TL norms, thus intrinsically managing the utterance by deleting the addressing term completely:

ST:

بخير ياعم جواد سألت عليك العافية

TT:
"*Fine, Gawad*", said Abda. I hope you are well".

> **Comment:**
>
> As can be seen, the ST employs an addressing term عم 'lit. *paternal uncle*'. Given full consideration to the norms of politeness in the TL, regardless of the politeness strategy itself, whether an honorific is used or not, the translator has opted for the deletion of the term عم, which affects the degree of respect to the referent. Translating it into *'Mr Gawad'*, for instance, instead of opting for the first name only would undoubtedly capture the degree of respect of the referential form. However, it changes the degree of intimacy between the two participants from intimate into formal, thus distorting the pragmatic function associated with the use of the term عم. Given that the employment of this addressing term by the speaker indicates that the speaker is relatively younger than the addressee and deleting the intimate term and addressing Gawad without a social honorific would be very face threatening; the "only way to solve this problem is to preserve the social honorific *'uncle'*

in translation" (Farghal and Almanna 2015: 123). They hold that "the relational use of the social honorific *'uncle'*, which is very familiar in Arabic, is not alien to 'young-elderly' interaction in English" (124). As such, translators need to strike a balance between the different constraints in translation activity in order to do justice to both languages/cultures and their signifying systems by zooming in and out to capture all details of the image.

Aspects of semiotics

In order to express their feelings, opinions, ideas and experiences of the world, people normally use language. However, in addition to the linguistic elements, they use signs, symbols, sounds and so on. Grutman (2009: 261) holds that in order to study "how people make sense of their experience of the world and how cultures share and give currency to this understanding", one needs to adopt a semiotic approach. Approached from such a perspective, Faiq and Sabry (2013: 47) state that semiotics is "the study of the methods in which local populations communicate through signs and symbols that are obviously influenced by cultural traditions".

The most common definition of 'semiotics' is that it is the study of signs, symbols, significance and sign-using behaviour, especially in language. Adopting a wider perspective, Stam and colleagues (1992: 1) define it as "the study of signs, signification and signifying systems". Further, for some semioticians (cf. Fiske and Hartley 1978), semiotics deals with "studying how meanings are constructed through certain sets of socio-cultural norms" (Al-Shehari 2001: 104). Building on such an assumption, Fiske and Hartley (1978) hold that the way in which signs are constructed into codes determines the meaning of a sign, not only the relationship between the sign and its meaning (1978: 37; Al-Shehari 2001: 104).

Semiotic analysis as a field of research was established by three scholars adopting three different models. The Swiss linguist Ferdinand de Saussure (1857–1913) adopted a *'structural semiotics'*, the American philosopher Charles Sanders Peirce (1839–1914) adopted an *'interpretive semiotics'* and the American semiotician and philosopher Charles William Morris (1901–1979) developed a *'behaviorist semiotics'*, which led to the emergence of semiotics as a method for examining phenomena in different fields, including aesthetics, anthropology, communications, psychology and semantics (for more details, see Grutman 2009: 260; Faiq and Sabry 2013: 47; Almanna 2013: 79–80; Farghal and Almanna 2015: 128–131). In this section, special attention will be paid to Peirce's *interpretive semiotics* and de Saussure's *structural semiotics*, as they provide translators with a systematic foundation through which they can approach the invisible or conventional meanings of signs.

Peirce's (1839–1914) *interpretive semiotics* considers a sign anything that is determined by an 'object' that invokes in a person's mind an idea, image and the like. Such invocation is what Peirce labels 'interpretant'. As such, a sign can be found in the physical form of words, phrases, images, symbols, wink, smile, odor, diagrams, sounds, acts or objects. Peirce further differentiates between the sign and its functions. According to him, each sign has three functions: **iconic**

176 *Pragmatic, semiotic, stylistic aspects*

function (i.e., the signifier is perceived as resembling or imitating the signified); **indexical** function, (i.e., the signifier is physically or causally connected in some way to the signified); and **symbolic** function, (i.e., the signifier does not resemble the signified, but it is learnt by having an agreement among people on it). These three functions of sign – iconic, indexical and symbolic – do not have to function independently from one another, as they sometimes function as an icon, an index and a symbol or any combination of these (cf. Al-Shehari 2001). To explain how (not) taking into account the sign's functions would affect the image resolution, let us discuss the following example quoted from Sāliḥ's (1966: 243) novel عرس الزين *The Wedding of Zein,* translated by Denys Johnston-Davies (1986: 81):

ST:

وقال عبد الصمد مستفزاً: أي فلوس! أنا عارفك كنت خال عينك عليها عشان مال أبوها. واحتدّ الناظر وهو يردّ التهمة عن نفسه: أنا خاف الله يا رجل هذه في عمر بناتي

TT:

"What money!" said Abdul Samad provocatively. "I know you had your eye on her because of her father's wealth".
"I have some shame, my dear fellow", said the Headmaster, furiously warding off the accusation. "She's no older than my daughters".

Comment:

(a) Here, the first sign that functions iconically is خال عينك عليها 'lit. *you put your eye on her*'. Semiotically speaking, such an expression recalls other signifiers (such as تحبها '*you love her*', تعجبك '*you like her*', تميل لها '*you are attracted to her*', etc.), which refer to the same signified. To put it differently, the expression خال عينك عليها in this context refers to physical referents in the real world ('*eye*', '*man*'/'*boy*' and '*woman*'/'*girl*') as well as invoking in the mind of the hearer/reader the idea of being attracted to somebody. It so happens that Arabic and English conceptualize such a world experience in a similar way, thus giving rise to 'optimal equivalence' in which both formal equivalent (i.e., the image conjured up in the mind of the reader) and functional equivalent (i.e., the function of the expression, independently of the form and its image conjured up in the mind of the reader) coincide (see Baker 1992: 72; Farghal 2012: 47).

(b) The second sign that needs special treatment is خاف الله يارجل 'lit. *Fear God, man*'. In Arabic, this formula is normally used to urge someone to fear God when s/he is in the course of or at the point of committing a mistake or metaphorically to urge someone to stop teasing you. As it is difficult to find a TL sign with the same three functions, that is iconic, indexical and symbolic, the translator has given the indexical and symbolic functions a front seat at the expense of the iconic function, thus preserving partially the expression's functions, that is, indexical and symbolic.

de Saussure's (1857–1913) *structural semiotics* sees languages as a system of signs. For him, a sign is composed of a signifier, the physical form of the sign, and signified, the mental concept of the sign. For de Saussure, the signified, which is not a material thing, can refer to physical objects in the real world, abstract concepts or fictional entities. Signifieds are often classified into two main types: a denotative signified and a connotative signified (Al-Shehari 2001: 151). The denotative meaning is the literal (direct) meaning that can be understood via a direct and clear relationship between the sign and the thing it refers to. The connotative meaning(s), on the other hand, are those that come into existence as a result of an interaction between the sign and the user's context (for more details on denotation and connotation, see Chapter 5 in this book). According to de Saussure, there are two ways in which signs are organized into codes: syntagmatic and paradigmatic (for more details, see Al-Shehari 2001: 159–173). The two ways of organizing signs into codes are described as two 'axes': the vertical axis is paradigmatic and the horizontal one is syntagmatic. While the main concern of paradigms is the selection of some signs and exclusion of others, syntagms focus on the combination of the selected signs. Further, these two ways can be used as an approach to testing the sign's significance on the one hand and the translation accuracy on the other. These two axes constitute the micro signs that form a mental image in the mind of the hearer/reader. By way of explanation, let us consider the following example quoted from Mahfuz's (1973: 90) novel اللص والكلاب *The Thief and the Dogs*, translated by Adel Ata Elyas (1987: 161):

ST:

فتح عينيه فرأى الدنيا حمراء ولا شيء فيها ولا معنى لها.

TT:

He opened his eyes to see a red world without meaning or significance.

Comment:

As can be observed, in the ST, the sign فتح عينيه 'lit. *opened his eyes*' is chosen from a set of possible words/expressions such as نهض, صحا, انتبه, فزّ, استيقظ من النوم and the like. The same holds true for other signs used, such as رأى (instead of أدرك (أن), لاحظ, أبصر, شاهد, etc.); الدنيا (instead of العالم, etc.); حمراء (instead of خضراء, صفراء, سوداء, وردية, etc.) and so on. A syntagm, on the other hand, is the linear arrangement into which the signs, which are chosen from paradigms, are combined. So the paradigmatic signs:

فتح، عينيه، ف، رأى، الدنيا، حمراء، و، لا، شيء، في، ها (الدنيا)، و، لا، معنى، لـ، ها

are combined to formulate the syntagm

فتح عينيه فرأى الدنيا حمراء ولا شيء فيها ولا معنى لها.

While translating, translators normally rely on the syntagmatic and paradigmatic axes to produce the final shape of the TT. Any change in these two axes will undoubtedly create a different mental image. For instance, had the translator opted for signs, such as *'when'* (instead of no connector); *'come to'* (instead of *'open his eyes'*); *'comma'* (instead of *'to'*); *'realize'* (instead of *'see'*); *'life'* (instead of *'world'*); *'colourless'* (instead of *'red'*); *'value'* (instead of *'meaning'*) and *'importance'* (instead of *'significance'*), as in:

When he came to, he realized that life is colourless, without value or importance.

he would have created a mental image different from that formed by other micro signs. This clearly shows how using different syntagmatic and paradigmatic axes dramatically change the mental image conjured up in the mind of the hearer/reader, thus affecting image resolution and translation quality.

To elaborate, let us consider the following example quoted from Choukri's novel الخبز الحافي (2000: 183; 6th edition), translated by Bowles into *For Bread Alone* (1993: 136):

ST:

ـ اجلس مكانك. لابد أن يكون قواد هو الذي يدق بهذا الشكل.

TT:

"Stay where you are", said Zailachi.

Comment:

In the ST, a number of signs are chosen out of a set of possible words, for example:

~ اجلس مكانك (instead of ابق, قف, لا تتحرّك, انبطح, خليك, etc.);
~ لابد (instead of لازم, يجب, يمكن, احتمال, يفترض, يتوقع, etc.);
~ قواد (instead of أحد الجيران, مستطرق, ضيف, الشرطة, etc.); and
~ يدق (instead of يطرق, يخبط (الجرس) يرن, يضرب, etc.); and
~ بهذا الشكل (instead of بهذه القسوة, بهذا الهدوء, بهذا الوقت, بهذه الساعة, بدون موعد, etc.).

So, the paradigmatic signs:

اجلس ـ مكانك ـ لابد أن ـ .ـ يكون ـ قواد ـ هو ـ الذي ـ يدق ـ بهذا ـ الشكل

are combined to formulate the syntagm:

اجلس مكانك. لابد أن يكون قواد هو الذي يدق بهذا الشكل.

Opting for other micro signs that constitute the paradigmatic axis would yield completely different syntagms, thus creating different images in the mind of the reader/hearer, as in:

ابق في مكانك، أتوقع أنه شخص مستطرق يطرق على الباب بهذا الشكل.

Back-translation: *Stay in your place. I think somebody passing by is knocking on the door in that way.*

خليك، أنا ذاهب لأرى أي قواد يدق الباب بهذا الشكل المفزع.

Back-translation: *Stay. I'm going to see. Only a pimp would knock in that horrible way.*

اجلس. هذا جاري فهو الذي يدق الباب بهذا الشكل.

Back-translation: *Sit down. He is my neighbour; he knocks in that way.*

The translator, however, has resorted to deleting some signs, such as:

- the modalized verb لا بد *'must'* used epistemically to express the speaker's opinion or point of view;
- the lexical item قواد *'pimp'*, which is used without tanween, i.e. قواد instead of قوادًا, although it is in the accusative case, used out of its denotative meaning to reflect the tenor of the text (informal) and reflect the speaker's social status;
- the material process (process of doing) along with its implied goal, *'door'*, and the circumstance of manner, *'in that way'* يدق بهذا الشكل *'someone is knocking (on the door) in that way'*.

Further, the translator has changed the sign اجلس 'lit. *sit down*' into another sign, ابق اينما تكون whose denotative meaning is wider and less specific than that of the sign used in the ST. Having different micro signs means yielding different syntagmatic and paradigmatic axes, thus creating different mental images. Had the translator given full consideration to the syntagmatic and paradigmatic axes, he could have suggested something like:

Keep still. Only a pimp would knock like that.

To further demonstrate how news items can be structurally constructed on these two axes or how different micro signs may affect the overall meaning of the text, let us consider the following example along with its translation (Farghal 2008: 3–4):

ST:
In an interview with Newsweek *yesterday, the Israeli Defense Minister said that the Palestinian suicide operations constitute the main cause for the Israeli troops' entering cities in the West Bank.*

TT:
ادعى وزير الحرب الصهيوني في مقابلة مع مجلة النيوزويك أمس أن العمليات الاستشهادية الفلسطينية هي السبب الرئيس في اجتياح قوات الاحتلال الإسرائيلي للمدن الفلسطينية في الضفة الغربية المحتلة.

Comment:

As can be observed, in the ST, signs such as *'the 'Israeli Defense', 'said', 'Palestinian suicide operations', 'Israeli troops', ' entering'* and *'the West Bank'* are chosen from a set of possible words. So the paradigmatic signs:

In – an – interview – with – Newsweek – yesterday –, – the – Israeli – Defense – Minister said – that – the – Palestinian – suicide – operations – constitute – the – main – cause – for – the – Israeli – troops – entering – cities – in – the – West – Bank.

> are combined to formulate the syntagm:
> *In an interview with* Newsweek *yesterday, the Israeli Defense Minister said that the Palestinian suicide operations constitute the main cause for the Israeli troops' entering cities in the West Bank.*
>
> However, in an attempt to create a narrative dimension familiar to the TL readers, the translator has used different paradigmatic signs and a particular syntagmatic structure by changing a neutral verb *'said'* into evaluative verb ادعى *'claim'*, *'Israeli'* into صهيوني *'Zionist'*, *'defense'* into حرب *'war'*, *'suicide'* into استشهادية *'martyrdom'*, *'entering'* into اجتياح *'annihilation or invasion'*. Similarly s/he has added the noun احتلال *'occupation'* and the adjective محتلة *'occupied'*.

Aspects of stylistics

In any language, the same idea can be expressed differently, thus creating various linguistic forms or styles. This is because each language has its own linguistic system (phonetics, graphology, semantics, morphology, syntax and pragmatics) that enables language users to opt for a particular linguistic form and exclude others (cf. McEnery and Wilson 2001; Murphy 2006). This goes in line with the definition of style provided by Crystal (1989: 66):

> Style is seen as the (conscious or unconscious) selection of a set of linguistic features from all the possibilities in a language. The effects these features convey can be understood only by intuitively sensing the choices that have been made [. . .] and it is usually enough simply to respond to the effect in this way.

In the field of Translation Studies, a great number of attempts have been made to define 'style' for some time now (cf. Nida 1964; Venuti 2000/2004; Zyngier 2001; Bassnett 2002; Ghazala 2011; Huang 2011; Makokha *et al.* 2012; Almanna 2013). However, formulating a rigorous definition of what style exactly is remains ambiguous in nature, and the investigation is still unsystematic. Since the early attempts about writing on translation made by Cicero, Horace and St. Jerome, style has often been touched on, but "its role has rarely been systematically explored. Yet style is central to the way we construct and interpret texts" (Boase-Beier 2006: 1).

Style is defined by Literary Devices Net as a "technique which an individual author uses in his writing. It varies from author to author and depends upon one's syntax, word choice, and tone". In a direct link with written texts, as opposed to oral texts, it "can also be described as a voice that readers listen to when they read the work of a writer" (literarydevices.net). However, style can be defined in this study as a kind of deviation either from the ordinary expected patterns of structures or from the direct literal meanings of words. Such a deviation occurring within any language system normally creates marked and unexpected dominations of sounds, ways of writing, meanings, structures and so forth. These marked and unexpected combinations are often divided into two main types: 'tropes' and 'schemes' (cf. Corbett 1971; Leech and Short 1981; Abrams 1988/1993; Al-Rubai'i 1996, 2005; Teilanyo 2007). Schemes (from the Greek word *schēma*, which means 'form' or 'shape') are expressions in which there is a deviation from the ordinary or expected pattern of words, such as ellipsis, parallelism, apposition, alliteration, anastrophe, assonance, asyndeton, chiasmus, enallage, anadiplosis, zeugma, hyperbation and so forth. By contrast, tropes (from the Greek *tropein*, 'to turn'), refer to a type of language that involves a deviation from its basic, straightforward meaning, such as metaphor, irony, metonymy, neologism, onomatopoeia, paradox, personification, simile, zoomorphism, litotes, euphemism and so on.

To demonstrate the impact of failing to reflect certain stylistic features in authentic translation practice, let us consider the following example quoted from Karīm 'Abid's story (ع) غرام السيدة *'the Passion of Lady A'* translated by Eric Winkel (2010: 63–64):

ST:

ظلّتْ الفتاتان الملائكيتان تسيران أمامه من دون أن يرى وجهيهما، كانتا عايتين ورشيقتين ومثيرتين لكن لم يكن هذا قصده، كان في حالة من لذة غريبة لم يكن يفهم كنهها.

TT:

The two lady angels kept walking in front of him, without him being able to see their faces. They were graceful, stimulating, but this was not his aim. He was in a strange pleasure he couldn't grasp completely.

Comment:

In this example, the suffix repetition that leads to the assonance in عايتين, مثيرتين and رشيقتين and the assonance in الملائكيتان and الفتاتان is lost in the TT. In this regard, Al-Rubai'i (1996: 111) rightly comments that it is not an easy task to reflect "schemes of construction which depend upon similarity of sound" in the TT. As for the combination of both assonance and alliteration in لكن لم يكن هذا قصده, the translator has utilized the sound '*S*' in his rendering *'but this was not his aim'* as compensation for the lost assonance. However, had he done the same with لم يكن يفهم كنهها, he could have produced a translation such as *'he couldn't grasp its essence'* to make up for the assonance and alliteration.

To further demonstrate how not taking into account the deliberate and conscious selections made by the original writer may create a misleading mental image in the minds of the TL readers, let us consider the following example quoted from Choukri's novel الخبز الحافي (2000: 191; 6th edition), translated by Bowles into *For Bread Alone* (1993: 143):

- إرادة الحياة، هذا هو معنى ما يقوله.
- وما معنى إرادة الحياة؟

182   *Pragmatic, semiotic, stylistic aspects*

- إرادة الحياة معناها هو أنه إذا كان هناك شعب مستعبد أو إنسان ما وأراد أن يتحرر فإن الله له، والفجر يستجيب والقيد يستجيب يتهرس بقوة إرادة الحياة.

"He's talking about the desire to live".
"And what does the desire to live mean?"
"It means that if a man or a country is enslaved and decides to try and get free, Allah will help. He says: the dawn will respond and the chains will break because men will make it happen".

Comment:

In this example, there is a phrasal repetition إرادة الحياة, which is used by the original writer four times. It is fronted at the first and third utterances and repeated at the second and fourth utterances. Such a repetition is quite natural and acceptable in Arabic – it is one of the devices for emphasis in Arabic. Taking into account such a stylistic feature on the one hand and TL linguistic and stylistic norms on the other, the translator has opted for reflecting it in the first and second utterances only. In the third utterance, he has resorted to anaphoric-*it*, and in the final clause, it is not referred to explicitly, but its sense is incorporated into the clause. Further, there is an example of climax, arranging words يستجيب يتهرس according to their increasing importance, which is accompanied by the deliberate omission of connectors and/or punctuation marks. Paying no attention to such stylistic features, the translator has opted for deleting the second word يتهرس 'lit. *be smashed* or *crushed*' completely. Had the translator adopted a stylistic approach to analyzing and appreciating the stylistic peculiarities utilized by the original writer and relating them to their artistic functions, he could have resorted to a *wh*-cleft in the first clause, an anaphoric-*it* in the second clause, a phrasal repetition in the third clause and the prepositional phrase 'by virtue of' that can accommodate the repetition of the phase 'the desire to live' smoothly, as in:

What he's trying to emphasize is 'the desire to live'.
What does it mean?
'The desire to live' means if a man or a country is enslaved and decides to get free, Allah will help, and the dawn will respond and the chains will break . . . will be smashed by virtue of 'the desire to live'.

To cast more light on the importance of appreciating and then reflecting the ST stylistic features in the TT, let us consider the following example quoted from Greene's (1980: 10) *The Bomb Party*:

ST:
From the sale of their chocolate my employers paid me three thousands francs a month which I suppose may have represented half an hour's income to Doctor Fischer who many years before had invented Dentophil Bouquet, a toothpaste

Pragmatic, semiotic, stylistic aspects 183

which was supposed to hold at bay the infections caused by eating too many of our chocolates.

TT:

ومن بيع الشوكولاتا كان رؤسائي يدفعون لي ثلاثة آلاف فرنك شهريا، وأظنّها تساوي إيراد نصف ساعة من إيرادات الدكتور فشر الذي ابتكر قبل عدّة سنوات دنتوفل بوكيه، وهو معجون أسنان يفترض به أن يقاوم النخر الذي يسببه تناول الكثير من الشوكولاتا التي ننتجها.

Annotation:

(a) Here, in an attempt to maintain the complexity of the sentence and in order to avoid any ambiguity that might arise out of a straightforward rendering on the one hand and to make it read smoothly on the other, a syntactic reordering to the relative clause *'which I suppose may have represented half an hour's income to Doctor Fischer'* is needed, as in: وأظنّها تساوي إيراد نصف ساعة من إيرادات الدكتور فشر الذي ابتكر قبل عدّة سنوات دنتوفل بوكيه

(b) The marked prepositional phrase *'From the sale of the chocolate, . . .'* lends itself to a marked prepositional phrase in the TT ومن بيع الشوكولاتا. Also, in order not to charge the prepositional phrase with extra stylistic features, namely alliteration, an attempt is made to resist the strong temptation of using the word ريع *'income'* in the above prepositional phrase, although it is a finer style, as in ومن بيع ريع الشوكولاتا.

(c) Here, in order to avoid any sort of generalization that might result from leaving شوكولاتا without a possessive pronoun, and for fear of having an ambiguous phrase, such as شوكولاتتنا, that comes from using the possessive pronoun *'our'*, on the one hand, and to avoid the difficulty in reading and pronouncing the word شوكولاتتنا on the other, we resort to a relative clause التي ننتجها in our rendering.

Following is another example extracted from Maḥmūd Saīd's story البديلة *The Stand-in* (2009: 67):

ST:

أصبح العالم قرية صغيرة يشرب فيها الكل الكوكاكولا ويأكلون "الهم" بركر ويلبسون نفس الزي ويحلقون رؤوسهم بنفس الطريقة وو.. ونحن ما زلنا متخلفين.. يا ويلي علينا..

TT:

The world is now a small village where everybody drinks Coca Cola and eats the bloody hamburger, wears the same clothes and has the same haircut . . . we are so behind the times, God help us!

Annotation:

In this extract, a certain degree of rhetorical devices, such as alliteration (in the repetition of the sound-cluster الكل at the beginning of the words

184 *Pragmatic, semiotic, stylistic aspects*

> ـل and ك, و) and assonance (in the repetition of the letters الكوكاكولا and الكل) along with the pun (in the words هم '*grief*' and همبركر '*hamburger*') have been used to convey the author's tone of indignation. It would be sensible for the TT to retain as much as possible this effect. To convey the author's tone of indignation and minimize the loss in the phonic effect, the addition of an adjectival expletive, such as *'damn'*, *'damned'*, *'confounded'* or, more informally, *'bloody'* is needed.

To demonstrate how translators, by adopting a style-based approach, can have a better understanding and appreciation of texts, let us discuss the following example extracted from Lubna Maḥmūd Yāsīn's story بصمة مواطن *A Citizen's Fingerprint* (n.d.):

ST:

يبتلعه المساء . . . فيوغل في أحشاء الصمت . . . ومن ذا الذي يستطيع فرارا إذا عسعس الألم داخل النفس . . . وتوغلت الأحزان في حنايا الفؤاد . . . يتآكل قلبه . . . تتساقط أشلاؤه . . . يتمزق صوته على حدود الزمان ولا من مجيب . . .

TT:

The night swallows him so he delves ever deeper into the heart of silence. Who can, then, escape if the pain is densely settled inside the self and sadness penetrates the depths of the heart? . . . His heart erodes; his limbs fall off; his voice gets torn away at the boundaries of time, yet no response comes.

> **Annotation:**
>
> (a) Here, in rendering the marked collocation in أحشاء الصمت *'the bowels of silence'*, an attempt is made to resist the temptation of opting for an unmarked collocation, viz. *'wall of silence'* or *'a vow of silence'*. This is exactly what Trotter (2000: 351) tries to lay emphasis on when he states: "Translation requires invariance in the markedness of collocates, rather than replacing abnormal usage in an original with normal usage in translation".
>
> (b) As can be observed, there is an example of parallelism . . . يتمزق صوته تتساقط أشلاؤه . . . يتآكل قلبه. Further, the original writer deliberately produces his above parallel structures without connectors, thus creating an example of asyndeton. Asyndeton, according to Corbett (1971: 469) is the "deliberate omission of connective particles between series of related clauses". Al-Rubai'i (1996: 111) distinguishes between schemes of construction which depend upon similarity of sound, viz. alliteration and assonance and other schemes of construction that do not rely on sound, such as asyndeton and climax. She adds that the former "are very frequently untranslatable", while the latter "can sometimes be retained

> through translation". Thus, such parallel structures lend themselves to *'his heart erodes; his limbs fall off; his voice gets torn away'* to maintain parallelism as well as asyndeton in the TT.
> (c) Further, attention is paid to the formal structure in ومن ذا الذي which is supported by an archaic lexical item عسعس that has a religious connotation as well as the deliberate use of the rhyme ـس in: ومن ذا الذي يستطيع فرارا إذا عسعس الألم داخل النفس, thus it is translated into:
>
> '*who can, then, escape if the pain is densely settled inside the self and sadness penetrates the depths of the heart?*'

Further reading on pragmatics

Austin, J. L. (1962). *How to Do Things With Words.* Oxford: Oxford University Press.
Grice, H. P. (1975). "Logic and Conversation." In P. Cole and Morgan, J. L. (eds.), *Syntax and Semantics, 3: Speech Acts*, pp. 41–58. New York: Academic Press.
Leech, G. N. (1983). *Principles of Pragmatics*. London: Longman.
Levinson, S. C. (1983). *Pragmatics*. Cambridge: Cambridge University Press.
Lin, G.H.C., & Perkins, L. (2005). "Cross-Cultural Discourse of Giving and Accepting Gifts," *International Journal of Communication*, 16, 1–2, 103–112 (ERIC Collections in ED 503685 http://www.eric.ed.gov/PDFS/ED503685.pdf)
Robinson, D. (2003). *Performative Linguistics: Speaking and Translating as Doing Things With Words*. London/New York: Routledge.
———. (2006). *Introducing Performative Pragmatics*. London and New York: Routledge.
Sperber, D., & Wilson, D. (2005). "Pragmatics." In F. Jackson and M. Smith (eds.), *Oxford Handbook of Contemporary Philosophy*, pp. 468–501. Oxford: Oxford University Press.
Thomas, J. (1995). *Meaning in Interaction: An Introduction to Pragmatics*. London: Longman.
Verschueren, J. (1999). *Understanding Pragmatics*. London/New York: Arnold Publishers.
———, Jan-Ola, Ö., & Jan B. (eds.). (1995). *Handbook of Pragmatics*. Amsterdam: Benjamins.
Wierzbicka, A. (1991). *Cross-Cultural Pragmatics. The Semantics of Human Interaction*. Berlin/New York: Mouton de Gruyter.
Yule, G. (1996). *Pragmatics*. Oxford: Oxford University Press.

Further reading on semiotics

Adab, B. J. (1997). *Translation Strategies and Cross-Cultural Constraints: A Case Study of the Translation of Advertising Texts*. Unpublished PhD thesis: Aston University.
Al-Rubai'i, A. (2005). *Translation Criticism*. Durham, UK: Durham Modern Languages Series.
Al-Shehari, K. (2001). *The Semiotics and Translation Advertising Texts: Conventions, Constraints and Translation Strategies with Particular Reference to English and Arabic*. Unpublished PhD thesis: University of Manchester.
Faiq, S., & Sabry, R. (2013). "Altered Semiotics through Translation," *STJ: Sayyab Translation Journal*, Vol. 5, pp. 45–56.

Farghal, M., & Bloushi, N. (2012). "Shifts of Coherence in Quran Translation," *STJ: Sayyab Translation Journal*, Vol. 4, pp. 1–18.
Hatim, M., & Mason, I. (1990). *Discourse and the Translator*. London: Longman.
Grutman, R. (2009). "Multilingualism." In M. Baker and G. Saldanha (eds.), *Routledge Encyclopedia of Translation Studies* (2nd ed.), pp. 182–85. London/New York: Routledge.
Pertilli, S. (1992). "Translation, Semiotics and Ideology," *TTR: traduction, terminologie, redaction*, Vol. 5 (1), pp. 233–264.
Saussure, F. de. (1916/1983). *Cours de linguistique générale*. Paris: Editions Payot. Translated (1983) by R. Harris as Course in General Linguistics. London: Duckworth.

Further reading on stylistics

Abrams, M. (1988/1993). *A Glossary of Literary Terms*. London: Harcourt Brace Jovanovich College Publishers.
Boase-Beier, J. (2006). *Stylistic Approaches to Translation*. St. Jerome Publishing. Manchester, UK.
Bragina, J. (2012). *A Cognitive Stylistic Analysis of J.R.R. Tolkien's Fantasy World of Middle-Earth*. Unpublished PhD dissertation: University of Glasgow.
Ghazala, H. (2011). *Cognitive Stylistics and the Translator*. London: Sayyab Books Ltd.
Harris, R. (2000, July). *Will Stylistics Ever Grow Up?* Paper delivered at the XX International Poetics and Linguistics Association Conference at Goldsmiths College, London.
Leech, G., & Short, M. (1981). *Style in Fiction: A Linguistic Introduction to English Fictional Prose*. London: Longman.
Toolan, M. (1998). *Language in Literature*. London: Hodder.
Zyngier, S. (2001). "Towards a Cultural Approach to Stylistics." *CAUCE, Revista de Filología ysu Didáctica*, Vol. 24, pp. 365–380.

Companion website and online resources

http://cw.routledge.com/textbooks/translationstudies/
www.est-translationstudies.org/

Assignment 1: *Instructors*: Select an English or Arabic text (depending on your students' translation directionality whether they translate out of Arabic or into Arabic) from BBC (no more than 500 words). Then ask them to translate the text to be published in one of the local newspapers by paying special attention to pragmatic, semiotic and stylistic issues.

Assignment 2: *Students*: Select an English text (no more than 500 words) and translate it to be published in one of the local newspapers in your country. Before embarking on the actual act of translating the text, adopt the most appropriate global strategy. In no more than 300 words:

(i) tell us in your introduction why you have opted for this particular global strategy.
(ii) annotate any pragmatic, semiotic and stylistic issues that you have faced while translating the text.

Assignment 3: *Students*: In no more than 150 words, comment on the translation offered by an MA student, giving full consideration to pragmatic, semiotic and stylistic dimensions. The ST extracted from a book entitled في نيبال: بلاد الجبال (1989) by a famous Saudi traveller whose name is Muḥammed bin Nāṣir al-ʿbūdī (Al-Hakmani 2013: 11–15).

Pragmatic, semiotic, stylistic aspects 187

ST:

نهضت هذه الطائرة الصغيرة التي لم نكن نعلم أنها هي التي سنسافر عليها وإنما كنا نظن أنها من طراز بوينج ٧٣٧ لأن هذه رحلة خارجية وهي بعيدة نوعاً ما فأعلن مكبر الصوت فيها أن السفر سيدوم ساعتين وربعاً. وبدت أرض البنغال مليئة بالأنهار ومجاري المياه والمستنقعات التي تربى فيها السمك وحياض الأرز واستمر الأمر كذلك حوالي خمسين دقيقة.

وقد قدموا لنا عصيرَ الفاكهة ثم وجبة جيدة من الغداء أكثر وأسخى مما يقدم في الطائرات الهندية التي ركبت معها في عشراتِ الرحلات. فكان مؤلفاً من الأرز واللحم والسمك وطبق من خضارِ السلطة ثم صحناً من الحلوى والقهوة أو الشاي تماماً مثلما يقدم في الطائرات الكبيرة.

TT:

I did not know that this plane would be the one I would travel on. That is because I thought it would be a Boeing 737 plane, for the flight was international and somewhat long. It was announced through the megaphone that the flight would last for two and a quarter hours. The land of Bengal started to appear full of rivers, watercourses, swamps in which fish grow, and rice fields. That view lasted for almost 50 minutes.

They served us fruit juice, and then a good lunch that was more generous than what is served in the Indian planes on which I flew tens of times. Just as served in big planes, the lunch consisted of rice, meat, fish and a dish of salad. Then a plate of dessert along with tea or coffee was served.

Assignment 4: *Instructors*: Discuss with your students the strengths and weaknesses of the comments offered by one of the translation students with respect to translating taking into account Grice's (1975) maxims. In your discussion, you may touch on whether:

(i) there is an external coherence in the translator's comment. In other words, does s/he link his/her comment to others' studies?
(ii) there are other examples that need to be commented on.

ST:

After Mohammed's death in 632, the military and later the cultural and religious hegemony of Islam grew enormously. First Persia, Syria and Egypt, then Turkey, then North Africa fell to the Muslim armies; in the eighth and ninth centuries Spain, Sicily and parts of France were conquered.

TT:

فبعد وفاة محمد – صلى الله عليه وسلم- في عام ٦٣٢، ازدادت هيمنة الإسلام العسكرية، وازدادت في وقت لاحق هيمنته الثقافية والدينية زيادة هائلة. فقد فتحت جيوش المسلمين أولاً بلاد فارس، وسوريا، ومصر ثم تركيا ثم شمال إفريقيا، كما فتحت في القرنين الثامن والتاسع إسبانيا وجزيرة صقلية وأجزاء من فرنسا.

188 *Pragmatic, semiotic, stylistic aspects*

Comment:

(a) In the source text, the author is discussing the Islamic religious hegemony that grew after the death of Prophet Mohammed. He explains that Persia, Syria, Egypt, Turkey and North Africa fell to the Muslims. Using the word 'fell' implies that these regions were originally non-Muslim countries and were taken by Muslims to come under Islamic rule.

In the TT, the translator has added the phrase صلى الله عليه وسلم, which means *'peace be upon him'*, after the name of Prophet Mohammed. By adding this phrase, the translator has not complied with Grice's maxims of conversation. He breaches the maxim of quantity by delivering more than required (Grice 1975: 26). The expression صلى الله عليه وسلم is usually used by Muslims to follow the name of the Prophet as sign of great respect and honor. It reflects a religious affiliation to Islam and to Prophet Mohammed. The translator's breach of Grice's maxims might have been carried out to produce a domesticated translation that meets the expectations of the majority of the receptor.

(b) Another religious inclination in Enani's translation is marked by using the word فتحت, which means *'conquered'*, to stand for the word *'fell'*. His translation submits that Persia, Syria, Egypt, Turkey and North Africa were conquered by Muslims. The word فتحت tones down the meaning. In this instance, Enani has not observed Grice's maxims of conversation. He has violated the maxim of quality by delivering what lacks adequacy. Seemingly, Enani has used euphemism to generate a milder meaning. The translation gives eligibility to Muslims which is not evoked in the source text. Additionally, it gives Muslims legitimacy to control and govern others' lands. It seems that Enani's affiliation to Muslims and Islam has motivated him to change the implied meaning of the translation. Another reason for this violation of Grice's maxims might be to generate a domesticated translation that can be more engaging for the target reader. In light of this, it can be argued that Enani has been influenced by norms related to religion in this example.

Assignment 5: *Students*: translate the following text taken from 'Abdul-Raḥmān al-Rubai'ī's story ذلك الأنين *Dhālik al-Anīn* *'Groaning'* (for more details on the story, see Chapter 1 in this book):

ST:
وكنت ذاهلة طول الطريق. تركتك مع نفسك، مع ما رأي ومضيت في قيادة السيّارة. كانت السيّارة تخرج بنا من المدينة في طريق مبلط إلا أنه يمتد في فلاة خالية، وكان السراب يلوح فوق أسفلت الطريق على إمتداد بصرنا وكأنه بحيرة ماء تنادينا لأن نعوم فيها

Pragmatic, semiotic, stylistic aspects 189

وبعد أن إبتعدنا عن المدينة قرابة العشرة كيلومترات فوجئنا بأفواج هائلة من الغربان السوداء الناعقة ، غربان في كل مكان، في السماء، في الطريق ولا تغادر أماكنها إلا بعد أن تقترب السيارة منها حتى تكاد تهرسها بعجلاتها، تهب طائرة ونعيقها يزداد وهي تدور حول السيارة المنطلقة.
علقت على هذا المشهد بعد أن غاب صوتك عني:
- ماذا لوكنا نمشي بدون سيارة؟
- وتابعت تعليقك دون أن تنظري إليّ وكأنك تكلمين إنسانا آخر غيري.
لربما إفترستنا بمناقيرها ، كأننا في مشهد من ذلك الفلم الهتشكوكي الذي رأيته طفلة ولم تغب عن ذاكرتي أحداثه.

آلاف الغربان، تنعق، تطير، تحط، تتكوم فوق جثث حيوانات، جوار برك مياه، وعلى جانبي الطريق لايبدو أي أثر للحياة، لا نخلة، لابيت، لاسيارة، لاضريح ولي.

Assignment 6: *Students*: select an English text (no more than 500 words) and translate it to be published in one of the local newspapers in your country. Before embarking on the actual act of translating the text, adopt the most appropriate global strategy. In no more than 300 words:

(i) tell us in your introduction why you have opted for this particular global strategy.
(ii) annotate any pragmatic, semiotic and stylistic issues that you have faced while translating the text.

Assignment 7: *Students*: select a literary text (no more than 500 words) and translate it for publication. Before embarking on the actual act of translating the text, adopt the most appropriate global strategy. In no more than 300 words:

(i) tell us in your introduction why you have opted for this particular global strategy.
(ii) annotate any pragmatic, semiotic and stylistic issues that you have faced while translating the text.

The Routledge Course in Translation Annotation website at www.routledge.com/cw/almanna contains:

- A video summary of the chapter
- PowerPoint slides
- Further reading links
- Further assignments
- More research questions
- Further annotated texts

9 Annotating cultural and ideological issues

> **In this chapter...**
>
> The previous chapter has discussed how to annotate the different aspects of language, such as aspects of pragmatics, stylistics and semiotics. In this chapter, special attention will be paid to **cultural** and **ideological** issues. To this end, ample authentic data drawn from existing translations or translated for the purposes of this study will be used to drive home relevant theoretical constructs.
>
> **Key issues**
>
> - Culture
> - Culture-specific terms
> - Ideology
> - Insider
> - Outsider
> - Narrative

Culture

Over the past five decades, there has been a series of shifts from word to sentence, from sentence to text, from text to context, from language to culture and/or society, from prescriptive to descriptive approaches, from micro to macro approaches in describing the translation process and from colonially exclusive to postcolonially inclusive paradigms. More recently, however, over the last 20 years or so, the focus of translation studies has shifted from such issues as accuracy, acceptability, faithfulness, (un)translatability and so forth that beg close attention to language to border issues such as "treating translation as social, cultural and political acts taking place within and attached to global and local relations of power and dominance" (Faiq 2008: 33). Some scholars have stressed that as translation involves the process of reflecting cultures that are mirrored in languages, it needs to be approached as a cross-cultural transfer (Snell-Hornby 1988/1995; Bassnett 1991; Niranjana 1992; Carbonell 1996; Faiq 2004, 2007, 2008). In this act of cross-cultural communication, the two fundamental components of translation are culture and language. Because it brings the two together, translation is by necessity a multifaceted and multiproblematic process with different manifestations, realizations and ramifications (Faiq 2008: 35).

In his oft-cited book *A Textbook of Translation*, Newmark (1988: 94) defines culture as "the way of life and its manifestations that are peculiar to a community that uses a particular language as its means of expression". In a similar vein, Faiq (2008: 35) defines culture as "shared knowledge: what the members of a particular community ought to know to act and react in specific almost preformatted ways and interpret their experience, including contact with other cultures, in distinctive ways". Cast in less technical terms, culture involves all walks of life, such as people's way of talking, nodding, smiling, queuing, sitting, eating, drinking, greeting, inviting, asking, answering and the like and the totality of attitudes and assumptions towards events, peoples, other cultures and so on. In order for people in a given society to communicate properly, it is not enough that they rely on language alone (superficial level), but rather there should be an agreement (symbolic level) among them toward a particular belief, behaviour, custom, moral, habit, emotion and so on. It is this agreement at the symbolic level that makes people interpret, for instance, the act of smiling or staring differently. When translating between languages with little cultural affinity, such as Arabic and English, there will be gaps, thus creating ample space for negotiating. Cultural gaps have always "produced the most far-reaching misunderstandings among readers" (Nida and Reyburn 1981: 2). This requires translators to take utmost care of such cultural asymmetries between the interfacing languages. Such cultural asymmetries place extra efforts on translators, requiring them to figure out the symbolic level of the text in order to "capture the cultural implications meant by the source author". To this end, these cultural issues should be dealt with from the perspective of a cultural insider (Al-Masri 2004: 112). In an attempt to distinguish between an insider (emic) perspective and outsider (etic) perspective, Almanna and Farghal (2015: 152) comment that the outsider (or etic) perspective

> relies on the extrinsic concepts and categories that make sense to scientific observers – it has next to nothing to do with native speakers/society members' reactions towards an issue. Therefore, in order to be able to study the intrinsic phonological distinctions that are meaningful to native speakers of a given language, one needs to do phonemic analysis. The same holds true for studying the intrinsic cultural distinctions that make sense to the members of a given society, s/he needs to adopt an emic or insider perspective.

The Holy Qur'an is a great source of culture-specific expressions. Therefore, to understand the ST and its symbolic level, translators need to be insiders in the SL culture and the TL culture. To this end, they activate a bottom-up process (i.e., forming a mental image of the text by working on the linguistic elements by

192 *Cultural and ideological issues*

consulting their own knowledge of vocabulary, morphology, syntax and all aspects of language, such as textual, pragmatic, semiotic, stylistic etc.) and top-down process (i.e., working the other way round from the mental image conjured up in their own minds when they have activated the bottom-up process of reading in order to understand some linguistic elements that they have failed to comprehend by relying on the bottom-up process). By way of illustration, let us consider the following example from the Holy Qur'an (Luqman, 31, 17) translated by different translators:

ST:

وَلَا تُصَعِّرْ خَدَّكَ لِلنَّاسِ وَلَا تَمْشِ فِي الْأَرْضِ مَرَحًا ۖ إِنَّ اللَّهَ لَا يُحِبُّ كُلَّ مُخْتَالٍ فَخُورٍ

TT1:
And turn not thy cheek away from people in [false] pride, and walk not haughtily on earth: for, behold, God does not love anyone who, out of self-conceit, acts in a boastful manner. (Muhammad Asad 1980/2003)

TT2:
Turn not thy cheek in scorn toward folk, nor walk with pertness in the land. Lo! Allah loveth not each braggart boaster. (M. M. Pickthall 1930/2005)

TT3:
And do not turn your face away from people in contempt, nor go about in the land exulting overmuch; surely Allah does not love any self-conceited boaster. (M. H. Shakir 1995)

TT4:
And swell not thy cheek (for pride) at men, nor walk in insolence through the earth; for Allah loveth not any arrogant boaster. (Y. A. Ali 1934/2006)

TT5:
Do not sneer down your cheek at other men nor walk brashly around the earth: God does not love every swaggering boaster. (T. B. Irving 1930/2006)

Comment:

Here, the word that needs to be fully understood before any attempt to transfer it into the TL is تُصَعِّرْ. It is worth noting that there are many words in the Holy Qur'an that are hardly understood by even Arabs without trying their utmost to be insiders in their own culture. This is because of the difference between the modern standard Arabic used currently and the classical Arabic used at the time of revealing the Qur'an. Etymologically speaking, the verb صَعَّرَ is derived from the noun الصَّعَرُ, which refers to a disease that afflicts camels, thus causing their necks to twist. An attempt is made in the ST to liken the haughty to the camel in that shape by way of demoralizing people behaving in a haughty way (cf. Sadiq 2008: 53–54). Having probed the deep symbolic levels of the language/culture in the ST and captured the cultural implications, the translators have reflected the intended meaning in their translations.

Cultural and ideological issues 193

In an attempt to render the ST and its symbolic level, translators adopt different local strategies. Consider the following extract quoted from Mahfouz's novel أولاد حارتنا *Children of Gebelawi* (1959/1986: 214; 6th edition), along with its translation offered by Philip Stewart (1981: 190):

ST:

فبصق الرجل متأففاً وقال محنقاً:
أسياد الحارة! ما نحن إلا عبيد أذلاء يا عبده، ذهب جبل وعهده الحلو، وجاء زنفل أجحمه الله، فتوتنا وهو علينا لا لنا، يلتهم أرزاقنا ويفتك بمن يشكو.

TT:
The man spat angrily:
Lords of the Alley indeed! We are just miserable slaves, Abda; Gebel and his happy times have gone, and 'Snarler' has come, damn him, our strongman who is against us and not for us, who gobbles up our earnings and destroys anybody who complains.

Comment:

To reflect the communicative effect of the ST, the translator has offered a range of effective choices of idioms and expressions, such as *'Lords of the Alley indeed!'*, *'happy times'* and *'damn him'*. As far as the religious expression أجحمه الله is concerned, it is apparent that the translator has succeeded in being an insider in the source culture, understanding the cultural experience in the SL, and being an insider in the target culture, encoding the cultural experience in the TL. In other words, the translator has succeeded in intrinsically managing it by opting for the neutral imprecation *'damn him'*.

To shed more light on these cultural asymmetries between Arabic and English, let us consider the following example quoted from Choukri's (2000: 176–168; 6th edition) الخبز الحافي *For Bread Alone*, translated by Paul Bowles (1993: 126):

ST:

- ها أنا جئت. خير إن شاء الله.

TT:
"Here, I am".

Comment:

In the original text, the religious expression إن شاء الله is not meant to express hope or communicate commitment conditioned on God's permission. Rather, it is used here by the speaker to encourage the addressee to tell him/

194   *Cultural and ideological issues*

> her what is happening. Being aware of this, the translator has intrinsically managed the text by opting for deleting the whole formulaic expression to have it meet the TL reader's expectations, thus guaranteeing the acceptability and accessibility. However, had the translator taken into account the fact that such a formulaic expression contributes to the essential illocutionary force and implicature of the original utterances, he could have suggested expressions like *'Here, I am. What's up?'*, *'Here, I am. What's the matter?'* or, at least, *'Here, I am. Yes, please'*.

To demonstrate the translator's inability to cope with cultural asymmetries between Arabic and English, let us consider the following example quoted from Mahfouz's novel أولاد حارتنا *Children of Gebelawi* (1959/1986: 213), along with its translation offered by Philip Stewart (1981: 189):

ST:

فتوقف الرجل عن المسير وهو يقول في غيظ:
- استريحي، ربنا يتعب المتعب.

TT:
The man stopped and said gruffly:
Take a rest then, and damn those who caused your tiredness!

> **Comment:**
>
> Here, taking into account that the use of literal translation, *'May Allah tire those who tired you'*, would fail to capture the cultural implications meant by the original writer and instead would linger within the bounds of literalness, the translator has opted for the simple, agentless *'damn'* to lead and carry the imprecation, thus reflecting the ST expression functionally. To put this differently, the translator has succeeded in being an insider in the source culture, understanding the cultural experience in the SL, and being an insider in the target culture, encoding the cultural experience in the TL. Further, the translator has succeeded in reproducing in the TT the poetic form and effect of the Arabic idiom that occurs quite naturally ربنا يتعب المتعب.

To further demonstrate how relying on the TL denotational equivalent without doing any sort of explication might seriously affect the intentionality of the ST sign, let us consider the following three examples quoted from Mahfuz's (1961/1973) novel اللص والكلاب *The Thief and the Dogs*, translated by Adel Ata Elyas (1987):

ST:

وجاء صوت من ورائه يقول: سعيد مهران: ألف نهار أبيض (11)

TT:

Suddenly a voice came from behind, "Sa'eed Mahran: what a pleasant surprise. (89)

ST:

ليلة بيضاء بالصلاة على النبي (63)

TT:
By the prophet, it is a lovely surprise (35).

Comment:

In many cultures, the colour *'white'* is linked to light, purity, cleanliness, piety, peace and so on; it mostly has a positive connotation. However, it sometimes refers to cowardice and fear, as in expressions like *'to show the white feather'*, which means *'to be afraid or frightened'*. The original writer, in an attempt to invoke the intended readers and make them physically involved in the text, injects his text with expressions used by Egyptian people in their daily life, such as: ليلة بيضاء '*lit. a white night*' and خبر أبيض '*lit. white news*'. Taking into account the symbolism of colour terms and their differences from one language/culture into another, the translator, in rendering the colour *'white'* in these two examples, has succeeded in intrinsically managing the text to be in line with the TL linguistic and stylistic norms. A white night in English is different from ليلة بيضاء '*lit. white night*' in Arabic, as the former refers to a sleepless night, while the latter indicates something good happens. Further, relying on the TL denotational equivalent of the ST phrase خبر أبيض '*white news'*, without any sort of explication, would seriously affect the intentionality of the ST sign, thus creating a completely different sign and striking the TL reader as unusual.

Following is another example (Ibid.):

ST:

قلبه أبيض كقلبك وستجده إنشاء الله من الطيبين (p. 129)

TT:
His heart is as yours, and with God's help you will live to see him a good man (187).

Comment:

In this example, paying extra attention to the linguistic and stylistic norms of the TL, the translator has opted for deleting the colour term أبيض *'white'*. In Arabic, قلب أبيض *'white heart'* refers to a person who is kind, with a good and pure heart. Being aware that some colour terms may lose their colourness while being transferred from one language/culture into another, the translator has resorted to a functional equivalent in which special attention is paid

196 *Cultural and ideological issues*

> to the function of the SL expression, independently of the form and its image conjured up in the mind of the SL reader, thus guaranteeing acceptability, naturalness and readability. However, his rendering *'His heart is as yours'* gives rise to implicature, as he has not specified whether it is a positive or a negative way, thus leaving the reader to rely on the context and co-text.

To show how not being content with the denotational equivalent of the SL sign may lead to a different sign in the TT, thereby affecting the overall meaning of the text, let us consider the following example quoted from Choukri's (2000: 176–177; 6th edition) الخبز الحافي *For Bread Alone*, translated by Paul Bowles (1993: 131):

ST:

ـ الغزال! فين ماشي؟
ـ شغلك؟

TT:

"Where are you off to, handsome?"
"What do you care where I'm going?"

> **Comment:**
>
> In this example, the sign that functions iconically is the word الغزال 'lit. gazelle'. In Arabic, such a word, in addition to its denotative meaning, a type of animal, refers to a beautiful woman or girl (connotative meaning). So the relationship between the denotative meaning and connotative meaning is what Peirce called 'interpretant' that works as a sign. Being aware of the differences between the signifying systems of the interfacing languages/cultures on the one hand and taking into account that giving priority to the sign's iconic function would linger within the bounds of literalness on the other, the translator has opted for a functional equivalent, *'handsome'*, thus preserving partially the sign's functions, indexical and symbolic.

Before we come to close this section, let us consider the following example from Mahfouz's novel ثرثرة فوق النيل (1966) translated by Frances Liardet as *Adrift on the Nile* (quoted in Al-Saeghi 2014b: 22):

ST:

فقال خالد عزوز:
نحن نعاني نقصا في المحتويات لا في الأفراد.
وجاء بوليس النجدة!
كان يجب أن يجي أيضا بوليس الآداب.

TT:

"That's what we care about, the contents," said Khalid, "not the individuals!"
"And the rescue police came", continued AmmAbduh.
"The arts police should have come as well".

> **Comment:**
>
> In this example, the phrase بوليس الآداب refers to a type of police that fight various forms of vice. As can be seen, the translator has adopted a literal translation in rendering بوليس الآداب into *'The arts police'*. Here, it is quite clear that the translator has adhered to the superficial level of the text, thus failing to probe into its symbolic level and capture the cultural implications meant by the original writer. Had she been an insider in the SL culture to understand what the phrase بوليس الآداب exactly means, she could have suggested something like *'vice squad'*, which refers to a police division charged with enforcing laws dealing with various immoral acts, such as gambling, prostitution, narcotics and the like.

Ideology

The term 'ideology' was first coined by the French Philosopher Antoine Destutt de Tracy (1754–1836) about two centuries ago to simply refer to a theory of ideas conceived within a particular view of mind (cf. Van Dijk 2004). Tracy separated three aspects, 'ideology', 'general grammar' and 'logic'. While he used the term 'ideology' to refer to the first of his three aspects, namely: 'science of ideas', he used the other two aspects to refer to the means and reasons, respectively.

In general, the term 'ideology' refers to a set of opinions, assumptions or beliefs of a group of people or an individual. However, in a political context, it sometimes refers to a set of political beliefs, assumptions or ideas that characterize a particular culture. Within the scope of traditional Marxist definitions, for example ideology refers to the "form of cognitive distortion, a false or illusory representation of the real" (Gardiner 1992: 60). Emphasizing both the issue of patterning and contingent claims to truth, Steger and James (2010: ix–xxvii) hold that the term 'ideology' refers to patterned clusters of normatively imbued ideas and concepts, including particular representations of power relations. These conceptual maps help people negotiate the complexity of their political universe and carry claims to social truth.

In translation studies, the term 'ideology' has been employed by many scholars from different perspectives to study various issues. Munday (2007: 195–217) casts light on how ideology can be linked to manipulation and power relations. In touching on the local strategies that a translator may resort to, Kelly (1998: 57) demonstrates how these strategies adopted by translators may well "introduce ideological elements, in particular positive self and negative other representation, which reproduce and reinforce myths or stereotypes existing in the target culture regarding the source culture". In a similar vein, Hatim and Mason (1997: 143–163)

198   *Cultural and ideological issues*

hold that translators, being influenced whether consciously or subconsciously by their own ideologies, opt for the employment of some linguistic devices, such as 'transitivity', 'cohesive device', 'over-lexicalization', 'style-shifting' and so on to superimpose certain directionality on the text in order to have it meet their own accumulated value systems.

Some scholars (Lefevere 1992; Bassnett and Lefevere 1998; Hatim and Munday 2004; Xiao-jiang 2007, among others) stress that ideology influences every single aspect of translation and that the translation product is shaped whether consciously or subconsciously by ideologies. Ideologies manifest themselves in the way texts are consciously or unconsciously "brought into line with dominant world views and/or dominant literary structures (Hatim and Munday 2004: 100). Lefevere (1992: 12–18) states that the translator's own ideology and the dominant TL poetics are the apparent determiners of the translated work. Ideology therefore plays an important role in forming the final shape of translation; it influences every single stage of the selection of the ST and the author up to transferring, representing and consuming the foreign materials.

Following Lefevere (1998: 41), this study considers ideology as an approach through which 'readers' in general and 'translators' in particular approach texts. To cast some light on how ideology, as an essential element of cultural context, influences the process of transfer and how ideology, which resides in texts is rendered into culturally different environments, let us consider the following extract taken from a joint press conference held at the presidential palace in Cairo on July 20, 2013, between EU foreign policy chief Catherine Ashton and Egyptian Vice President Mohammed El-Baradei:

ST:
I met with many people including general El-Sisi, President Mansour . . . with you Vice President, foreign affairs minister, with representatives from Nour Party . . . from Tamarod Group and others. Particularly I met with representatives from Freedom and Justice Party [and] Mohammed Morsi last evening.

TT1:
اني تقابلت وتشاورت مع عدد من الفصائل بما في ذلك اللواء السيسي ونائب الرئيس بجانب وزير الخارجية أيضا إلى جانب حزب النور وحركة تمرد إلى جانب أحزاب سياسية أخرى. وعلى وجه التحديد لقد حظيت بمقابلة مع حزب الحرية والعدالة ومع الرئيس السابق محمد مرسي.

> **Comment:**
> Here, EU foreign policy chief Catherine Ashton has repeatedly referred to the ousted President Mohammed Morsi by name only, without any title. Such a conscious refusal to go for other available options, such as *'ousted president'*, *'deposed president'*, *'former president'* *'toppled president'* or *'ex-president'*, clearly reflects her own attitude or at least the attitude of the body that she is affiliated with, thus sending an implicit message to all conflicting parties that there seems to be a strong will on all parties to find a peaceful way forward, though they had very different views and starting

points. However, the interpreter has referred to him as the deposed President (and later, in another example, Dr. Morsi). Taking into account that first she was interpreting Ashton's speech consecutively, that is, she did not have enough time to ponder the message and, consequently, extrinsically manage the original text to have it meet her own beliefs, assumptions and accumulated value system, and second, the conference was held in Cairo a few days after Morsi had been ousted, one can readily conclude that her decision was habitus oriented. In a similar vein, the interpreter has extrinsically managed the text when interpreting the verb *'meet'* in *'I met with representatives from Freedom and Justice Party [and] Mohammed Morsi last evening'* as حظيت بـ in لقد حظيت بمقابلة مع حزب الحرية والعدالة ومع الرئيس السابق محمد مرسي 'lit. *I had the honour to meet representatives from Freedom and Justice and the former President Mohammed Morsi*', thus subconsciously superimposing certain directionality on the text to approximate it to her unswerving loyalty to her country, represented in this context by representatives from Freedom and Justice Party and the ousted President Mohammed Morsi.

Now let us compare the interpreter's version with the subtitling offered by Al-Nile Chanel on July 30, 2013:

TT2

تعلمون أنني قابلت شخصيات كثيرة بينها الجنرال السيسي، الرئيس منصور، معك نائب الرئيس، ووزير الخارجية ومع ممثلين من حزب النور وحركة تمرد وآخرين. تحديدا قابلت ممثلين من حزب الحرية والعدالة، وتقابلت مع محمد مرسي مساء أمس.

Comment:

Here, the subtitler has reflected the original text accurately and faithfully when referring to Mohammed Morsi by name only. The subtitler's local strategy might be motivated by his/her being a member of a specific body that has its own political attitude and has its own criteria and descriptions that form established systems with specific norms and conventions for selecting, representing, producing and consuming the foreign materials; it is a habitus-motivated decision. Or one may argue that s/he might be motivated by his/her own political attitude toward the ousted President Morsi, which so happens to be in line with Aston's, so it is an ideologically motivated decision.

To demonstrate how the political commitment and attitude a particular body adopts influence selecting, representing and consuming the translated materials, let us have a look at two BBC news items on the same topic (one in English and the other in Arabic):

ST:
EU foreign policy chief Catherine Ashton says Egypt's ousted President Mohammed Morsi is "well", but that she does not know where he is being held.

TT:

قالت مسؤولة السياسة الخارجية بالاتحاد الأوروبي كاثرين اشتون إن الرئيس المصري المعزول محمد مرسي يتمتع بـ "صحة جيدة" ولكنها لا تعرف المكان المحتجز به.

> **Comment:**
>
> As can be seen, the translators and/or editors of both versions have extrinsically managed the texts by inserting *'ousted President'* and الرئيس المعزول, thereby reflecting a neutral attitude toward such a sensitive political issue.

To observe how changing lexical items can twist the message to varying degrees, let us consider the following BBC news item extracted from a text sent to a number of translation students:

ST:

He [Jihad] had just had a call from a friend to tell him the Israeli military had bombed his house and that his 11-month-old baby boy Omar was dead.

TT 1:

استلم اتصالا هاتفيا من صديق له يخبره بأن الجيش الإسرائيلي قد فجر منزله وإن طفله البالغ من العمر أحد عشر شهراً قد مات.

TT 2:

لقد تلقى جهاد أتصالا من أحد أصدقائه يفيد بأن ألقوات ألاسرائيلية قصفت منزله و أن ابنه ذي ال 11. شهراً قد قتل

TT 3:

لقد تلقى للتو اتصالا من صديق أخبره بأن الجيش الإسرائيلي قد فجر منزله و إن ابنه عمر البالغ من العمر احد عشر شهراً قد مات.

TT 4:

حينها تلقى جهاد اتصالاً هاتفياً من احد أصدقائه اخبره انا القوات الاسرائيليه قد دمرت بيته وان طفله عمر ذو الحادية عشر شهراً قد استشهد.

TT 5:

إن ما دفع جهاد للتصرف بهذا الشكل هو تلقيه لاتصال من صديق له يخبره بأن الجيش الإسرائيلي قد قام بتفجير منزله مما تسبب باستشهاد ابنه الذي يبلغ عمره احد عشر شهراً.

TT 6:

إذ تلقى جهاد للتو مكالمة من صديق يخبره إن الجيش الإسرائيلي قصف بيته وإنَّ طفلهُ ـ عُمَر ـ ذو الإحدى عشر شهراً قد لقيَّ حتفهُ!

TT 7:

إن ما جعل جهاد يتصرف بهذه الطريقة هو تلقيه لاتصال من صديق له يبلغه بتفجير بيته من قبل القوات الإسرائيلية مما تسبب باستشهاد ابنه عمر ذو الإحدى عشر شهراً.

Cultural and ideological issues 201

> **Comment:**
>
> As can be observed, three students (TT4), (TT5) and (TT7) have extrinsically managed the text to approximate it or have it meet their own political attitudes, religious and cultural commitment and accumulated value systems – they have changed the neutral lexical item *'dead'* into politically and religiously loaded lexical items, استشهد *'be martyred'* in (TT 4), استشهاد *'martyrdom'* in (TT5) and (TT7). Here, it is clearly evident that they have been motivated by their own ideology, since they are not affiliated with any specific body that might impose on them certain editorial translation guidelines.

To show how changing the participant's degree of commitment to the truth of propositions toward the knowledge constructed in events may well promote a different narrative, let us consider the following example (Farghal 2008: 11):

ST:
The Head of the International Investigation Commission in the assassination of the Lebanese former Prime Minister Rafiq Al-Hariri said that some Syrian officials may have been involved in this crime.

TT:
قال رئيس لجنة التحقيق الدولية في اغتيال رئيس الوزراء اللبناني السابق رفيق الحريري إن بعض المسئولين السوريين متورطون في هذه الجريمة.

> **Comment:**
>
> As can be observed, in the original text, the modal verb *'may'* is used epistemically, indicating a mere possibility. However, such a mere possibility becomes an absolute certainty in the Arabic text. To reflect the same degree of commitment to the truth made by the participant toward the knowledge constructed in such a political event, one can resort to modalized particles, such as قد, ربما or a modalized verb, such as يحتمل and the like (for more details on modality, see Chapter 4 in this book).

To observe how removing the doer of the action can twist the message to varying degrees, let us have a look at two BBC news items on the same topic (one in Arabic and the other in English; 30 November 2014):

ST:
كشف تحقيق أجرته الحكومة العراقية في شأن الفساد بالجيش أن هناك 50 ألف "جندي شبح" في قائمة الرواتب التي تدفعها الحكومة العراقية لقواتها.

202 *Cultural and ideological issues*

TT:
An investigation into corruption in the Iraqi army has revealed that there were 50,000 false names on its payroll.

> **Comment:**
>
> As can be seen, the doer of the action, *'the Iraqi government'*, is removed in the English version either to express least solidarity with the Iraqi government, to minimize the overt solidarity found in the original Arabic text or to promote a different narrative. Removing any element or participant in a given narrative, then, provides the reader with a different interpretive frame that would guide their interpretations and responses to the narrative at hand.

Now, let us compare the two BBC news items discussed earlier with two versions offered by Aljazeera Net (on November 31, 2014) and *Azzaman Newspaper* (on December 1, 2014) on the same event:

ST1:
في أول اعتراف رسمي عراقي بحجم الفساد في المؤسسة العسكرية، أعلن رئيس الوزراء حيدر العبادي الكشف عن وجود 50 ألف اسم وهمي في سجلات الرواتب بوزارة الدفاع. وكشف خلال استضافته الأحد في مجلس النواب عن "وجود 50 ألف اسم وهمي في أربع فرق عسكرية"، في إطار إصلاح المؤسسة العسكرية، بحسب بيان رسمي.

ST2:
كشف رئيس وزراء العراق حيدر العبادي عن وجود خمسين الف جندي وهمي في اربع فرق عسكرية، في خطوة جديدة في اطار مكافحة الفساد التي يجريها في المؤسسة العسكرية منذ توليه المنصب.

> **Comment:**
>
> Here, in an attempt to create solidarity with the newly nominated Iraqi prime minister, Haidar al-Abadi, on the one hand and create distance and hostility toward the ex-prime minister, Nori al-Maliki, the two versions opt for explicitly naming the person, Haidar al-Abadi, thus providing the reader with "an interpretive frame that guides and constrains [their] response to the narrative in question" (Baker 2006: 122). Such a strategy is supported by phrases like في أول اعتراف رسمي 'lit. *in the first official admission*' and في خطوة جديدة 'lit. *in a new step*'. Accordingly, one would not hesitate to conclude that in a politically sensitive discourse, it could make a big difference whether the actor of the process of doing, كشف *'reveal'* is removed, explicitly framed or implicitly framed.

Cultural and ideological issues 203

Finally, let us consider the following example in which a politically loaded phrase is used (Samhat 2014: 38–39):

ST:

The 2006 Lebanon Campaign opened when Hezbollah ambushed an Israeli Defense Force (IDF) patrol and captured two Israeli soldiers on July 12. The Israeli Air Force (IAF) quickly retaliated against 30 targets in Lebanon. Before dawn on July 13, the IAF executed Operation SPECIFIC GRAVITY, destroying more than 50 of Hezbollah's long-range rocket launchers in a pre-planned, 34-minute strike.

TT:

بدأت حرب لبنان 2006 عندما قام حزب الله بنصب كمين لدورية تابعة للقوات الإسرائيلية وأسر جنديين إسرائيليين في 12 تموز/يوليو، الأمر الذي دفع القوات الجوية الإسرائيلية إلى الردّ السريع على هذه العملية؛ إذ قامت باستهداف ثلاثين هدفاً في لبنان. وقبل بزوغ فجر نهار 13 تموز/يوليو، نفذت القوات الجوية الإسرائيلية عملية الثقل النوعي (Specific Gravity)، ودمرت أكثر من 50 قاذفة صواريخ بعيدة المدى تابعة لحزب الله في ضربة مخطط لها مسبقا استمرت 34 دقيقة.

Annotation:

Here is an example of 'counter-naming', to use Baker's (2006: 123) term, in which the phrase *'Israeli Defense Force'*, which is a politically loaded phrase, has been translated into القوات الإسرائيلية *'Israeli Forces'*. Counter-naming is the person's "responses to the systemic use of euphemisms in the political sphere" (123). In politically sensitive discourse, it is believed that it is not enough for translators to reflect the content of the message, take into account the purpose of translation and demands of text type and generic convention and live up to the TL readers' expectations. However, they need to pay extra attention to what has been legitimate in the Arab institutional context as long as they translate into Arabic and try to secure social acceptance, thus avoiding a foreign hegemony that contradicts theirs.

Approached from the narrative theory, although phrases like *'Israeli Defense Force', 'Israeli Force', 'Zionist War Force'* and so on refer to the same signified in the real world, they promote different narratives. For example, *'Israeli Defense Force'* is embedded in a Zionist narrative, while other alternatives signal a pro-Palestine narrative (for more details, see Baker 2006). Thus, translating such politically sensitive issues for Arabs in hopes of securing social acceptance, translators tend to avoid as much as possible describing, for instance, *'Israeli Defense Force'* as قوات الدفاع الإسرائيلي, but rather they tend to render it into قوات الاحتلال الصهيوني, قوات الجيش الصهيوني or قوات الجيش الإسرائلي, thereby reflecting the prevalent political order in the Arab world, which commonly believes that Israel is the attacker not a defender. This is exactly what Bennett and Edelman (1985: 160) try to say: "The awareness that every acceptance of a narrative involves a rejection of others makes the issue politically and personally vital".

Further reading on culture

Al-Masri, H. (2004). *Semantics and Cultural Losses in the Translation of Literary Texts.* Unpublished PhD thesis: Purdue University.
Anderson, M. (2003). "Ethnography as Translation." In S. Petrilli (ed.), *Translation Translation: Approaches to Translation Studies*, Vol. 21, pp. 389–396. Amsterdam: Rodopi.
Carbonell, O. (1996). "The Exotic Space of Cultural Translation." In R. Álvarez & M. Vidal (eds.), *Translation, Power, Subversion*, pp. 79–98. Clevedon: Multilingual Matters.
Faiq, S. (2004). "The Discourse of Intercultural Translation," *Intercultural Communication Studies* XIII: 3, pp. 35–46.
———. (2007). *Trans-Lated: Translation and Cultural Manipulation.* New York: Roman & Littlefield Publishing Group.
———. (2008). "The Master Discourse of Translation From Arabic." *STJ: Sayyab Translation Journal*, Vol. 1, pp. 27–36.
Farghal, M. (2004). "Literary Translation: A Schema-theoretic Model," *Al-Arabiyya*, Vol. 37, pp. 21–35.
Katan, D. (1999). *Translating Cultures: An Introduction for Translators, Interpreters and Mediators.* Manchester: St. Jerome Publishing.
Newmark, P. (1988). *A Textbook of Translation.* New York/London/Toronto/Sydney/Tokyo: Prentice Hall.
Pike, K. L. (1990). "On the Emics and Etics of Pike and Harris." In T. N. Headland, K. L. Pike, &and M. Harris (eds.), *Emics and Etics: The Insider/Outsider Debate.* Frontiers of Anthropology 7, pp. 28–47. Newbury Park: Sage.
Snell-Hornby, M. (1988/1995). *Translation Studies: An Integrated Approach.* Amsterdam/Philadelphia: John Benjamins.

Further reading on ideology

Álvarez, R., & Vidal, M. C. (1996). "Translating: A political Act." In R. Álvarez & M. C. Vidal (eds.), *Translation, Power, Subversion*, pp. 1–9. Philadelphia: Multilingual Matters.
Baker, M. (2006). *Translation and Conflict: A Narrative Account.* London/New York: Routledge.
Bennett, W. L., & Edelman, M. (1985). "Toward a New Political Narrative," *Journal of Communication*, Vol. 35 (4), pp. 156–171.
Kelly, D. (1998). "Ideological Implications of Translation Decision: Positive-Self and Negative-Other Presentation," *Quaderns, Revista de traduccio*, Vol. 1, pp. 57–63.
Mannheim, K. (1936). *Ideology and Utopia.* New York: Harcourt, Brace & World, Inc.
Mason, I. (1994). "Discourse, Ideology and Translation." In R. A. Beaugrande de, Shunnaq & M. H. Heliel (eds.), *Language, Discourse and Translation in the West and Middle East*, pp. 23–34. Amsterdam: John Benjamins.
Munday, J. (2007). "Translation and Ideology: A Textual Approach," *The Translator*, Vol. 13 (2), pp. 195–217.
Steger, M. B., & James, P. (2010). "Ideologies of Globalism." In P. James & M. B. Steger (eds.), *Globalization and Culture, Vol. 4: Ideologies of Globalism*, pp. ix–xxxi. London: Sage Publications Ltd.
Van Dijk, T. A. (1996). "Discourse, Opinions and Ideologies." In C. Schäffner & H. Kelly-Holmes (eds.), *Discourse and Ideologies*, pp. 7–37. Philadelphia: Multilingual Matters.

Companion website and online resources

http://cw.routledge.com/textbooks/translationstudies/
www.est-translationstudies.org/

Assignment 1: *Instructors*: select an ideology-loaded text (no more than 300 words). Then ask your students to translate the text to be published in one of the local newspapers by paying special attention to ideological issues.

Assignment 2: *Students*: select an Arabic text (no more than 500 words) and translate it to be published in one of the local newspapers in your country. Before embarking on the actual act of translating the text, adopt the most appropriate global strategy. In no more than 300 words:

(i) tell us in your introduction why you have opted for this particular global strategy.
(ii) annotate any cultural or ideological issues that you have encountered while translating the text.

Assignment 3: *Instructors*: discuss with your students the strengths and weaknesses of the annotations offered by an MA student with respect to translating ideological issues. In your discussion, you may touch on:

(i) Is there an external coherence in the translator's annotation? In other words, does s/he link his/her annotation to others' studies?
(ii) Are there other examples of ideological issues that need to be annotated?

ST:
Other early targets included Hezbollah observation posts along the border, Hezbollah compounds in the Dahyia section of Beirut, and roads and bridges that Israel believed might be used to exfiltrate the abducted soldiers. Over the course of the campaign, the IAF flew roughly 5,000 strike missions, primarily directed at the Dahyia, the Beqaa Valley near the Syrian border, and the region south of the Litani River.

TT:
ومن بين الأهداف المبكرة الأخرى مراكز مراقبة تابعة لحزب الله على طول الحدود، ومجمعات حزب الله في الضاحية في بيروت، إضافةً إلى طرقات وجسور اعتقدت اسرائيل أنه سيتم استخدامها لنقل الجنديين المخطوفين. على مدار الحرب، نفذت القوات الجوية الإسرائيلية 5000 ضربة جوية تقريباً تركزت بشكل أساسي على الضاحية، ووادي البقاع قرب الحدود السورية، والمنطقة الواقعة جنوب نهر الليطاني.

Annotation:

Although in Lebanon it is not believed to have borders with Israel, but with occupied Palestine, as a means to avoid recognizing Israel, I chose to translate it as "الحدود الإسرائيلية" first to highlight who the other part of the war is, which is Israel and not Palestine, and second to preserve the viewpoint of the authors and not interfere in the ideology of the text as much as possible.

206 *Cultural and ideological issues*

Assignment 4: *Instructors*: discuss with your students the strengths and weaknesses of the comments provided by an MA student with respect to translating cultural issues (highlighted for you). In your discussion, you may touch on:

(i) Is there an external coherence in the translator's comments? In other words, does s/he link his/her comments to others' studies?
(ii) Are there other examples of cultural issues that need to be commented on?

ST:

- أأنت جاد يا عم عبده؟
- أووه..
- ألم تعلم بأن سمارة نبية جديدة؟
- **أستغفر الله العظيم.**

TT:
"Are you a serious man, AmmAbduh?" he asked, still teasing.
"Ah!"
"Do you not know that Samara is a new Prophet?"
"Almighty God forgive you!"

Comment:

The phrase أستغفر الله العظيم is used when somebody says something religiously unacceptable or when gets annoyed by hearing or seeing something (Almaany Dictionary, http://www.almaany.com). Here, the translator has succeeded to be an insider in both SL culture and TL culture by opting for *'Almighty God forgive you!'*.

Assignment 5: *Instructors*: discuss with your students the strengths and weaknesses of the comments provided by an MA student with respect to translating cultural issues (highlighted for you). In your discussion, you may touch on:

(i) Is there an external coherence in the translator's comments? In other words, does s/he link his/her comments to others' studies?
(ii) Are there other examples of cultural issues that need to be commented on?

أنت الليلة عصبي على غير عادتك..
المعسل زفت!
لكنه كثيرا ما يكون كذلك.

TT:
"You're unusually touchy tonight!" Ahmad observed of him.
"This filthy tobacco."
"But it is often like that".

Cultural and ideological issues 207

Comment:

The word معسل in this context means a special type of tobacco, and the denotative meaning of زفت is *'asphalt'* (Almaany Dictionary, http://www.almaany). However, in this context زفت means the tobacco is bad. Normally, زفت is used in our daily life to describe something bad. Here, the translator has succeeded to be an insider in both cultures when opting for *'this filthy tobacco'*.

Assignment 6: *Instructors*: discuss with your students the strengths and weaknesses of the comments provided by an MA student with respect to translating cultural issues (highlighted for you). In your discussion, you may touch on:

(i) Is there an external coherence in the translator's comments? In other words, does s/he link his/her comments to others' studies?
(ii) Are there other examples of cultural issues that need to be commented on?

ST:

ضبطته يغازل جارة جديدة!
يا خبر أحمر ..
ولعلع صوتي حتى سمعه سابع جار!

TT:

She puffed voraciously and said, to satisfy the curiosity around her: "I caught him flirting with the new neighbor!"
"Salacious news!"
"And I should think they heard me on the seventh floor!"

Comment:

(a) In this example, the colour أحمر *'red'* usually refers to love. The first expression يا خبر أحمر is used figuratively. Here, the translator has succeeded in being an insider in both source culture and target culture. The colloquial Egyptian expression يا خبر أحمر has a completely different connotative meaning from its denotative meaning. In this context, the colour أحمر is used to describe a surprise or a shameful issue. Also, the speaker can say يا خبر without using any colour term to express his/her reaction towards the bad news. Being an insider in both cultures, the translator has transferred the exact meaning in the target culture *'Salacious news!'*

208 *Cultural and ideological issues*

(b) The original writer uses the expression سابع جار 'lit. *the seventh neighbour'* to indicate the reaction of the lady whose louder voice was heard in a long distance. The Islamic religion cares a lot about neighbors; it recommends everyone be kind with his/her neighbors and not bother them in any way. The Prophet Muhammad (peace be upon him) said: "Whoever believes in God and the Last Day should be generous to his neighbor" (Al-Muwatta n.y., Volume 49, Hadith 22).

Assignment 7: *Instructors*: discuss with your students the strengths and weaknesses of the annotation offered by one of my BA students with respect to translating ideological issues (highlighted for you). In your discussion, you may touch on:

(i) Is there an external coherence in the translator's annotation? In other words, does s/he link his/her annotation to others' studies?
(ii) Are there other examples of ideological issues that need to be commented on?

ST:
Women are encouraged in Islam to contribute their opinions and ideas. There are many traditions of the Prophet which indicate that women would pose questions directly to him and offer their opinions concerning religion, economics and social matters.

TT:
فالإسلام يدعم المرأة دائمًا ويشجّعها على الإسهام في آرائها وأفكارها. وهناك العديد من الأدلة المأخوذة من الأحاديث النبوية التي تشير إلى أن المرأة تمتلك حرية إبداء الرأي في شتّى المسائل الدينية والاجتماعية وحتى الاقتصادية.

Annotation:

As can be observed, I have managed the text to meet my own religious commitment. Here, in the target text, I have added some words, like يدعم,أدلة and مأخوذة, and deleted *'to him'*. Further, I have reordered the last part of the text and added حتى. These are examples of modulation. Modulation refers to "a variation of the form of the message obtained by changing point of view" (Vinay and Darbelnet 1958, cited in Almanna 2014: 77). According to Vinay and Darbelnet 1958 (cited in Ibid.), modulation can be 'optional' or 'obligation'.

The Routledge Course in Translation Annotation website at www. routledge.com/cw/almanna contains:

- A video summary of the chapter
- PowerPoint slides
- Further reading links
- Further assignments
- More research questions
- Further annotated texts

10 Annotation into action

In this chapter . . .

A short text (407 words) will be translated from Arabic into English. Prior to translating the text and annotating it from different perspectives, an introduction in which the ST is analyzed in terms of the field of discourse, main linguistic and stylistic features, register, language function, text type, genre and so on will be presented. Further, in order to adopt the appropriate global strategy, issues such as the reasons behind translating this particular text, translation purpose and readership will be given full consideration.

Key issues

- Genre
- Global strategies
- Language function
- Readership
- Register
- Skopos
- Text typology
- Translation brief

Title: Translating and annotating Muḥammed Khuḏayyir's story حكايات يوسف *'Joseph's Tales'*.

Introduction

The source text (ST) is part of a short story written by Muḥammed Khuḏayyir. He is a prominent Iraqi storyteller, novelist, critic and writer. He was born in 1942 in the Iraqi city of Basra, where he still lives, and has worked as a teacher for many years. Khuḏayyir is the author of several collections of short stories and a well-known novel, بصرياثا *Basriyatha*, published in 1996. He was awarded the prestigious Oweiss prize in 2004.

The story حكايات يوسف '*Joseph's Tales*' selected here was published in 1995 in a collection of short stories under the title رؤيا خريف '*Autumnal Vision*' and then republished by Sayyab Books (2011). The text is taken from the beginning of the story. It tells of a giant publishing-and-writing building that was constructed in the narrator's city after the war. A wide plot of land on the riverbank, two kilometers in area, was chosen to be the site of a printing house, rising 12 storeys, so high that anyone approaching could see it glinting in the sun before its dazzling rays reached the lofty marble walls of the city towers. Work on this real-imagined printing house has carried on, day and night, for years. In the story, the city authorities gathered together from the neighboring cities blacksmiths, smelters, builders, carpenters and engineers, which enhanced their importance among the people. They also placed printers, copyists and writers in high positions, assigning to them the highest printing house in the city, and put in charge a skilled man, known to the locals as 'Joseph the Printer'. It is a scene-based story, taking its theme and details from realistic situations in an ironic way with a view to engaging the reader and also the authorities that have neglected the city after the war. It is an implicit invitation to the authorities to look after their people: blacksmiths, smelters, builders, carpenters, engineers, printers, copyists, writers and so on – they have to put the right person in the right place.

Rationale

I have chosen this text for three reasons: (1) it presents translation challenges that require full consideration of relevant translation theory and methodology, (2) I know the author personally, and that will help a lot in terms of taking permission from him to translate his text into English and the possibility of discussing any ambiguous issues that need clarification and (3) the text describes a city in which I have spent most of my life; therefore, there will be a certain degree of familiarly with concepts, objects, entities and events that may be used in the story.

Language role and register

The story is characterized by its formal lexical items (such as رقعة, طبقات, ساطع, حام, أقفل, فطن, هاجس, نشوى, ناور, اغذ, مشرق, خصّ, احتفى, تبدد, رنين, سفور, بهيج, شاهق, و هاج, مرآب, انسكب, لدائن, رحابة, مغمورا, ذاب, فاض, برق, ترجرج, بريق, عكف, دلف etc.) and complex sentences, as in:

حامت عيناي على سطح الجدارية الواسعة المرسومة فوق عقد البوابة بألوان طباشيرية راسخة، والتقطت وأنا أدلف في موعدي اليومي الثابت جزئية صغيرة من اللوحة لنساخ عربي يعكف على مخطوط مفتوح بين يديه.

كنت قد رفعت عيني إلى الجدارية لأتأكد من بريق الحبر في دواة الناسخ وترجرجه بضوء الشمس في مثل هذه الثانية من كل صباح، كما تبرق جزئيات آخر من اللوحة بريقاً خاصاً بفيض الاشعة في أوقات معلومة من النهار.

212 *Annotation into action*

Such syntactic structures and lexical items require the reader of the original Arabic to ponder the lexical items, structuring and punctuation in order to grasp the exact meaning intended by the writer. As such, the tenor of the story is formal. The formality of a given text can be measured by the amount of the attention that text producers (be they writers or speakers) give to their lexical items (formal lexis vs. informal lexis), syntactic structures (complex sentences vs. simple sentences), punctuation and the like. This accords well with Bell's (1991: 186) view: "Greater attention leads to more care in writing and this marks the text as possessing a higher degree of formality and signals a more distant relationship between sender and receiver(s)".

Further, the original text is characterized by a number of marked collocations (such as ينسكب عليها الضوء) and unmarked collocations (such as رفعت شأنهم). Therefore, extra attention is paid to markedness, as opposed to unmarkedness, while translating. As such, paying special attention to the unmarked collocation in the ST, رفعت شأنهم, one may well suggest something like *'raised their profile'*, *'enhance their importance'* or *'increased their importance'*. In an attempt to reflect the marked collocation ينسكب عليها الأضواء, one may suggest a rendering like *'light . . . is streaming down on them'*. The language function is a combination of referential and expressive, focusing on the message and its implicit references.

Text type and genre

It is a literary text, as it shares certain characteristics, such as the frequency of occurrence of particular lexical items or syntactic structures, with other literary texts. These linguistic features are of crucial importance to the language user to identify the text type. Therefore, "any attempt to explain how texts are created and used must include an answer to the question 'How is it, given that each text is unique, that some texts are treated as the same?'" (Bell 1991: 202). Despite that, there is a substantial difficulty in working with such a text typology, in particular when we come to the act of defining a particular text type. For instance, what is meant by a literary text? In this regard, Bell (Ibid.: 203) is of a view that in defining a text type according to such a text typology, there will be some degree of overlapping that "suggests that content, *per se*, is inadequate as discriminator" (Ibid.). Such a classification may "work with some highly ritualized genres (some types of poetry, for example) but not in the case of the majority of texts where again, and now at the formal level, there is overlap" (Ibid.).

Let us build on the premise that even though texts are essentially characterized by their hybrid nature, one particular function tends to predominate over the others. Approached from such a perspective, one may suggest that the original text is expository, sharing particular features with descriptive texts, focusing on objects spatially viewed and narrative texts focusing on events temporally viewed (cf. Hatim 2001: 197). As stated in Chapter 2, Hatim and Mason (1990, 1997) proposed a model of text typologies in translation. In their model, texts are divided into three main types: exposition (be they descriptive, narrative or conceptual), argumentation (be they counter-argumentative or through-argumentative) and instruction (be they with options or without). With respect to expository texts, in which writers tend to present concepts, states, events, entities, relations and so on in a nonevaluative manner, they are subdivided into:

(i) descriptive texts in which the text producers focus on objects, which are spatially viewed;
(ii) narrative texts in which text producers shift their focus of attention to events which are temporally viewed; and
(iii) conceptual texts in which text producers concentrate on the detached analysis of concepts, thereby introducing a number of text forms (for more details, see Hatim and Mason 1990, 1997; Hatim 1997b, 2001).

As can be observed, the original writer presents his objects, events and entities in a nonevaluative manner, focusing on describing objects spatially (descriptive) and narrating events temporally (narrative). Consider the first lines of the story as an example:

عندما اعدنا بناء المدينة، بعد الحرب [**narrative**]، اخترنا رقعة واسعة على ضفة النهر [**descriptive**]، مساحتها كيلومتران [**descriptive**]، واقمنا عليها داراً للطباعة [**descriptive**]، ورفعنا طبقاتها الاثنتي عشرة الحجرية الملساء [**descriptive**]، كي يراها القادم من بعيد ساطعة بالشمس [**descriptive**]، قبل ان تستدير اشعتها الوهاجة [**narrative**] الى الجدران الرخامية الشاهقة لابراج المدينة [**descriptive**].

As such, special attention is given to the text type focus in the process of translation, as in:

When we reconstructed the city after the war [**narrative**], *we chose a wide plot of land on the river bank* [**descriptive**], *two kilometres in area* [**descriptive**], *where we built a printing house* [**descriptive**]. *We erected twelve smooth, stone storeys so high* [**descriptive**] *that anyone approaching could see it glinting in the sunlight* [**descriptive**] *before the dazzling rays reached* [**narrative**] *the lofty marble walls of the city towers* [**descriptive**].

Any text should belong to a genre or a combination of more than one genre. As such, this expository text belongs to a literary genre, which is subclassified to a number of subgenres – poetry, fiction, drama and so on. More accurately, it belongs to a fictional genre in which the world is created autonomously through imaginative texts sharing certain characteristics and having more or less a weak relationship with the real world (Dickins *et al.* 2002: 178). Like other subgenres in this literary genre such as poetry, novel, novella, play and so on, this subgenre, short-story telling, is characterized by its excessive use of expressive language:

- يراها القادم من بعيد ساطعة بالشمس قبل ان تستدير اشعتها الوهاجة الى الجدران الرخامية الشاهقة لابراج المدينة. . .
- يستقبلون أشعة الصباح الاولى، ويستذكرون أيام العمل البهيجة. . .
- مع سفور الفجر تدق ساعة المدينة الكبيرة دقات التنبيه. . .
- في هذا الصباح الربيعي المشرق، . . .

- مناوراً بين الاجساد النشوى . . .
- حامت عيناي على سطح الجدارية الواسعة المرسومة فوق عقد البوابة بألوان طباشيرية راسخة . . .
- بريق الحبر في دواة الناسخ وترجرجه بضوء الشمس في مثل هذه الثانية من كل صباح، كما تبرق جزئيات آخر من اللوحة بريقاً خاصاً بفيض الاشعة في أوقات معلومة من النهار . . . .
- ووجدت نفسي مغموراً برحابة الصالة الداخلية . . .
- تنسكب عليها أضواء مصابيح مدفونة في السقف . . . .

It is worth noting that translating such an expressive language in a literary genre can be substantially different from its treatment in nonliterary genres. As stated, such a feature is part and parcel of a literary genre; hence the importance of reflecting it in the TL. Unlike other texts, such as birth certificates, death certificates, marriage contracts and the like that need to be accommodated to the target culture conventions of a given genre, the original text at hand easily lends itself to the generic conventions of the target culture. It does not utilize any signaling devices (such as كان يا ما كان في سالف العصر أو الآوان, يُحكى أن, عاشوا عيشة سعيدة, etc.) or contextualization cues. In touching on genre-specific signaling devices, Baker (2006: 87) writes that signalizing devices or contextualization cues "may also be visual, including typographical features such as the use of italics, the choice of colour, or a particular style of drawing that might signal the genre as a cartoon, hence encoding a nonfactual and humorous or satirical narrative".

Readership

One of the translation norms proposed by Chesterman (1997/2000: 86) is 'expectancy norm', that is, translators, in addition to taking into account the TL grammaticality, acceptability, appropriateness, and so on in a certain text type need to give full consideration to the TL readers' expectations. While translating the text at hand, a number of fundamental decisions concerning the levels of acceptability and accessibility have been taken. A number of local strategies have been taken in order to superimpose certain directionality on the text to bring it into line with the TL linguistic and stylistic norms, thus guaranteeing acceptability and accessibility. To live up to the TL readers' expectations, I have opted for *'to fan out'* instead of *'to separate'*, *'storey'* instead of *'floor'*, *'to enjoy the sunshine of the early morning'* instead of *'to receive the first rays of morning'*, *'increased their importance'* instead of *'upgraded their importance'* or *'raised their importance'* and so on.

Purpose of translation

The translation purpose or 'skopos', as it is known in the literature, is a crucial factor that determines, among other factors, the final shape of the translation. Translating a text for publication purposes, for instance, is different from translating the same text for pedagogical purposes or informing others of the main ideas of the text. While translating the text, I have assumed that the text will be translated for publication purposes. As far as the purpose of each local strategy is concerned, it is determined to be in line with the global strategy adopted to deal with the text (see the global strategy in what follows). The aim is to produce an adequate translation. Unlike some scholars, such as Even-Zohar (1978) and Toury (1995), who relate the notion of adequacy to equivalence, adequacy is envisaged here as a link between translation brief and strategies. It is achieved when translators take into account the translation brief (i.e., the purpose of translation, text type, readership, etc.) before adopting their global strategy (be it reader-oriented or text-/author-oriented). Then, their local strategies (i.e., reasoned decisions, such as addition, omission, deviation, lexical choice, maintaining or ignoring some stylistic features, etc.) should be in line with their global strategy adopted earlier.

Global strategy

Having taken into account the readership (those who are interested in literature in general and Arabic literature in particular, the purpose of translation (for publication), text type (expository), genre (literary/fiction), the tenor of text (formal), the language function (referential and expressive with special focus on the message and its implicit references) and generic conventions (neither signaling devices nor contextualization cues), I have opted for a global strategy that stands somewhere between a reader-oriented translation and a text-/author-oriented translation. In other words, I have adopted a combination of a translation that is based on the principle of equivalent effect, thus producing on the TL reader the same effect that the ST produced on its readers (Nida 1964; Nida and Taber 1969/1982; Newmark 1981) and a translation that tries "to render, as closely as the semantic and syntactic structures of the second language allow, the exact contextual meaning of the original" (Newmark 1981: 39). Newmark (Ibid.) suggests that communicative translation is recommended for texts with informative and vocative functions, as the main language function of such texts is to produce the same effect on the TT reader as that produced on the ST reader. On the other hand, semantic translation is the most appropriate translation for literary and religious writing, as well as works of outstanding value in which individualistic expression of the original author is given priority.

Translation

Target Text (TT)	Source text (ST)
Joseph's Tales *When we reconstructed the city after the war, we chose a wide plot of land on the river bank, two kilometres in area, where we built a printing house. We erected twelve smooth, stone storeys so high that anyone approaching could see it glinting in the sunlight before the dazzling rays reached the lofty marble walls of the city towers.*	حكايات يوسف عندما اعدنا بناء المدينة، بعد الحرب، اخترنا رقعة واسعة على ضفة النهر، مساحتها كيلومتران، واقمنا عليها داراً للطباعة، ورفعنا طبقاتها الاثنتي عشرة الحجرية الملساء كي يراها القادم من بعيد ساطعة بالشمس قبل ان تستدير اشعتها الوهاجة الى الجدران الرخامية الشاهقة لابراج المدينة.

(Continued)

Target Text (TT)	Source text (ST)
Work on this printing house has carried on day and night for years. You can see today dozens of skilled workers sitting on the broad steps to the yard surrounding the building to enjoy the sunshine of the early morning and remember the happy days spent working there, before going off to another construction site.	استمر العمل في بناء الدار ليلاً ونهاراً طوال سنوات، وانك لترى اليوم عشرات العمال المهرة جالسين على درجات السلالم العريضة للساحة المحيطة بالبناء، يستقبلون أشعة الصباح الاولى، ويستذكرون أيام العمل البهيجة، قبل الانصراف إلى موقع بناء آخر.
With dawn breaking, the big city clock chimes fifty times to wake the people up. Its loud echo resounds through the city and fades away in the fields. After a while, workers and craftsmen leave their houses outside the city heading for the main square before fanning out across the wide roads leading to their workplaces.	مع سفور الفجر تدق ساعة المدينة الكبيرة دقات التنبيه الخمسين، فينتشر رنينها العالي حول المدينة ثم يتبدد في الحقول، وبعد لحظات يغادر العمال والحرفيون منازلهم خارج المدينة ويتوجهون الى الساحة الرئيسة، قبل ان يتفرقوا في الطرقات الواسعة الى اعمالهم.
Blacksmiths, smelters, builders, carpenters and engineers were gathered together from the neighbouring cities by our city authorities, who welcomed them. They increased their importance among the people. They, also, placed printers, copyists and writers in lofty positions, assigned them to the highest printing house in the city, and put over them a skilled man, known to us as 'Joseph, the Printer'.	حدادون وسباكون وبناؤون ونجارون ومهندسون، جمعتهم سلطات مدينتنا من المدن المجاورة، واحتفت بهم، ورفعت شأنهم بين السكان، ووضعت الطباعين والنساخين والكتاب في منزلة عليا، وخصتهم باعلى دار في المدينة، رأست عليهم رجلاً ماهراً يدعى بيننا (يوسف الطباع).
On that shining, spring morning, I hastened to the printing house; I went up one of the many flights of stairs around the house, manoeuvring among the bodies of drunks lying on the stone steps beside different work tools. I was occupied with one idea, so I was not aware of my colleagues who had strolled with me from the high southern gate. 'Joseph, the Printer' had promised to acquaint me with a secret he had kept locked in one of the rooms of the building.	في هذا الصباح الربيعي المشرق، اغذ السير الى دار الطباعة، وارتقي احد السلالم الكثيرة حول الدار، مناوراً بين الاجساد النشوى، المستلقية على الدرجات الحجرية بجوار عدد العمل المختلفة. كنت مشغولاً بهاجس واحد، فلم أفطن إلى زملائي الذين دلفوا معي من البوابة الجنوبية العالية. كان (يوسف الطباع) قد وعدني بالاطلاع على سر أقفل عليه في إحدى حجرات الدار.
My eyes scanned the wide mural painted on the gate arch in unfading chalk colours, and as I strolled on my regular daily journey, I picked out a small detail in the mural showing an Arab copyist busy with an open manuscript in his hands.	حامت عيناي على سطح الجدارية الواسعة المرسومة فوق عقد البوابة بألوان طباشيرية راسخة، والتقطت وأنا أدلف في موعدي اليومي الثابت جزئية صغيرة من اللوحة لنساخ عربي يعكف على مخطوط مفتوح بين يديه.

Annotation into action 217

Target Text (TT)	Source text (ST)
I raised my eyes towards the mural to check the gloss of the ink in the copyist's inkpot and its quivering in the sunlight at that very moment every morning. They were just as other details of the mural that gave off a special glitter in the flood of rays at particular times of the day.	كنت قد رفعت عيني إلى الجدارية لأتأكد من بريق الحبر في دواة الناسخ وترجرجه بضوء الشمس في مثل هذه الثانية من كل صباح، كما تبرق جزئيات آخر من اللوحة بريقاً خاصاً يفيض الاشعة في أوقات معلومة من النهار.
But that detail slipped my mind when I crossed the printing house's outer hall that contains the information offices and public services. I found myself overwhelmed by the vastness of the inner hall overlooking the printing presses in the workshop on the floor beneath.	لكن هذه الجزئية ذابت من ذاكرتي عندما اجتزت الصالة الخارجية للدار التي تضم مكاتب الاستعلامات والخدمات العامة، ووجدت نفسي مغموراً برحابة الصالة الداخلية القائمة على ورشة المطابع في الطبقة تحت الارضية.
The hall is a thousand square metres in area, with a huge pillar in the middle built of metal supports and plated with thick glass. This pillar, within which the electric lifts operate, penetrates the floors of the building.	كانت الصالة بمساحة ألف متر مربع، يتوسطها عمود ضخم مبني من دعائم معدنية مصفحة بزجاج سميك، يخترق طبقات الدار، وتتحرك فيه مصاعدها الكهربائية.
I crossed the hall floor made of solid vitreous plastic and walked in my rubber shoes to one of the lifts. The coloured plastic seats in the hall were empty at that time, and light from the bulbs recessed into the ceiling streamed down on them.	قطعت أرض الصالة المصنوعة من لدائن زجاجية صلبة، وسرت بحذائي المطاطي إلى أحد المصاعد. كانت المقاعد البلاستيكية الملونة في أرض الصالة فارغة في مثل هذا الوقت، تنسكب عليها أضواء مصابيح مدفونة في السقف.
Below the transparent floor is the hall of the printing presses, which is as spacious as the upper hall. It can be accessed through individual outer passageways. It is joined to the processing and bookbinding departments, the paper stores, the mechanical repair workshop, and the garage for the mini vehicles that carry the paper and printed books along the corridors of the floor.	أسفل الارضية الزجاجية كانت قاعة المطابع باتساع الصالة العليا، ينفذ إليها من منافذ خارجية خاصة، وتتصل بها أقسام التوضيب والتجليد، ومخازن الورق، وورشة التصليح الميكانيكية، ومرأب العجلات الصغيرة التي تنقل الورق والكتب المطبوعة عبر ممرات أرضية.

Annotation

ST:
عندما اعدنا بناء المدينة، بعد الحرب، اخترنا رقعة واسعة على ضفة النهر، مساحتها كيلومتران، واقمنا عليها داراً للطباعة، ورفعنا طبقاتها الاثنتي عشرة الحجرية الملساء كي يراها القادم من بعيد ساطعة بالشمس قبل ان تستدير اشعتها الوهاجة الى الجدران الرخامية الشاهقة لأبراج المدينة.

218 *Annotation into action*

TT:

When we reconstructed the city after the war, we chose a wide plot of land on the river bank, two kilometres in area, where we built a printing house. We erected twelve smooth, stone storeys so high that anyone approaching could see it glinting in the sunlight before the dazzling rays reached the lofty marble walls of the city towers.

Annotation

(a) The length of the sentences and the way in which they are presented in the ST should be taken into account in translating the above extract (cf. Ghazala 2011: 164; Shen 1987: 184). The original writer opts to subordinate the first two clauses by using the connector عندما *'when'*, thereby emphasizing the action of 'choosing' over the other action, i.e. 'reconstructing'. However, in the next two sentences, viz. أقمنا عليها دارا and كيلومترا ن مساحتها للطباعة, he opts for simplicity of language structuring. It is worth noting that the complexity and simplicity of the structures of language used in the text reflect the degree of formality that, in turn, determines among other parameters the tenor of discourse, hence the importance of reflecting such a characteristic in the TT, which can be achieved most effectively by presenting the passage in two complementary complex sentences focusing on the two main issues.

(b) As it is not preferable to have two participles next to each other, referring to different things as in *'approaching shining'*, it is proposed to rewrite this particular clause using the active voice.

ST:

استمر العمل في بناء الدار ليلاً ونهاراً طوال سنوات، وانك لترى اليوم عشرات العمال المهرة جالسين على درجات السلالم العريضة للساحة المحيطة بالبناء، يستقبلون أشعة الصباح الاولى، ويستذكرون أيام العمل البهيجة، قبل الانصراف إلى موقع بناء آخر.

TT:

Work on this printing house has carried on day and night for years. You can see today dozens of skilled workers sitting on the broad steps to the yard surrounding the building to enjoy the sunshine of the early morning and remember the happy days spent working there, before going off to another construction site.

Annotation

(a) The sequence of the collocated words sometimes requires the translator to reorder them in the TT. For instance, in Arabic, when one talks about a day–night succession or any similar expressions involving *'day and night'*, ليل *'night'* preferably comes before نهار *'day'*, while in English the opposite is true. As such, the sequence of ليلا ونهارا in the original

Annotation into action 219

needs to be reordered prior to transferring it into the TL. Divergence in the sequence of the collocates between Arabic and English occurs in expressions like أبر ودبابيس 'pins and needles', بالماء والصابون 'with soap and water', أخذ وعطاء 'giving and taking', الخطأ والصواب 'right and wrong', ذهابا وآيابا 'coming and going', الماء والزاد 'food and water', بالشوكة والسكين 'sooner or later', آجلا أم عاجلا 'with knife and fork' and the like (cf. Shamaa 1978; Trotter 2000; Ghazala 2011).

(b) Here, the original verb يستقبل 'i.e. *to receive*' collocates, to a certain degree, with أشعة الشمس 'i.e. *the rays of the sun*', or الضياء 'i.e. *the light*', on the one hand, and has a positive overtone, i.e. *'happily'*. As such, taking these two elements into account, one may well suggest a rendering, such as *'to enjoy the sunshine of the early morning'*.

(c) Unlike the expression *'working in it'*, the expression *'work on'* emphasizes that the workers are involved in the construction of the printing house. In this context, it is also recommended to use the present perfect tense in the opening clause, viz. *'has carried on'*, as this emphasizes continuity and the unfinished nature of the construction work.

ST:
مع سفور الفجر تدق ساعة المدينة الكبيرة دقات التنبيه الخمسين، فينتشر رنينها العالي حول المدينة ثم يتبدد في الحقول، وبعد لحظات يغادر العمال والحرفيون منازلهم خارج المدينة ويتوجهون الى الساحة الرئيسة، قبل ان يتفرقوا في الطرقات الواسعة الى اعمالهم.

TT:
With dawn breaking, the big city clock chimes fifty times to wake the people up. Its loud echo resounds through the city and fades away in the fields. After a while, workers and craftsmen leave their houses outside the city heading for the main square before fanning out across the wide roads leading to their workplaces.

Annotation

(a) The length of sentences again should be taken into account. For example the connector و *'and'* before *'after a while'* can be deleted to break down the long complex sentence into shorter sentences. It is worth noting that the connector و *'and'* in Arabic appears with most other connectors as in ولكن lit. *'and but'*, أضف إلى ذلك lit. *'and furthermore'*, وعلاة على ذلك lit. *'and add to this'*, ولذلك lit. *'and therefore'*, وعليه *'and thus'*, وبسبب *'lit. and because'* and so on. In this case, it is the other connector that links incoming and ongoing discourse units rather than و *'and'*.

(b) The original writer uses the lexical item تفرّق *'lit. to separate or part'*. However, according to the context, it is used in the sense of انتشر, i.e. *'to spread'*. It is felt that the phrasal verb *'to fan out'* reflects the same mental image conjured up in the mind of the original reader.

220 *Annotation into action*

ST:

حدادون وسباكون وبناؤون ونجارون ومهندسون، جمعتهم سلطات مدينتنا من المدن المجاورة، واحتفت بهم، ورفعت شأنهم بين السكان، ووضعت الطباعين والنساخين والكتاب في منزلة عليا، وخصتهم بأعلى دار في المدينة، رأست عليهم رجلاً ماهراً يدعى بيننا (يوسف الطباع).

TT:

Blacksmiths, smelters, builders, carpenters and engineers were gathered together from the neighbouring cities by our city authorities, who welcomed them. They increased their importance among the people. They, also, placed printers, copyists and writers in lofty positions, assigned them to the highest printing house in the city, and put over them a skilled man, known to us as 'Joseph, the Printer'.

Annotation

(a) The syntactic choices need to be taken into account. Failure to account for the length of sentences and the way in which they are presented, for instance, may lead to the loss of various stylistic and aesthetic values. The translator's success depends on the correct contextual inference and determining the appropriate syntactic choice. In this regard, Shen (1987: 184) rightly comments:

Syntax is often chosen or manipulated to generate literary significance. [. . .] in contrast to the translation of ordinary discourse where critical attention is focused on syntactic errors, syntactic stylistics in literary translation goes beyond question of mere grammaticality.

(b) From a textual perspective, the original writer uses a particular thematic pattern where he deliberately uses the same theme *'they'* in almost all his clauses: وضعت, خصتهم, جمعتم, احتفت بهم, رفعت شأنهم, and رأست عليهم. As such, the constant theme pattern, to use Bloor and Bloor's term (1995), the consistency in the use of the past tense as well as parallelism need to be given full consideration by the translator in a way that the TL stylistically accommodates such structuring.

(c) Here, paying special attention to the unmarked collocation in the ST, viz. رفعت شأنهم, one may well suggest something like: *'raised their profile'*, *'enhanced their importance'* or *'increased their importance'*.

ST:

في هذا الصباح الربيعي المشرق، اغذ السير الى دار الطباعة، وارتقى احد السلالم الكثيرة حول الدار، مناوراً بين الاجساد النشوى، المستلقية على الدرجات الحجرية بجوار عدد العمل المختلفة. كنت مشغولاً بهاجس واحد، فلم أفطن إلى زملائي الذين دلفوا معي من البوابة الجنوبية العالية. كان (يوسف الطباع) قد وعدني بالاطلاع على سر أقفل عليه في إحدى حجرات الدار.

TT:

On that shining, spring morning, I hastened to the printing house; I went up one of the many flights of stairs around the house, manoeuvring among the bodies of drunks lying on the stone steps beside different work tools. I was occupied with one idea, so I was not aware of my colleagues who had strolled with me from the high southern gate. 'Joseph, the Printer' had promised to acquaint me with a secret he had kept locked in one of the rooms of the building.

Annotation

(a) Here, it is clear from the context and co-text that the defined word الدار, i.e. *'the house'* in the original text refers to the printing house. As such, translating it into *'the building'*, will definitely entail 'a degree of loss' as the meaning of the original lexical item is narrower and more specific than that of *'the building'* (Dickins *et al.* 2002: 56). Adopting such a 'generalizing translation' in which the denotative meaning of the TL word is wider and less specific than its counterpart in the ST is not acceptable as long as "the TL does in fact offer a suitable alternative" (Ibid.: 57). Generalizing translation is only opted for if the TL offers no alternative and if the omitted details do not clash with the overall context of the ST (Ibid.). However, unless this passage is treated in total isolation from the other passages in this section, which are integral parts of one narrative, the degree of loss in translation will not be so significant. As such, to avoid over repetition, the use of a more general term would be quite acceptable in English.

(b) The original writer uses a particular thematic pattern where he deliberately uses the same theme in these sentences: كنت مشغولا, ارتقي أحد السلالم, لم أفطن, and أغذ السير. From a textual perspective, the thematic progression in a text, i.e. "what its themes are, how they stay the same, how they change and so on over the course of the text" (Stillar 1998: 17), needs to be taken into account as it plays a significant role in building cohesion within a text (also see Halliday and Hasan 1976; Al-Jabr 1987; Baker 1992).

(c) In the opening time phrase, it is preferable to opt for *'that'* in place of *'this'* as long as the simple past tense is used throughout the translation of the above extract.

ST:

حامت عيناي على سطح الجدارية الواسعة المرسومة فوق عقد البوابة بألوان طباشيرية راسخة، والتقطت وأنا أدلف في موعدي اليومي الثابت جزئية صغيرة من اللوحة لنساخ عربي يعكف على مخطوط مفتوح بين يديه.

TT:

My eyes scanned the wide mural painted on the gate arch in unfading chalk colours, and as I strolled on my regular daily journey, I picked out a small detail in the mural showing an Arab copyist busy with an open manuscript in his hands.

222   *Annotation into action*

> **Annotation**
>
> Here, a careful re-structuring in *'I picked out a small detail of the mural of an Arab copyist busy with an open manuscript in his hands'* is needed as it is not clear whether the mural is created by the Arab copyist or it refers to a small detail picked out by the narrator. According to the context and co-text, what is meant is that the Arab copyist is part of the detail picked out by the narrator. Therefore, the addition of the participle *'showing'*, or a precise choice of prepositions in the TT as in *'I picked out a small detail in the mural of an Arab copyist busy with an open manuscript in his hands'* should be sufficient to transmit the intended message/picture and remove such confusion.

ST:

كنت قد رفعت عيني إلى الجدارية لأتأكد من بريق الحبر في دواة الناسخ وترجرجه بضوء الشمس في مثل هذه الثانية من كل صباح، كما تبرق جزئيات آخر من اللوحة بريقاً خاصاً بفيض الاشعة في أوقات معلومة من النهار. لكن هذه الجزئية ذابت من ذاكرتي عندما اجتزت الصالة الخارجية للدار التي تضم مكاتب الاستعلامات والخدمات العامة، ووجدت نفسي مغموراً برحابة الصالة الداخلية القائمة على ورشة المطابع في الطبقة تحت الارضية.

TT:

I raised my eyes towards the mural to check the gloss of the ink in the copyist's inkpot and its quivering in the sunlight at that very moment every morning. They were just as other details of the mural that gave off a special glitter in the flood of rays at particular times of the day. But that detail slipped my mind when I crossed the printing house's outer hall that contains the information offices and public services. I found myself overwhelmed by the vastness of the inner hall overlooking the printing presses in the workshop on the floor beneath.

> **Annotation**
>
> (a) Attention should be paid to verb aspects, particularly in the opening clause كنت قد رفعت عيني. Here, although the particle قد is used in the original opening clause which is normally used to indicate that an event had occurred before the other in a specific period of time, the emphasis is on the completion of the action rather than the sequence of events, thus a simple past tense is sufficient here.
>
> (b) Here, the relationship between these chunks of information, i.e. لكن هذه الجزئية . . . and . . . . ووجدت نفسي needs to be taken into account by careful reading. It is a cause–effect relation despite the fact that in the original text the connector و *'lit. and'* is used. In such a context, the connector و can be smoothly replaced by the connector ف. The connector و can signal different relations, such as a temporal relation, addition relation,

contrast relation and simultaneous action (cf. Holes 1984: 234; Baker 1992: 193). As stated earlier, some Arabic connectors perform more functions than some of their English counterparts, and *vice versa*. Several relations can be expressed by the same connector depending on the context in which it is used. As such, decontextualizing the original conjunctive element and translating it literally may distort the relationship itself between the two chunks of information.

(c) Again, the length of the sentences and the way in which they are presented in the ST should be given full consideration in translating the above extract so that the result can be considered elegant English.

ST:

كانت الصالة بمساحة ألف متر مربع، يتوسطها عمود ضخم مبني من دعائم معدنية مصفحة بزجاج سميك، يخترق طبقات الدار، وتتحرك فيه مصاعدها الكهربائية.

TT:

The hall is a thousand square metres in area, with a huge pillar in the middle built of metal supports and plated with thick glass. This pillar, within which the electric lifts operate, penetrates the floors of the building.

Annotation

(a) Here, attention needs to be paid to verb tenses. In the ST, a combination of past (or perfect) tense, expressed by كانت and present (or imperfect) tense, expressed by verbs such as يتوسط, يخترق and تتحرك is used. However, the emphasis in the original sentences is on continuity and permanence rather than the time element. As such, one can argue that the present tense is more appropriate throughout this passage. Such a shift in aspect from a perfect tense to an imperfect tense should be taken into consideration by the translator as it does produce a change in time reference and continuity, which in turn will affect the pragmatic communicative effect. It is worth noting here that the decision on TT tenses can be crucial. The decision is up to the translator, but s/he must be consistent throughout and ensure his/her reasoning is sound.

(b) Further, to make the description clear and effective to the TT reader, a careful restructuring is needed as in *'This pillar, within which the electric lifts operate, penetrates the floors of the building'*.

ST:

أسفل الارضية الزجاجية كانت قاعة المطابع باتساع الصالة العليا، ينفذ إليها من منافذ خارجية خاصة، وتتصل بها أقسام التوضيب والتجليد، ومخازن الورق، وورشة التصليح الميكانيكية، ومرأب العجلات الصغيرة التي تنقل الورق والكتب المطبوعة عبر ممرات أرضية.

224 *Annotation into action*

TT:

Below the transparent floor is the hall of the printing presses, which is as spacious as the upper hall. It can be accessed through individual outer passageways. It is joined to the processing and bookbinding departments, the paper stores, the mechanical repair workshop, and the garage for the mini vehicles that carry the paper and printed books along the corridors of the floor.

Annotation

(a) The length of the sentences and thematic progression need to be taken into account. They are too wordy and the readers need a map to find their own way around. The long sentence in the final version lends itself to three sentences, thereby facilitating the reader's task in understanding the text, on the one hand, and reflecting the structuring as well as thematic progression of the original text on the other.

(b) Further, attention is paid to verb tenses. In the ST, a combination of both past (or perfect) tense, expressed by كانت and present (or imperfect) tense, expressed by verbs such as تتصل, ينفذ and تنقل is used. However, the emphasis in the original sentences is on continuity and permanence rather than the completion of actions. As such, the present tense is more appropriate throughout this passage. Such a shift in aspect from a perfect tense to an imperfect tense is given full consideration here as it does produce a change in time reference and continuity, which in turn will affect the pragmatic communicative effect.

References

Al-Jabr, A. M. (1987). *Cohesion in Text Differentiation: A Study of English and Arabic*. Unpublished PhD thesis. England: University of Aston.

Baker, M. (1992/2011). *In Other Words: A Coursebook on Translation*. London/New York: Routledge.

———. (2006). *Translation and Conflict*. London/New York: Routledge.

Bell, R. T. (1991). *Translation and Translating: Theory and Practice*. London/New York: Longman.

Bloor, T., & Bloor, M. (1995). *The Functional Analysis of English: A Hallidayan Approach*. London: Arnold.

Chesterman A. (1997/2000). *Memes of Translation: The Spread of Ideas in Translation Theory*. Amsterdam/Philadelphia: John Benjamins.

Dickins, J., Hervey, S., & Higgins, I. (2002). *Thinking Arabic Translation*. London/New York: Routledge.

Even-Zohar, I. (1978/2004). *The Position of Translated Literature within the Literary Polysystem*. In L. Venuti (ed.), *The Translation Studies Reader* (2nd edition). London/New York: Routledge, pp. 192–197.

Ghazala, H. (2011). *Cognitive Stylistics & the Translator*. London: Sayyab Books Ltd.

Halliday, M.A.K., & Hasan, R. (1976). *Cohesion in English*. London: Longman Group Ltd.

Hatim, B. (1997). *English-Arabic/Arabic-English Translation: A Practical Guide.* London: Saqi Books.
———. (2001). *Teaching & Researching Translation.* Edinburgh: Pearson Education Limited.
———, & Mason, I. (1990). *Discourse and the Translator.* London: Longman.
———, & Mason, I. (1997). *The Translator as Communicator.* London/New York: Routledge.
Holes, C. (1984). "Textual Approximation in the Teaching of Academic Writing to Arab Students: A Contrastive Approach." In J. Swales & H. Mustafa (eds.), *English for Specific Purposes in the Arab World.* Birmingham: University of Aston, pp. 228–242.
Newmark, P. (1981). *Approaches to Translation.* Oxford: Pergamon.
Nida, E. (1964). *Towards a Science of Translation, With Special Reference to Principles and Procedures Involved in Bible Translating.* Leiden: E. J. Brill.
———, & Taber, C. R. (1969). *The Theory and Practice of Translation.* Leiden: Brill.
Shamaa, N. (1978). *A Linguistic Analysis of Some Problems of Arabic into English Translation.* Unpublished PhD thesis. Oxford: Oxford University Press.
Shen, D. (1987). *Literary Translation and Translation: With Particular Reference to English Translations of Chinese Prose Fiction.* Unpublished PhD thesis. UK: University of Edinburgh.
Stillar, G. R. (1998). *Analysing Everyday Texts: Discourse, Rhetoric and Social Perspectives.* Thousand Oaks/London/New York/New Delhi: Sage Publications.
Toury, G. (1995). *Descriptive Translation Studies and Beyond.* Amsterdam: John Benjamins.
Trotter, W. (2000). *Translation Salience: A Model of Equivalence in Translation (Arabic/English).* Unpublished PhD thesis. Australia: University of Sydney.

The Routledge Course in Translation Annotation website at www.routledge.com/cw/almanna contains:

- A video summary of the chapter
- PowerPoint slides
- Further reading links
- Further assignments
- More research questions
- Further annotated texts

References

Abdel-Fattah, M. M. (2005). "On the Translation of Modals from English into Arabic and Vice Versa: the Case of Deontic Modality," *Babel*, Vol. 51 (1), pp. 31–48.

Abdel-Hafiz, A. (2003). "Pragmatic and Linguistic Problems in the Translation of Naguib Mahfouz's: *The Thief and The Dogs*: a Case Study," *Babel*, (3), pp. 229–252.

Abdulla, A. (2001). "Rhetorical Repetition in Literary Translation," *Babel*, Vol. 47 (4), pp. 289–303.

'Abid, K. (2010). Layālī al-Saīd Salmān *'Nights of Mr Salman.'* London: Sayyab Books Ltd.

Abrams, M. (1988/1993). *A Glossary of Literary Terms*. London: Harcourt Brace Jovanovich College Publishers.

Adab, B. J. (1997). *Translation Strategies and Cross-Cultural Constraints: A Case Study of the Translation of Advertising Texts*. Unpublished PhD thesis: Aston University.

Al-Hakmani, M. (2013). *The Country of Mountains: Nepal: A Journey and Talk about the Affairs of Muslims*. MA Translation Project. England: University of Durham.

Al-Hinai, M. (2009). *Translating the Agreement Between the Government of Ireland and the Government of the United Kingdom of Great Britain and Northern Ireland (April 1998) and annotating it*. MA Translation Project. England: University of Durham.

Al-Māni', S. (1997). Al-Qāmi'ūn *'Oppressors'*. London: Al-Ightirāb Al-Adabī.

Ali, Y. (1934/2006). *The Meaning of the Glorious Quran*. Vol. 1. Beirut and Cairo: Dār Al-Kitāb al-Lubnani wa Dār Al-Kitāb Al-Masrī.

Al-Ismail, Y. A. (2009). *Arabic Translation of the Secret Daily Teaching by Rhonda Byrne*. MA Translation Project. England: University of Durham.

Al-Jabr, A. M. (1987). *Cohesion in Text Differentiation: A Study of English and Arabic*. Unpublished PhD thesis. England: University of Aston.

Al-Khafaji, R. (2011). *Essays in Arabic Text Linguistics and Translation Studies*. Amman: Amwaj for Publication and Distribution.

Almanna, A. (2005). *Aspects of Cohesion in Translating Legislative Texts from Arabic into English*. Unpublished MA thesis: University of Westminster.

———. (2010). "A Decoding-Encoding Approach to Translating Simile between English and Arabic." In S. Faiq & A. Clark (eds.), *Beyond Denotation in Arabic-English Translation*, pp. 108–125. London: Sayyab Books Ltd.

———. (2013). *Quality in the Translation of Narrative Fictional Texts from Arabic into English for the Purposes of Publication: Towards a Systematic Approach to (Self-)Assessing the Translation Process*. Unpublished PhD thesis: University of Durham.

———. (2014). *Translation Theories Exemplified from Cicero to Pierre Bourdieu*. München: Lincom Europa Academic Publishers.

——— & Almanna, F. (2008). *Translation: History, Theory and Practice* (in Arabic). London: Sayyab Books Ltd.

——— & Farghal, M. (2015). "An Emic-etic Approach to Translating Cultural Expressions between Arabic and English," *ASUJ, Applied Science University Journal*, Vol. 17, pp. 51–60.

Al-Masri, H. (2004). *Semantics and Cultural Losses in the Translation of Literary Texts*. Unpublished PhD dissertation. USA: Purdue University.

Al-Qaradaghi, A. (n.d.). Nahnu wa al-Aakhar '*We and the Other*'. No Publisher.

Al-Qinai, J. (2000). "Translation Quality Assessment: Strategies, Parameters & Procedures," *Meta*, Vol. 45 (3), pp. 497–519.

———. (2008). "Translating Modals between English and Arabic," *Translation and Interpreting Studies*, Vol. 3.1/3.2, pp. 30–67.

Alqunayir, A. (2014). *Islamophobia: The Challenge of Pluralism in the 21st Century*. MA Translation Project. England: University of Durham.

Al-Ramlī, M. (2009). *Al-Bahith 'an Qalb Haī 'Search for a Live Heart.'* London: Sayyab Books Ltd.

Al-Rubai'i, A. (1996). *Translation Criticism: A Model for Assessing the Translation of Narrative Fictional Texts*. Unpublished PhD thesis. Iraq: Al-Mustansiriya University.

———. (2005). *Translation Criticism*. Durham, UK: Durham Modern Languages Series.

Al-Rubai'ī, 'A. M. (2009). *Dhālik al-Anīn 'Groaning.'* Sayyab Books Ltd.

Al-Saeghi, S. (2014a). "Register and Translation: Mahfouz's Novel 'Adrift on the Nile' as a Sample." Assignment 1 (MA programme). Oman: University of Nizwa.

———. (2014b). "A Cultural Approach to Translating Literary Texts: Mahfouz's Novel 'Adrift on the Nile' as a Sample." Assignment 2 (MA programme). Oman: University of Nizwa.

Al-Sayyāb, B. S. (1971). *Dīwān Badr Shākir al-Sayyāb*. Beirut: Dār al-'Aūda.

Al-Shehari, K. (2001). *The Semiotics and Translation Advertising Texts: Conventions, Constraints and Translation Strategies with Particular Reference to English and Arabic*. Unpublished PhD thesis. UK: University of Manchester.

Álvarez, R., & Vidal, M. C. (1996). "Translating: A Political Act." In R. Álvarez & M. C. Vidal (eds.), *Translation, Power, Subversion*, pp. 1–9. Philadelphia: Multilingual Matters.

Anderson, M. (2003). "Ethnography as Translation." In S. Petrilli (ed.), *Translation Translation: Approaches to Translation Studies*, Vol. 21, pp. 389–396. Amsterdam: Rodopi.

Asad, M. (1980/2003). *The Message of the Qur'an*. England: The Book Foundation.

Austin, J. L. (1962). *How to Do Things with Words*. Oxford: Oxford University Press.

Aziz, Y. (1989). *A Contrastive Grammar of English and Arabic*. Iraq: Mosul University Press.

Baker, A. E., & Hengeveld, K. (eds.). (2012). *Linguistics*. Oxford: Wiley-Blackwell.

Baker, M. (1992/2011). *In Other Words: A Coursebook on Translation*. London/New York: Routledge.

———. (2006). *Translation and Conflict*. London/New York: Routledge.

——— & Malmkjær, K. (1998). *Routledge Encyclopaedia of Translation Studies*. London/New York: Routledge.

Bassnett, S. (1980/1991/2002). *Translation Studies*. London/New York: Routledge.

——— & Lefevere, A. (1998). *Constructing Cultures: Essays on Literary Translation*. Clevedon: Multilingual Matters.

Bayar, M. (2007). *To Mean or Not to Mean*. Damascus: Kadmous Cultural Foundation.

Beaugrande, R. de (1980). *Text, Discourse and Process: Toward a Multidisciplinary Science of Texts*. Norwood. Norwood, NJ: Ablex.

Beaugrande, R. de & Dressler, W. (1981). *Introduction to Text Linguistics*. London: Longman.
Belhaaj, A. E. (1998). *The Process of Translation: Factors, Tasks and Challenges*. Saudi Arabia: Umm Al-Qura University Press.
Bell, R. T. (1991). *Translation and Translating: Theory and Practice*. London/New York: Longman.
Bennett, W. L., & Edelman, M. (1985). "Toward a New Political Narrative," *Journal of Communication*, Vol. 35 (4), pp. 156–171.
Bloor, T., & Bloor, M. (1995). *The Functional Analysis of English: A Hallidayan Approach*. London: Arnold.
Boase-Beier, J. (2006). *Stylistic Approaches to Translation*. Manchester: St. Jerome Publishing.
Borrillo, J. M. (2000). "Register Analysis in Literary Translation," *Babel*, Vol. 46 (1), pp. 1–19.
Bowles, P. (trans.). (1993). *For Bread Alone*. London: Saqi Books.
Bragina, J. (2012). *A Cognitive Stylistic Analysis of J.R.R. Tolkien's Fantasy World of Middle-Earth*. Unpublished PhD dissertation. Glasgow: University of Glasgow.
British Standards Institution. (2006). *Translation Services: Service Requirements (BSEN-15038 European Quality Standard for Translation Services)*. London: BSI.
Brown, T., & Yule, G. (1983). *Discourse Analysis*. Cambridge: Cambridge University Press.
Brunette, L. (2000). "Towards a Terminology for Translation Quality Assessment: A Comparison of TQA Practices," *The Translator*, Vol. 6 (2), pp. 169–182.
Bybee, J., & Fleischman, S. (1995). "Modality in Grammar and Discourse: An Introductory Essay." In J. Bybee & S. Fleischman (eds.), *Modality in Grammar and Discourse*, pp. 1–14. Amsterdam/Philadelphia: Benjamins, Amsterdam.
Carbonell, O. (1996). "The Exotic Space of Cultural Translation." In R. Álvarez & M. Vidal (eds.), *Translation, Power, Subversion*, pp. 79–98. Clevedon, UK: Multilingual Matters.
Catford, J. C. (1965). *A Linguistic Theory of Translation*. Oxford: Oxford University Press.
Celce-Murcia, M., & Larsen-Freeman, F. D. (1999). *The Grammar Book: An ESL/EFL Teacher's Course*. Boston: Newbury: Heinle and Heinle Publishers.
Chakhachiro, R. (2005). "Revision for Quality," *Perspectives Studies in Translation*, Vol. 13 (3), pp. 255–238.
———. (2011). *Translating Irony: An Interdisciplinary Approach with English and Arabic as a Case in Point*. London: Sayyab Books Ltd.
Chesterman, A. (1997/2000). *Memes of Translation: The Spread of Ideas in Translation Theory*. Amsterdam/Philadelphia: John Benjamins.
Chomsky, N. (1957). *Syntactic Structures*. The Hague, Netherlands: Mouton.
Choukri, M. (2000). *al-Khubz al-hafī* (6th ed.). London: Saqi Books.
Coates, J. (1983). *The Semantics of the Modal Auxiliaries*. London: Croom Helm.
Corbett, E. P. (1971). *Classical Rhetoric for Modern Student*. Oxford: Oxford University Press.
Crystal, D. (1980). *A Dictionary of Linguistics and Phonetics*. Cambridge: Basil Blackwell.
———. (1989). *The Cambridge Encyclopedia of Language*. Cambridge: The University Press.
———. (1997). *The Cambridge Encyclopedia of Language* (2nd ed.). Cambridge: Cambridge University Press.

——— & Davy, D. (1969). *Investigating English Style*. London: Longman.
Cutting, J. (2002). *Pragmatics and Discourse: A Resource Book for Students*. London: Routledge.
Dagut, M. (1976). "Can Metaphor Be Translated?" *Babel*, Vol. 32, pp. 21–33.
Dickins, J., Hervey, S., & Higgins, I. (2002). *Thinking Arabic Translation*. London/New York: Routledge.
Downing, A., & Locke, P. (1992). *A University Course in English Grammar*. Hemel Hempstead: Phonix ELT.
Eggins, S. (1994). *An Introduction to Systematic Functional Linguistics*. London/New York: Continuum.
Elyas, A. E. (trans.). (1987). *The Thief and the Dogs*. Jeddah: Dār Al-Shurūq.
Emery, P. G. (1989). "Legal Arabic Texts: Implications for Translation," *Babel*, Vol. 35 (1), pp. 1–11.
Emery, P. G. (2004). "Translation, Equivalence and Fidelity: A Pragmatic Approach," *Babel*, Vol. 50 (2), pp. 143–167.
Even-Zohar, I. (1978/2004). "The Position of Translated Literature within the Literary Polysystem." In L. Venuti (ed.), *The Translation Studies Reader* (2nd ed.), pp. 192–197. London/New York: Routledge.
Faiq, S. (2004). "The Discourse of Intercultural Translation," *Intercultural Communication Studies*, XIII (3), pp. 35–46.
———. (2007). *Trans-Lated: Translation and Cultural Manipulation*. New York: Roman & Littlefield Publishing Group.
———. (2008). "The Master Discourse of Translation from Arabic." *STJ: Sayyab Translation Journal*, Vol. 1, pp. 27–36.
——— & Sabry, R. (2013). "Altered Semiotics through Translation," *STJ: Sayyab Translation Journal*, Vol. 5, pp. 45–56.
Farghal, M. (2004). "Literary Translation: A Schema-Theoretic Model," *Al-Arabiyya*, Vol. 37, pp. 21–35.
———. (2008). "Extrinsic Managing: An Epitaph to Translational Ideological Move," *STJ: Sayyab Translation Journal*, Vol. 1, pp. 1–26.
———. (2012). *Advanced Issues in Arabic-English Translation Studies*. Kuwait: Kuwait University Press.
——— & Al-Shorafat, M. (1996). "The Translation of English Passives into Arabic: An Empirical Perspective," *Target*, Vol. 8 (1), pp. 97–118.
——— & Almanna, A. (2015). *Contextualizing Translation Theories: Aspects of Arabic–English Interlingual Communication*. England: Cambridge Scholar Publishing.
——— & Borini, A. (1996). "Pragmalinguistic Failure and the Translatability of Arabic Politeness Formulas into English: A Case Study of Mahfouz's *'awlaadu haaratinaa*," *INTERFACE: Journal of Applied Linguistics*, Vol. 11 (1), pp. 3–23.
——— & Borini, A. (1997). "Pragmareligious Failure in Translating Arabic Politeness Formulas into English, Evidence from Mahfouz's *'awlaadu haaratinaa*," *Multilingua*, Vol. 16 (1), pp. 77–99.
——— & Shakir, A. (1994). "Kin Terms and Titles of Address as Relational Social Honorifics in Jordanian Arabic," *Anthropological Linguistics*, Vol. 36 (2), pp. 240–253.
——— & Shunnaq, A. (1999/2011). *Translation with Reference to English and Arabic: A Practical Guide (1ST edition)*, Jordan: Dār al-Hilāl for Translation.
Fawcett, P. (1997). *Translation and Language: Linguistic Theories Explained*. Manchester: St. Jerome Publishing.
Fiske, J., & Hartley, J. (1978). *Reading Television*. London: Methuen.

Francis, G. (1993). "A Corpus-Driven Approach to Grammar: Principles, Methods and Examples." In M. Baker, G. Francis, & E. Tognini-Bonelli (eds.), *Text and Technology: In Honour of John Sinclair*, pp. 137–156. Amsterdam/Philadelphia: John Benjamins.
Fraser, J. (1996). "The Translator Investigated," *The Translator*, Vol. 2 (1), pp. 65–79.
Gadalla, H. (2000). *Comparative Morphology of Standard and Egyptian Arabic*. Muenchen, Germany: Lincom Europa.
———. (2006). "Arabic Imperfect Verbs in Translation: A Corpus Study of English Renderings," *META: Journal des Traducteurs, Les Presses de l'Universite de Montreal*, Vol. 51 (1), pp. 51–71.
Gardiner, M. (1992). *The Dialogics of Critique: M. M. Bakhtin and the Theory of Ideology*. London: Routledge.
Ghazala, H. (2011). *Cognitive Stylistics & the Translator*. London: Sayyab Books Ltd.
———. (2012). "Translating Media Style and Counter Styles: A Cognitive Approach," *STJ: Sayyab Translation Journal*, Vol. 4, pp. 19–45.
Graham, J. D. (1983). "Checking, Revision and Editing." In C. Picker (ed.), *The Translator's Handbook*, pp. 99–105. London: Aslib, the Association for Information Management.
———. (1989). "Checking, Revision and Editing." In C. Picker (ed.), *The Translator's Handbook*, pp. 99–105. London: Aslib, the Association for Information Management.
Greene, G. (1980). *The Bomb Party*. Harmondsworth, UK: Penguin Books.
Gregory, M. (1988). "Generic Situation and Register: A Functional View of Communication." In J. D. Benson, M. J. Cummings, & W. S. Graves (eds.), *Linguistics in a Systemic Perspective*, pp. 301–329. Amsterdam/Philadelphia: John Benjamins.
——— & Carroll, S. (1978). *Language and Situation: Language Varieties and Their Social Contexts*. London: Routledge and Kegan Paul.
Grice, H. P. (1975). "Logic and Conversation." In P. Cole & J. L. Morgan (eds.), *Syntax and Semantics, 3: Speech Acts*, pp. 41–58. New York: Academic Press.
Grutman, R. (2009). "Multilingualism." In M. Baker & G. Saldanha (eds.), *Routledge Encyclopedia of Translation Studies* (2nd ed.), pp. 182–185. London/New York: Routledge.
Gutt, E.-A. (1991). *Translation and Relevance: Cognition and Context*. Oxford: Blackwell.
Hall. M. F. (2008). *Discourse Analysis of Fictional Dialogue in Arabic to English Translation*. Unpublished PhD thesis. London: University of London.
Halliday, M.A.K. (1964). "Comparison and Translation." In M.A.K. Halliday, M. McIntosh, & P. Strevens (eds.), *The Linguistic Sciences and Language Teaching*, pp. 111–134. London: Longman.
———. (1970). "Functional Diversity in Language as Seen from a Consideration of Modality and Mood in English. Foundations of Language." *International Journal of Language and Philosophy*, Vol. (6), pp. 322–361.
———. (1976). "Notes on Transitivity and Theme in English. Part 2." *Journal of Linguistics*, Vol. 3 (1), pp. 199–244.
———. (1978). *Language as a Social Semiotic*. London: Edward Arnold.
———. (1994). *An Introduction to Functional Grammar*. London: Edward Arnold.
——— & Hasan, R. (1976). *Cohesion in English*. London: Longman Group Ltd.
——— & Matthiessen, C. (2004). *An Introduction to Functional Grammar*. London: Edward Arnold.

Harris, R. (2000). "Will Stylistics Ever Grow Up?" Paper delivered at the XX International Poetics and Linguistics Association Conference at Goldsmiths College: London, on July 1st.

Haroun, Y. (2013). *Translating and Annotating an Extract from Muḥammad al-ʿArabī Zubayrī, Book 'Tārīkhal-Jazāʾiral-muʿāṣir: dirāsah' (1999)*. MA Translation Project. England: University of Durham.

Hatim, B. (1997a). *Communication across Cultures: Translation Theory and Contrastive Text Linguistics*. England: University of Exeter Press.

———. (1997b). *English-Arabic/Arabic-English Translation: A Practical Guide*. London: Saqi Books.

———. (2001). *Teaching & Researching Translation*. Edinburgh: Person Education Limited.

——— & Mason, I. (1990). *Discourse and the Translator*. London: Longman.

——— & Mason, I. (1997). *The Translator as Communicator*. London/New York: Routledge.

——— & Munday, J. (2004). *Translation: An Advanced Resource Book*. London/New York: Routledge.

Haynes, J. (1995). *Style*. London/New York: Routledge.

Hervey, S., & Higgins, I. (1992). *Thinking Translation. A Course in Translation Method: French to English*. London/New York: Routledge.

Hoey, M. (1991). *Patterns of Lexis in Text*. Oxford: Oxford University Press.

Holes, C. (1984). "Textual Approximation in the Teaching of Arabic Academic Writing to Arab Students: A Contrastive Approach." In J. Swales & H. Mustafa (eds.), *English for Specific Purposes in the Arab World*. Birmingham, UK: University of Aston.

Holmes, J. H. (1970/2004). "The Name and Nature of Translation Studies." In L. Venuti (ed.), *The Translation Studies Reader*, pp. 172–185. London/New York: Routledge.

House, J. (2001). "Translation Quality Assessment: Linguistic Description versus Social Evaluation," *Meta*, Vol. 46 (2), pp. 243–257.

Hoye, L. (1997). *Adverbs and Modality in English*. London: Longman.

Huang, X. (2011). *Stylistic Approaches to Literary Translation: With Particular Reference to English-Chinese and Chinese-English Translation*. Unpublished PhD dissertation. University of Birmingham.UK.

Human Rights Watch. (2014, August). Retrieved on February 12th, 2014, from www.hrw.org

Husni, R., & Newman, D. (2008). *Modern Arabic Short Stories*. London: Saqi Books.

Irving, T. B. (1930/2006). *The Qurʾan; the Noble Reading*. Iowa: The Mother Mosque Foundation.

Jääskeläinen, R. (1993). "Investigating Translation Studies." In S. Tirkkonen-Condit & J. Laffling (eds.), *Recent Trends in Empirical Translation Research*, pp. 99–116. Joensuu: University of Joensuu, Faculty of Arts.

Jarjour, M. (2006). *A Relevance-Theoretic Account of the Translation of Ideological Assumptions in the Language of the News with Specific Reference to Translation from English into Arabic*. Unpublished PhD thesis. England: University of Salford.

Jarvie, G. (1993). *Grammar Guide: The Way the English Language Works*. Great Britain: Bloomsbury Publishing Ltd.

Jayyusi, S. K. (ed.). (1987). *Modern Arabic Poetry: An Anthology*. New York: Columbia University Press.

Johnston-Davies, D. (trans.). (1986). *The Wedding of Zein*. Boulder/London: Lynne Reiner.

Kashmiri, S.B.A. (trans.). (2014). *We and the Other*. Doha: DICISD.
Katan, D. (1999). *Translating Cultures: An Introduction for Translators, Interpreters and Mediators*. Manchester: St. Jerome Publishing.
Kelly, D. (1998). "Ideological Implications of Translation Decision: Positive-Self and Negative-Other Presentation," *Quaderns, Revista de traduccío*, Vol. 1, pp. 57–63.
Khalil, A. (1999). *A Contrastive Grammar of English and Arabic*. Amman: Jordan Book Centre.
Khuḍayyir, M. (2011). Ḥikaīāt Yūsif '*Joseph's Tales.*' London: Sayyab Books Ltd.
Kress, G. (1985). *Linguistic Processes in Sociocultural Practice*. Geelong, Australia: Deakin University Press.
Lakoff, G., & Johnson, M. (1980). *Metaphors We Live By*. Chicago: University of Chicago Press.
Lauscher, S. (2000). "Translation Quality Assessment: Where Can Theory and Practice Meet?" *The Translator*, Vol. 6 (2), pp. 149–168.
Leech, G. (1983). *Principles of Pragmatics*. London: Routledge.
——— & Short, M. (1981). *Style in Fiction: A Linguistic Introduction to English Fictional Prose*. London: Longman.
Lefevere, A. (ed.). (1992). *Translation/History/Culture: A Sourcebook*. London/New York: Routledge.
Lefevere, A. (1998). "Translation Practice(s) and the Circulation of Cultural Capital: Some Aeneids in English". In S. Bassnette and A. Lefevere (eds.) *Constructing Cultures*. Clevendon: Multilingual Matters, pp. 40–56.
Levinson, S. (1983). *Pragmatics*. Cambridge: Cambridge University Press.
Liardet, F. (trans.). (1993). '*Adrift on the Nile.*' Nobel Laureates in Search of Identity and Integrity: Voices of Different Cultures. Available at www.termspdf.org/files/2tjhw_adrift-on-the-nile-paperback-.pdf
Lin, G.H.C., & Perkins, L. (2005). "Cross-Cultural Discourse of Giving and Accepting Gifts," *International Journal of Communication*, Vol. 16, pp. 1–2, 103–112 (ERIC Collections in ED 503685, www.eric.ed.gov/PDFS/ED503685.pdf)
Literary Devices Net. (n.y.). *Literary Devices: Definitions and Examples of Literary Terms*. Retrieved on February 12th, 2014, from http://literarydevices.net/style/
Löescher, W. (1991). *Translation Performance, Translation Process and Translation Strategies: A Psycholinguistic Investigation*. Tubingen: Guten Narr.
Longman Dictionary of Contemporary English. (1987/1995). German: Longman Group Ltd.
Lyons, J. (1977). *Semantics*. Cambridge: Cambridge University Press.
Mahfouz, N. (1959/1986). '*Awlād Hāratina*. Beirut: Dār Al-Adab.
———. (1961/1973). *el-Lis wal-Kilāb*. Cairo: Maktabat Misr.
———. (1966). *Tharthara Fawq al-Nīl*. Cairo: Dār Misr liltibāʻa.
———. (1973). *Bain l-Qasrayn*. Cairo: Maktabat Misr.
Maier, C. (2000). "Introduction," *The translator*, Vol. 6 (2), pp. 137–148.
Makokha, J.K.S., Ogone, J. O., & West-Pavlov, R. (2012). *Style in African Literature: Essays on Literary Stylistics and Narrative Styles—Internationale Forschungen zur Allgemeinen und Vergleichenden Literaturwissenschaft*. Amsterdam and New York: Rodopi.
Malone, J. L. (1988). *The Science of Linguistics in the Art of Translation*. Albany: State University of New York Press.
Mandelblit, N. (1995). "The Cognitive View of Metaphor and Its Implications for Translation Theory." *Translation and Meaning*. Part 3. Maastricht: Universitaire Press.

Mannheim, K. (1936). *Ideology and Utopia: An Introduction to the Sociology of Knowledge (translated by Louis Wirth and Edward Shils)*. New York: Harcourt, Brace & World, Inc.
Mason, I. (1994). "Discourse, Ideology and Translation." In R. Beaugrande de, Shunnaq, A., & Heliel, M. H. (eds.), *Language, Discourse and Translation in the West and Middle East*, pp. 23–34. Amsterdam: John Benjamins.
Mason, K. (1982). "Metaphor and Translation," *Babel*, Vol. 28, pp. 140–149.
Matthews, P. H. (2005). *Oxford Concise Dictionary of Linguistics*. Oxford: Oxford University Press.
McCawley, J. (1968). "The Role of Semantics in a Grammar." In E. Bach & R. Harms (eds.), *Universals in Linguistic Theory*, pp. 125–170. New York: Holt, Rinehart, and Winston.
McEnery, T., & Wilson, A. (2001). *Corpus Linguistics*. Edinburgh: Edinburgh University Press.
Ministry of Information. (2008/2009). *Oman*. Muscat: the Ministry of Information, Sultanate of Oman. Available at: www.omannet.com.
Mizon, M. I., & Dieguez, M. I. (1996). "Self-Correction in Translation Courses: A Methodological Tool," *Meta*, Vol. 41 (1), pp. 75–83.
Mossop, B. (2007a). *Revising and Editing for Translators*. Manchester, UK: St. Jerome Publication.
———. (2007b). "Empirical Studies of Revision: What We Know and Need to Know," *The Journal of Specialised Translation* [on-line serial], Vol. 8, pp. 5–20. Retrieved on February 12th, 2014, from www.jostrans.org
Munday, J. (2007). "Translation and Ideology: A Textual Approach," *The Translator*, Vol. 13 (2), pp. 195–217.
———. (2001/2008/2012). *Introducing Translation Studies: Theories and Applications*. London/New York: Routledge.
Murphy, S. (2006). "Now I Am Alone: A Corpus Stylistic Approach to Shakespearian Soliloquies." In C. Gabrielatos, R. Slessor, & J. W. Unger (eds.), *Papers from the Lancaster University Postgraduate Conference in Linguistics & Language Teaching, Vol. 1. (Papers from LAEL PG)*, pp. 66–85. Lancaster, UK: University of Lancaster.
Myers-Scotton, C. (2005). *Multiple Voices: Introduction to Bilingualism*. London: Blackwell.
Nāṣir, 'A. (2009). *Thalath Qaṣaṣ laīsat lilnashir 'Three Stories Not for Publishing.'* London: Sayyab Books Ltd.
Newmark, P. (1981). *Approaches to Translation*. Oxford: Pergamon.
———. (1988). *A Textbook of Translation*. New York/London/Toronto/Sydney/Tokyo: Prentice Hall.
———. (1991). *About Translation*. Clevedon, UK: Multilingual Matters.
Nida, E. (1964). *Towards a Science of Translation, with Special Reference to Principles and Procedures Involved in Bible Translating*. Leiden: E. J. Brill.
——— & Reyburn, W. (1981). *Meaning across Cultures*. American Society of Missiology Series, No. 4. New York: Orbis Books.
——— & Taber, C. R. (1969/1982). *The Theory and Practice of Translation*. Leiden: Brill.
Niranjana, T. (1992). *Siting Translation: History, Poststructuralism and the Colonial Context*. Berkeley: University of California Press.
Nord, C. (1991). *Text Analysis in Translation: Theory, Methodology, and Didactic Application of a Model for Translation-Oriented Text Analysis* (1st edition) (C. Nord & P. Sparrow, Trans.). Amsterdam: Rodopi.

Nord, C. (1997). *Translating as a Purposeful Activity: Functionalist Approaches Explained.* Manchester: St. Jerome Publishing.

Oxford Wordpower. (2010). Oxford: Oxford University Press.

Palmer, F. R. (1976). *Semantics.* Cambridge: Cambridge University Press.

———. (1986). *Mood and Modality.* Cambridge University Press, Cambridge.

Peirce, C. S. (1931–58). "Collected Papers" (Volumes 1–6). In C. Hartshorne & P. Weiss (eds.), *Volumes 7–8.* Burks: A. W. Cambridge, MA: Belknap Press, Harvard University Press.

Perkins, M. R. (1983). *Modal Expressions in English.* London: Frances Pinter.

Pertilli, S. (1992). "Translation, Semiotics and Ideology," *TTR: traduction, terminologie, redaction,* Vol. 5 (1), pp. 233–264.

Pickthall, M. (1930/2005). *The Meaning of the Glorious Qur'an: An Explanatory Translation.* New Modern English Edition (2nd ed.). London: I.D.I.C.

Pierini, P. (2007). "Simile in English: From Description to Translation." *CICULO de linguistica aplicada a la comunicacion.* Retrieved on February 12th, 2014, from www.ucm.es/info/circulo

Pike, K. L. (1990). "On the Emics and Etics of Pike and Harris." In T. N. Headland, K. L. Pike, & M. Harris (eds.), *Emics and Etics: The Insider/Outsider Debate.* Frontiers of Anthropology 7, pp. 28–47. Newbury Park: Sage.

Pragnell, F. (2003). *A Week in the Middle East.* London: Pragnell Books.

Pym, A. (2010). *Exploring Translation Theories.* London/New York: Routledge.

Quirk, R., Greenbaum, S., Leech, G., & Svartvik, J. (1972). *A Grammar of Contemporary English.* London: Longman.

———, Greenbaum, S., Leech, G., & Svartvik, J. (1985). *A Comprehensive Grammar of the English Language.* Harlow: Addison Wesley Longman.

Radwan, R. (1975). *A Semantico-Syntactic Study of the Verbal Piece in Colloquial Egyptian Arabic.* Unpublished PhD thesis. University of London.

Rasmussen, K. W., & Schojoldager, A. (2011). "Revising Translations: A Survey of Revision Policies in Danish Translation Companies," *The Journal of Specialised Translation* [on-line serial], Vol. 15, pp. 87–120. Retrieved on February 12th, 2014, from www.jostrans.org

Reiss, K. (1977/1989). "Text Types, Translation Types and Translation Assessment" (translated by Chesterman, A.). In A. Chesterman (ed.), *Reading in Translation Theory,* pp. 105–115. Helsinki: Finn Lectura.

Reiss, K. (2000). *Translation Criticism—The Potentials & Limitations.* Manchester and New York: St. Jerome Publishing & American Bible Society. Translated into English by Erroll F. Rhodes.

Riemer, N. (2010). *Introducing Semantics.* Cambridge: Cambridge University Press.

Robert, I. (2008). "Translation Revision Procedures: An Explorative Study." P. Boulogne (ed.), *Translation and Its Others* (Selected Papers of the CETRA Research Seminar in Translation Studies 2007), pp. 1–25. Retrieved on February 12th, 2014, from www.kuleuven.be/cetra/papers/html

Robinson, D. (2003). *Performative Linguistics: Speaking and Translating as Doing Things With Words.* London/New York: Routledge.

———. (2006). *Introducing Performative Pragmatics.* London and New York: Routledge.

Sadiq, S. (2008). "Some Semantic, Stylistic and Cultural Problems of Translation with Special Reference to Translating the Glorious Qur'ân," *STJ: Sayyab Translation Journal,* Vol. 1, pp. 37–59.

Sager, J. C. (1994). *Language Engineering and Translation: Consequences of Automation*. Amsterdam: Benjamins.
Saīd, M. (2009). Al-Badīla *'The Stand-In.'* London: Sayyab Books Ltd.
Salih, G. (2013). *The balance realization between effect and effort of utterance in political texts: implications for English-Arabic translation*, unpublished MA thesis. England: University of Durham.
Sālih, T. (1966). 'Urs el-Zaīn *'The Wedding of Zein.'* Beirut: Dār al-'Aūda.
Samhat, M. (2014). *The 2006 Lebanon Campaign and the Future of Warfare: Implications for Army and Defense Policy*. MA Translation Project. England: University of Durham.
Samuelsson-Brown, G. (2004). *A Practical Guide for Translators* (4th ed.). Clevedon/Buffalo/Toronto: Multilingual Matters.
Santos, L., & Gomes, A. (2006). "Self-Assessment and Appropriation of Assessment Criteria." In J. Novotná, H. Moraová, M. Krátká, & N. Stehlíková (eds.), *Proceedings of the 30th Conference of the International Group for the Psychology of Mathematics Education*, Vol. 5, pp. 49–56. Prague: PME.
Saussure, F. de. (1916/83). *Cours de linguistique générale*. Paris: Editions Payot. Translated (1983) by R. Harris as *Course in General Linguistics*. London: Duckworth.
Schleiermacher, F. (1813/1992). "On the Different Methods of Translating." In R. Schulte and J. Biguenet (eds.), *Theories of Translation: An Anthology of Essays from Dryden to Derrida*, pp. 36–54. University of Chicago Press: Chicago and London.
Searle, J. (1969). *Speech Acts: An Essay in the Philosophy of Language*. Cambridge: Cambridge University Press.
Sedon-Strutt, H. (1990). "The Revision of Translation Work—Some Observations," *Language International*, Vol. 2 (3), pp. 28–30.
Shakir, M. H. (1995). *The Qur'an*. New York: Tahrike Tarsile Qur'an, Inc.
Shamaa, N. (1978). *A Linguistic Analysis of Some Problems of Arabic into English Translation*. Unpublished PhD thesis. Oxford: Oxford University Press.
Sharkas, H. (2005). *Genre and Translation Quality: Perspectives in Quality Assessment of English-Arabic Translations of Popular Science Genres*. Unpublished PhD thesis: University of Portsmouth.
———. (2009). "Translation Quality Assessment of Popular Science Articles: Corpus Study of the Scientific American and Its Arabic Version," *Trans-Com*, Vol. 2 (1), pp. 42–62.
Shen, D. (1987). *Literary Translation and Translation: With Particular Reference to English Translations of Chinese Prose Fiction*. Unpublished PhD thesis. UK: University of Edinburgh.
Sinclair, J. (1990). *Collins Cobuild English Grammar*. Glasgow: Harper Collins Publishers.
———. (1991). *Corpus, Concordance and Collocation*. Oxford: Oxford University Press.
———. (1998). "The Lexical Item." In E. Weigand (ed.), *Contrastive Lexical Semantics*, pp. 1–24. Amsterdam/Philadelphia John Benjamins,
———. (2008). "The Phrase, the Whole Phrase and Nothing but the Phrase." In S. Granger & F. Meunier (eds.), *Phraseology: An Interdisciplinary Perspective*, pp. 407–410. Amsterdam/Philadelphia: John Benjamins.
Snell-Hornby, M. (1988/1995). *Translation Studies: An Integrated Approach*. Amsterdam/Philadelphia, MA: John Benjamins.
Sperber, D., & Wilson, D. (2005). "Pragmatics." In F. Jackson & M. Smith (eds.), *Oxford Handbook of Contemporary Philosophy*, pp. 468–501. Oxford: Oxford University Press.
Stam, R., Burgoyne, R., & Flitterman-Lewis, S. (1992). *New Vocabularies in Film Semiotics: Structuralism, Post-Structuralism and Beyond*. London: Routledge.

Starkey, P. (trans.). (2008). *Oppressors*. [No publisher].
Steger, M. B., & James, P. (2010). "Ideologies of Globalism." In P. James & M. B. Steger (eds.), *Globalization and Culture, Vol. 4: Ideologies of Globalism*, pp. ix–xxxi. London: Sage Publications Ltd.
Stewart, P. (trans.). (1981). *Children of Gebelawi*. London: Heinemann.
Stillar, G. R. (1998). *Analysing Everyday Texts: Discourse, Rhetoric and Social Perspectives*. Thousand Oaks/London/New York/New Delhi: Sage Publications.
Sultan, H. (2007). *Translating a Chapter of 'State Crime: Governments, Violence and Corruption' and Analyzing the Linguistic Aspects of the Text*. MA Translation Project. London: University of Westminster.
Swales, J. (1993). *Genre Analysis. English in Academic & Research Settings*. Cambridge: Cambridge University Press.
Swan, M. (1995). *Practical English Usage*. Oxford: Oxford University Press.
Tawfik, K. M. (2011). "Rendering Body-Part Idioms in the Holy Qur'an: A Study of Three English Translations," *STJ: Sayyab Translation Journal*, Vol. 3, pp. 83–106.
Taylor, C. (1998). *Language to Language: A Practical and Theoretical Guide for Italian/English Translators*. Cambridge: Cambridge University Press.
Teilanyo, D. I. (2007). "Figurative Language in Translation: A Study of J. P. Clark's *The Ozidi Saga*," *Meta*, Vol. 52 (2), pp. 309–326.
Theroux, P. (trans.). (1996). *Children of the Alley*. New York: Anchor Books.
Thomas, J. (1995). *Meaning in Interaction: An Introduction to Pragmatics*. London: Longman.
Thompson, G. (1996). *Introducing Functional Grammar* (2nd ed.). London: Arnold.
Titscher, S., Meyer, M., Wodak, R., & Velter, E. (2000). *Methods of Text and Discourse Analysis*. Thousand Oaks/London/New York/New Delhi: Sage Publications.
Toolan, M. (1998). *Language in Literature*. London: Hodder.
Toury, G. (1995). *Descriptive Translation Studies and Beyond*. Amsterdam: John Benjamins.
Trotter, W. (2000). *Translation Salience: A Model of Equivalence in Translation (Arabic/English)*. Unpublished PhD thesis. Australia: University of Sydney.
Van Dijk, T. A. (1996). "Discourse, Opinions and Ideologies." In C. Schäffner & H. Kelly-Holmes (eds.), *Discourse and Ideologies*, pp. 7–37. Philadelphia: Multilingual Matters.
———. (2004). "Politics, Ideology and Discourse." In R. Wodak (ed.), *Encyclopedia of Language and Linguistics: Second Language and Politics* (2nd ver.). Retrieved on February 12th, 2014, from www.discourses.org/UnpublishedArticles/Politics,%-20ideology%20and%20discourse%20(ELL).htm
Venuti, L. (1995). *The Translator's Invisibility: A History of Translation*. London/New York: Routledge.
———. (eds.). (2000/2004). *The Translation Studies Reader*. London/New York: Routledge.
———. (n.y.) "How to Read Translation." Retrieved on June 1st, 2014, from http://wordswithoutborders.org/article/how-to-read-a-translation
Vermeer, H. J. (1989/2004). "Skopos and Commission in Translational Action." Translated by A. Chesterman in A. Chesterman (ed.), *Readings in Translation Theory*. Helsinki: OyFinnLectura Ab, pp. 173–87. Reprinted in L. Venuti (ed.), *The Translation Studies Reader* (2nd ed.), pp. 227–238.London/New York: Routledge.
Verschueren, J. (1999). *Understanding Pragmatics*. London/New York: Arnold Publishers.
———, Jan-Ola, Ö., & Jan, B. (eds.). (1995). *Handbook of Pragmatics*. Amsterdam: Benjamins.

Vinay, J. P., & Darbelnet, J. (1958/1995). *Stylistique comparée du français et de l'anglais. Méthode de traduction*. Paris: Didier (trans. and ed.) J. C. Sager & M. J. Hamel, *Comparative Stylistics of French and English: A Methodology for Translation*. Amsterdam/Philadelphia: John Benjamins.
Webster's New World Dictionary. (1991). New York: Warner Books.
Wierzbicka, A. (1991). *Cross-Cultural Pragmatics. The Semantics of Human Interaction*. Berlin/New York: Mouton de Gruyter.
Wilson, K. G. (1993). *The Columbia Guide to Standard American English*. Columbia: Columbia University Press.
Wilss, W. (1996). *Knowledge and Skills in Translator Behavior*. Amsterdam/Philadelphia: John Benjamins.
Winkel, E. (trans.). (2010). *Nights of Mr Salman* London: Sayyab Books Ltd.
Wright, W. (1975). *A grammar of Arabic Language*. Cambridge: Cambridge University Press.
Xiao-jiang, Y. (2007). "On the Role of Ideology in Translation Practice," *US-China Foreign Languages*, Vol. 5 (4), serial No. 43, pp. 63–65.
Yāsīn, L. M. (n.d.). Basmat Mūātin *'A Citizen's Fingerprint,"* unpublished short story.
Yi-yi Shih, C. (2006). "Revision from Translator's Point of View: An Interview Study," Vol. 18 (2), pp. 295–312.
Yule, G. (1996). *Pragmatics*. Oxford: Oxford University Press.
Zangana, H. (2009). *Mathwa 'Dwelling.'* London: Sayyab Books Ltd.
Zwicky, A., & Zwicky, A. (1982). "Register as a Dimension of Linguistic Variation." In R. Kittredge & J. Lehrberger (eds.), *Sublanguage: Studies of Languages in Restricted Semantic Domains*, pp. 213–218. Berlin/New York: Walter de Gruyter.
Zyngier, S. (2001). "Towards a Cultural Approach to Stylistics," *CAUCE, Revista de Filología ysu Didáctica,* Vol. 24, pp. 365–380.

Index

absolute object 105
acceptability 119; expense 47–8; guarantee 40, 196; levels 214
accessibility, inaccessibility (contrast) 157–8
action: annotation 210; completion/ progress, determination 92; face-threatening mode 173, 174; frequency 90; emphasis 61; regularity 90
active structures 157
active voice: annotation 89; expression 88; passive voice, contrast 86–9; resemblance 87
act, types 169
adaptation (borrowing type) 60
addition 115, 215; local strategy 45; usage 55
additive connector, deletion 137
addressing terms 173
adjective-noun sequences 70
adjuncts 131
adverbial clauses, examples 133
adverbial conjunct 134
adverbials, archaic adverbials 129
agentless clauses, construction 86
alliteration 181, 183; assonance, combination 181
al-Maliki, Nori 202
al-Rubai'i, Abdul-Rahman 17–18, 63, 88
Al-Sayyab 114
ambiguity, avoidance 183
amplification: local strategy 45; occurrence 67; reduction, contrast 64, 67–9; comment 67–9
anadiplosis 181
analysis, presentation method 17
anaphoric reference 127
anastrophe 181
annotation 6; action 210; branches 6–7; derivation 8; issues 8–12; lexical choices 103; local strategy 56; phraseological choices 103; place 6–8; procedure 13; purpose 11; revision, contrast 8
antonyms 126; introduction 105
antonymy 137
applied translation studies 6
apposition 181
Arabic language, free-word-order language 140
Arabic linguistics, review 128–9
archaic adverbials 129
Ashton, Catherine 198
aspect: annotation 90–1, 92, 145; comment 93, 144–6; continuity 143–6; information 90; pragmatic aspects, annotation 168; semiotic aspects, annotation 168; stylistic aspects, annotation 168; tense, contrast 90–3; translation 83; types 90
aspects of pragmatics 169–75
aspectual reference 91; determination, importance 92
assertive verbs 171
assessment 12; procedure 13
assonance 181; alliteration, combination 181
asyndeton 181, 184, 185
attention, impact 49–50
Austin, J.L. 169
author: author-oriented global strategy 215; explanation 17; intentions 39
auxiliary verbs, absence 129
axes 179

back-translation 178
Bahrain/United States of America (Article 9) 41–2
Baker, M. 71–7

bald on record strategy 174
behavioral process 152
Biddle, Stephen 98
body-related idiom 116–17
borrowing (local strategy) 56–60;
   adaptation 60; calque (through-
   translation) 57–8; core borrowings 75;
   literal strategy 58; modulation 59–60;
   transposition 59
Bowles, Paul 196
Byrne, Rhonda 85, 97
by-structure 57

calque (through-translation) 56, 57–8;
   lexical calque 57; structural calque
   57–8
cataphoric coreference 127
category shifts 61–4; class shifts 62;
   intrasystem shifts 63–4; rank shifts
   62–3; structure shifts 61–2; unit shifts
   62–3
Catford, J. C. 61–4
cause-result relation, suppression 134–5
changes 38
channel, usage 161–2
checking 10, 12; procedure 12; revision,
   contrast 10
chiasmus 181
Chomsky, Noam 110
class shifts 55, 62
clausal ellipsis 130, 131
clause: meaning, understanding 109;
   structure, types 141
climax 184
cognitive distortion 197
cognitive environment, direct access 41
coherence: cohesion, contrast 126–7;
   divergent patterns 126; external
   coherence 56
cohesion: achievement 126; annotating
   aspects 125; annotation 127; coherence,
   contrast 126–7; grammatical cohesion
   126; lexical cohesion 126, 137–8
cohesive device 198
cohesive function 129
collocated words, sequence 218–9
collocates, markedness (invariance
   requirement) 112
collocation 117–20, 126; annotation 120;
   comment 119; flexibility 115; marked
   collocation 114, 184; reference 137;
   sequences 70; translation 118; unmarked
   collocation 112, 119, 184, 212
commissive verbs 171

communication: act 158; motive 39; place/
   time 39
communicative dynamism, degree 139
communicative purpose (translation
   purpose) 40
communicative value 119
comparative reference 128
comparison 128; adverbial clause 133;
   elements 111
comprehensibility, increase 67
compressed simile 113
concept, lexicalization 75
conceptual texts 213
concession, adverbial clause 133
condensation, diffusion (contrast) 64, 69;
   comment 69
condition, adverbial clause 133
conjunction 126, 133–7; annotation 134;
   comment 135, 136–7
conjunctive elements 134;
   decontextualization 223
conjuncts: adverbial conjuncts 134; types
   133
connectors: omission 182; usage 218
connotative signified 177
constant theme pattern 139
constraints 169; cultural-pragmatic
   constraints 174
continuous past tense 93
contractions, presence 157
conventional simile 112; expression 114
convergence, divergence (contrast) 64,
   66–7; comment 66–7
conversational maxims, types 170
Cooperative Principle 170
coordinating conjuncts 133
core borrowings 75
countability, use 85
cultural allusion 113
cultural environment 16
cultural issues, annotation 190
cultural-pragmatic constraints 174
cultural racism 62
cultural-specific expressions 191–2
cultural substitution, usage 74; comment
   74
cultural translation 115
culture 190–7; comments 192–7; culture-
   specific terms 46; definition 191
culture-specific words 64

Darbelnet, J. 56–60
declarative verbs 171
deep structure 110

Index 241

deictic functioning 130
deletion, occurrence 131
demonstrative reference 128
denotative meaning 67, 74
denotative signified 177
deontic modality 94
derived theme 139
descriptive texts 213
Destutt, Antoine 197
deviant syntactic sequence 145
Dhalik al-Anin 'Groaning' example one 14, 18–19; comment 20; final version 19; first translation 18; native speaker's impression 19; reviser's version/comments 19; second translation 18; suggested version 20; translators, comments 19
Dhalik al-Anin 'Groaning' example two 20–3; comment 22–3; final version 22; first translation 21; native speaker's impression 21–2; reviser's version/comments 21; second translation 21; suggested version 23; translators, comments 21
Dhalik al-Anin 'Groaning' example three 23–5; comment 24–5; final version 24; first translation 23; impressions 24; native speaker's impression 24; reviser's version/comment 24; second translation 23; suggested version 25; translator's comments 23
Dhalik al-Anin 'Groaning' example four 25–8; comment 27; final version 27; first translation 25–6; native speaker's impressions 26–7; reviser's version/comments 26; second translation 26; suggested version 27–8; translators, comments 26
Dhalik al-Anin 'Groaning' example five 28–9; comment 29; final version 29; first translation 28; native speaker's impressions 28–9; reviser's version/comments 28; second translation 28; suggested version 29; translators, comments 28
Dhalik al-Anin 'Groaning' example six 29–31; comment 31; final version 31; first translation 29; native speaker's impressions 30; reviser's version/comments 30; second translation 30; suggested version 31; translators, comments 30
Dhalik al-Anin 'Groaning' example seven 31–3; comment 32–3; final version 32; first translation 31; native speaker's impressions 32; reviser's version/comments 31; second translation 31; suggested version 33; translator's comments 31
Dhalik al-Anin 'Groaning' example eight: comments 35; final version 34; first translation 33; native speaker's impressions 34; reviser's version/comments 34; second translation 33; suggested version 35; translator's comments 33
Dhalik al-Anin 'Groaning' explanation 17–22
dialectal features, usage 162
diffusion, condensation (contrast) 64, 69; comment 69
directives, usage 157
directive verbs 171
direct translation, types 56
discourse, field 151–6; annotation 153–5; circumstances 153–6; comment 155, 156; participants 152–3; process 151–2
discourse, mode 161–3; annotation 163; comment 162
discourse, paratactic nature 135
discourse, tenor 157–61; accessibility, inaccessibility (contrast) 157–8; formality, informality (contrast) 157; politeness 158–61; social distance, standing (contrast) 158–61
divergence, convergence (contrast) 64, 66–7; comment 66–7
drafts, finalization 106
duality 84; duality-indicated lexical terms 85
dynamic modality 95

editing, procedure 12
elaboration 56
El-Baradei, Mohammed 198
ellipsis 126, 130–3, 181; clausal ellipsis 130, 131; comment 132, 133; examples 132; lexical ellipsis 131; nominal ellipsis 130; operator ellipsis 131; propositional ellipsis 132; types 130; verbal ellipsis 130, 131
elliptical clauses, presence 157
eloquence, purpose 111
Elyas, Adel Ata 177, 194
emphasis, purpose 111
empirical genres 43
enallage 181
encyclopedic simile 113

242 *Index*

endnotes, usage 8
endophoric reference 127
English modals 94
entities, resemblance 110
epistemic modality 94
epithet functioning 130
equation: strategy 64–5; substitution, contrast 64–6; types 64–5
equivalence (borrowing type) 60
etic perspective (outside perspective), reliance 191
euphemism 173, 181
evaluation, procedure 13
exaggeration, impact 84
existential process 152
exophoric reference 127
expectancy norm 69
explication (local strategy) 45
expository texts, subdivisions 213
expressive verbs 172
external coherence 56
extraposition 50

factual situation, description 95, 98
features of spoken language, usage 162
field of discourse 151–6; annotation 153–5; circumstances 153–6; comment 155, 156; participants 152–3; process 151–2
field variable 151
first-person narrative 71
first-person pronoun, usage 157
first-person singular pronoun 71
Firthian linguistic models 61
footnotes, usage 8
forced passive voice 57
foreignization: approach 46; strategy 49
formal correspondent 61
formality: degree 41; informality, contrast 157
Fraser, Janet 39
free-word-order language 140
freshness, purpose 111
Friedman, Jeffrey A. 98
fronted theme 139
functional sentence perspective 139

general atmosphere, identification 44
General purpose (translation purpose) 40
general word (superordinate), translation 71–2; annotation 72; comment 71
genre 42–3; aims/properties 39; identification 44; types 43
global strategies 38; example 215

grammar, dimensions 82–3
grammatical cohesion 126
grammatical equivalence 82–4; comment 84
grammatical restraint, absence 110
graphological devices, usage 162
graphology 180
Grice, P. 170
groups, monolithic notions 62

habitus-oriented decision 199
Hallidayan approach 138, 140
Hallidayan linguistic models 61
Holy Qur'an: culture-specific expressions 191–2; extract 132
Holz-Manttari, Justa 40
Hussein, Saddam 18
hyperbation 181
hypernomy-hyponymy 137
hypertheme 139
hyponyms 126

iconic function 175–6, 196
idafa-construction 65, 145
identifying theme 139
ideological issues, annotation 190
ideology 197–203; annotation 203; comments 198–202; issue 48; term, coinage 197
idiomatic expression 60; function 116
idioms 114–20; body-related idiom 116–17; collocation 117–20; comment 115–17; idioms 114–17; metaphor 110–12; simile 112–14
illocutionary act 169; classification 171–2
illustration (translation) 77; comment 77
impersonalization, personalization (contrast) 157
inaccessibility, accessibility (contrast) 157–8
indexical function 176
informality, formality (contrast) 157
intended readership 39
interpretant 196
interpretive semiotics 175
intersentential instances 136–7
in-text participants 73; rhetorical questions, usage 157
intransitive verbs 86
intrasystem shifts 55, 63–4, 91
intrinsic managing, usage 88
irony 181

Johnston-Davies, Denys 176
Joseph's Tales 211; annotation 217–24; genre 212–14; global strategy 215;

language role/register 211–12;
readership 214; source text 215–17;
target text 215–17; text: selection,
rationale 211; type 212–14; translation
215–17; purpose 214–15

kernel sentences 110
Khuḏayyir, Muḥammed 210–11

language: choices 83; culture, interface
196; language-related issues 11;
language-specific rules 68; lexical
features 109; morphological resources
83, 91; phraseological features 109;
role/register 211–2; stretches 137; study
169; users 93–4
legal documents, translation 117
legal writing, quality 117
letters, repetition 184
level shifts 55, 61
lexical calque 57
lexical choices 103–9; annotation 104–5,
108; comment 107, 109
lexical cohesion 126, 137–8; comments 138
lexical ellipsis 131
lexical information 84
lexical items 103, 106; co-occurrence 117;
deletion 68; meaning 118; options 109;
repetition 126
lexical repetition, rendering 138
lexical term: denotative meaning 67;
translation 76
Liardet, Frances E. 69, 73, 156, 196
linear theme pattern 139
linguistic models 61
literal translation (borrowing type) 56, 58
Literary Devices Net 180
literary genres 43
litotes 181
loan word (loan word plus explanation),
translation 74–5; comment 75
loan word, usage 75
local strategies 55–6, 85; Baker
classification 71–7; borrowing 56–60;
classification 71; equivalence 60;
Malone list 64–71; reason, statement
55; stating 55; types 45, 55; type,
statement 55
locutionary act 169
lower-rank units, arrangement 62

Malone, J. L. 64–71
manner: adverbial clause 133;
circumstantials 153; maxim 170

marked collocation 184; example 114
marked prepositional phrase 183
marked theme 140; types 139
matching 64
material processes 151–4, 156, 158;
actors 89
Matthews, P. H. 93
maxim of manner 170
maxim of quality 170
maxim of quantity 170
maxim of relevance 170
maxims, types 170
meaning, sequence (creation) 126
medium, text transmission 39
mental image 156; problem 105
mental process 152
message: directionality 94; form, variation
59; parts, importance 155
metaphor 110–12, 181; annotation 111–12;
cognitive process 111; definition 110;
nonstructural metaphor 111
metaphorical expression 171
metonymy 181
micro signs 179
middle voice 87
mitigating features 173
modality 93–9; categories/classification
94–5; comment 96–9; deontic modality
94; dynamic modality 95; epistemic
modality 94; function 98; groups 95;
rendering, difficulty 96–7; root modality
95
modalized particles 95, 201
modalized prepositional phrases 95
modalized prepositions 95, 98
modalized verbs 95, 179, 201
modal verbs 98; usage 99
mode of discourse 161–3; annotation 163;
comment 162
Modern Iraqi Short Stories 18
mode variable 151
modulation: borrowing type 59–60;
local strategy 45; optional modulation
109
morphology 82–3, 180; asymmetries 83;
knowledge 192
morphosyntactic level 65
Morris, Charles William 175
Morsi, Mohammed 198–9
multiword units 109–14
myronyms 126

narrative texts 213
Nāṣir, Abdul-Sattar 127

244   *Index*

national passive 87
native speakers, distinctions 117–18
naturalness 63; level, desire 68, 77
neologism 181
neutral expressive words, usage 72–3
neutral/less expressive word, translation 72–4; annotation 73–4; comment 73
New Rhetoric 39
Nida, Eugene 110
nominal ellipsis 130
nonstructural metaphor 111
nonuniversal cross-cultural application 169
nonverbal factors 38
nouns: phrases, simplicity 157; translation 64, 108
number (grammatical category) 84–6; comments 85, 86

Obama, Barack (inaugural address) 143–4
objects, likeliness/unlikeliness 128
oblique translation 56
of-structure 65
omission 115, 215; local strategy 45; usage 55
omission (translation) 76–7; comment 77
one-to-one equivalent, absence 72
onomatopoeia 181
opening clause, usage 222
operator ellipsis 131
optimal equivalence 176
optimum orientation, achievement 11
optional modulation 109
Orwell, George 77
outside perspective (etic perspective), reliance 191
over-lexicalization 198

paradigmatic axes 179
paradox 181
parallelism 143–6, 181; annotation 145; comment 144–6; example 104–5
parallel structures: placement 143, 145; usage 144
paraphrase (related word usage), translation 55, 75–6; comment 76
paraphrase (unrelated word usage), translation 76; comment 76
paraphrasing 115
particles, modalized particles 95
passival 87
passive meaning, expression 87
passive voice: active voice, contrast 86–9; annotation 89; expression 88;

forced passive voice 57; meaning 87; national passive 87; usage, reasons 87; verbalized structure, marked use 89
passivization, usage 160; reasons 87
perfect aspect 90
perfect progressive aspect 90
perlocutionary act 169
persona, identification 9–10
personalization: degree 158, 159; impersonalization (contrast) 157
personal reference 128
personification 181; examples 114; usage 111
persuasive genres 43
philosophical genres 43
phonetics 180
phraseological choices, annotation 103
place: adverbial clause 133; circumstantials 153
plurality 84
politeness 158–61; annotation 160–1; comment 158–160; norms 173
power relationship 158
pragmatic aspects, annotation 168
pragmatic changes 38
pragmatic communicative effect 92, 223
pragmatics 180; annotation 174; aspects 169–75; comment 170–5
Pragnell, Fred 58
Prague School approach 138–40
predicated theme 139
predictability, speaker's assessment 93
prepositional phrases: marked prepositional phrase 183; modalized prepositional phrases 95
prepositions, modalized prepositions 95, 98
probability, speaker's assessment 93
progression, thematic progression 138–43
progressive aspect 90; feature 87; grammatical expression 83
pronouns: first-person pronoun, usage 157; reference 1257; second-person pronoun, usage 159; usage 127
proofreading, procedure 12
proofread, optimum orientation (achievement) 11
propositional elements 131
propositional ellipsis 132
propositional meaning 72
propositions, truth (commitment) 201
punctuation marks, omission 182
pure translation studies 6
purpose, adverbial clause 133

quality: maxim 170; perspectives 13
quantity, maxim 170

rank shifts 62–3; example 69
readability 119; expense 47–8
reader: identification 44; reader-oriented global strategy 215
readership 39, 41, 215; intended readership 39; *Joseph's Tales* 214
reason, adverbial clause 133
reasoned decisions 215
recrescence 64
reduction 68; amplification, contrast 64, 67–9; comment 67–9
reference 126–8; anaphoric reference 127; aspectual reference 91; cataphoric coreference 127; comparative reference 128; demonstrative reference 128; endophoric reference 127; exophoric reference 127; personal reference 128; temporal reference 91; textual reference 127; time reference 90; types 127
referential devices, sets 128
referential form, respect 174
referential items 144
reflexive meaning, example 87
register 154; analysis 127; annotation 150
Reid, Thomas Bertram 150
reiteration 126
related word, usage 75–6
relational process 152
relations, expression 136–7
relevance, maxim 170
religious genres 43
reordering 64, 70–1; annotation 70, 71; strategy 126
repackaging 64
representatives 171
researchers, strategic decisions (evaluation) 44–50
restructuring 223
result, adverbial clause 133
retranslation: procedure 13; terms 12
reviser: persona, identification 9–10; term, usage 17
revision 12; annotation, contrast 8; checking, contrast 10; perspectives 9; procedure 12; scholar's perspective 9; translator usage 9–10
rewriting: occurrence 12; procedure 13
rheme: split rheme pattern 139; theme-rheme notion 138, 139; theme-rheme relations, analysis 142

rhetorical devices 183–4
rhetorical questions, usage 157
root modality 95

Saīd, Maḥmūd 183
saying, processes 165
scene-based story 211
second-person pronoun, usage 159
self-assessment 10
self-image, expectations 174
self-revision 10
semantic changes 38
semantics 180
semantic units 70
semiotic aspects, annotation 168
semiotics: aspects 175–80; comments 176–80; interpretive semiotics 175; structural semiotics 175, 177
Semitic language 87
sentences: expression 88; functional sentence perspective 139; kernel sentences 110; length, impact 219; meaning, understanding 109; subordinate sentence 135
sequences, reordering 70
shifts 61–4; category shifts 61–4; class shifts 62; intrasystem shifts 63–4; level shifts 61; rank shifts 62–3; structure shifts 61–2; types, combination 77; unit shifts 62–3
signifieds, types 177
signs: functions 175–6; micro signs 179; organization methods 177
simile 112–14, 181; comment 114; translation, difficulty 113; types 112–13
simple aspect (zero aspect) 90
singularity 84
situational equivalence 60
skopos 40–1; translation purpose 39
slot and filler principle 109
social deixis 67
social distance: respect/deference description 173; standing, contrast 158–61
social honorific, usage 175
socio-cultural norms 175
source text (ST) 8; analysis 9; appearance 8; *Joseph's Tales* 215–17; linguistic slackening/tightening 69; translation, issues 52–3; word/expression, usage 76
speech: action 169; part, change 59
split rheme pattern 139
spoken language, features (usage) 162
spoken modes, employment 162

standing, social distance (contrast) 158–61
strategic decisions 40; evaluation 44–50; translation issues 52–3; translation student selections 45–50
strategies 37–40; local strategies 55–6
structural calque 57–8
structural methods 60
structural semiotics 175, 177
structure: balance 143; deep structure 110; element 61; repetition 130; shifts 61–2; variations, problems 86
style: definition 180–1; shifting 198
stylistic aspects, annotation 168
stylistic methods 60
stylistics, aspects 180–5; annotations 183–4; comments 181, 182
subjectivity, elements 13
subject-object sequences 70
subordinate conjuncts 133
subordinate sentence 135
subordinating conjuncts 133
substitution 65–6, 126, 128–30; annotation 130; comment 129; cultural substitution, usage 74; equation, contrast 64–6; verbal substitution 129
superordinate (general word), translation 71–2
symbolic function 176
synonyms 126
synonymy 50, 137
syntactic changes 38
syntactic structure 44, 57; occurrence 143
syntagmatic axes 179
syntagmatic patterns 70
syntax 82–3, 180; knowledge 192; selection/manipulation 220

target language 82
target text (TT) 8; aim 48; appearance 8; *Joseph's Tales* 215–17; naturalness 47
temporal information 90
temporal reference 91
tenor of discourse 157–61; accessibility, inaccessibility (contrast) 157–8; formality, informality (contrast) 157; personalization, impersonalization (contrast) 157
tenor variable 151
tense: annotation 90–1, 92; aspect, contrast 90–3; comment 93; continuity 126, 143–6; continuous past tense 93; information 90
text: author 39; binding 126; clarity, translator clarity 39; communication channel 39; conceptual texts 213;
decoration 112; descriptive texts 213; expository texts, subdivisions 213; function 39; meaning 107; narrative texts 213; organization 139; reception, time/place 39; sender/receiver, social distance 158; text-oriented global strategy 215; text-type focus 68; transmission, medium (usage) 39; type 42, 215; attention 213; identification 44; typology 41–2; demand 107
textual asymmetries 136–7
textual profile: consultation 17; first translation 14; first translator's comments 14–15; native speaker's impression 15–16; reviser's version/ comments 15; second translation 14; second translator's comments 15; translators, final translation 15
textual profile, example 14–16
textual reference 127
thematic pattern, usage 220
thematic progression 138–43; comment 141–3
theme: annotation 145; comment 144–6; constant theme pattern 139; derived theme 139; fronted theme 139; identifying theme 139; linear theme pattern 139; marked theme, types 139; predicated theme 139; theme-rheme relations, analysis 142
theme-rheme notion 138, 139
through-translation (calque) 57–8
time: adverbial clause 133; fronting, avoidance 155; circumstantials 153; relation 90
time reference 90; change 92
transitive verbs 86
transitivity 198; process, components 151
translation: accuracy 84; addition, usage 55; applied translation studies 6; author-oriented translation 44, 48; back-translation 178; brief 37–40; discussion 43–4; elements 39; calque 56; criticism, importance 7; cultural substitution 74; cultural translation 115; direct translation, types 56; editors, criteria (question form) 11; formal equivalence 49; generalization 221; general word (superordinate) 71–2; illustration, usage 77; *Joseph's Tales* 215–17; literal translation 58; loan word (loan word plus explanation) 74–5; neutral/less expressive word 72–4; oblique translation 56; occurrence 11;

omission 76–7; usage 55; paraphrase: related word usage 75–6; usage 55; paraphrase (unrelated word usage) 76; process: dynamic activity 13–4; focus 213; macro/micro levels 12; pure translation studies 6; purpose (skopos) 39; identification 44; types 40; purpose, example 214–15; quality control 17; reader-oriented translation 44; related word, usage 75–6; strategies 37; annotation 54; subcategories 38; strategy, purpose 40; structure variations, impact 86; text-oriented translation 38, 44; through-translation (calque) 57–8; translation-oriented analysis, usage 9; unrelated words, usage 76; word-for-word translation 49
translational action 40
translation student one, strategic decision 45–6
translation student two, strategic decision 46
translation student three, strategic decision 47–8
translation student four, strategic decision 48–49
translation student five, strategic decision 49–50
translation studies, map (Holmes) 7
translators, text clarity 39
transposition (borrowing type) 59

units: lower-rank units, arrangement 62; multiword units 109–14
unit shifts 55, 62–3; example 69
unmarked collocation 112, 119, 184, 212
unrelated words, usage 76
use-based variations 150
user-based variations 150

validation, procedure 13
verbal ellipsis 130, 131
verbalized structure, marked use 89
verbal process 152
verbal signs 67
verbal substitution 129
verbal system, morphological richness 87
verbs: aspects 91; assertive verbs 171; auxiliary verbs, absence 129; commissive verbs 171; declarative verbs 171; directive verbs 171; expressive verbs 172; intransitive verbs 86; modalized verbs 95, 179; modal verbs 98; transitive verbs 86; types 171–2; usage 105; verb-adverb sequences 70; weak verb 92
versions, assessment/evaluation 16
Vinay, J. P. 56–60
vocabulary, knowledge 192
voice (grammatical category) 86
vowels (pronunciation) 107

weak verb 92
Winkel, Eric 135, 181
words: collocated words, sequence 218–9; cultural specificity 67; culture-specific words 64; loan words, usage 75; neutral expressive words, usage 72–3; tendency 118; translation 66, 108; word-for-word translation 49

Yasin, Lubna Mahmud 184

zero aspect (simple aspect) 90
zeugma 181
zigzagging 64
zoomorphism 181